The Death of Prince George, Duke of Kent, 1942

The Death of Prince George, Duke of Kent, 1942

A New Investigation to Find the Truth

M.S. Morgan

AIR WORLD

First published in Great Britain in 2024 by
Pen & Sword Military
An imprint of
Pen & Sword Books Ltd
Yorkshire - Philadelphia

Copyright © M.S. Morgan, 2024

ISBN 978 1 03610 719 2

A CIP catalogue record for this book is available from the British Library.

Typeset in INDIA by IMPEC eSolutions
Printed and bound in the England by CPI Group (UK) Ltd, Croydon, CRO 4YY

Pen & Sword Books Ltd. incorporates the Imprints of Pen & Sword Archaeology, Atlas, Aviation, Battleground, Discovery, Family History, History, Maritime, Military, Naval, Politics, Railways, Select, Transport, True Crime, Fiction, Frontline Books, Leo Cooper, Praetorian Press, Seaforth Publishing, Wharncliffe, White Owl and After the Battle.

For a complete list of Pen & Sword titles please contact

PEN & SWORD BOOKS LIMITED
47 Church Street, Barnsley, South Yorkshire, S70 2AS, England
E-mail: enquiries@pen-and-sword.co.uk
Website: www.pen-and-sword.co.uk

or

PEN AND SWORD BOOKS
1950 Lawrence Rd, Havertown, PA 19083, USA
E-mail: uspen-and-sword@casematepublishers.com
Website: www.penandswordbooks.com

For my wife Kim with love,
for having to listen for many years to the findings of
my research before it finally got to print!

Contents

List of illustrations

Introduction

As a researcher, historian and author, I have written a number of books on military aviation and some lesser-known wartime incidents. I have always enjoyed the combination of history, mystery and intrigue, and one story that amply covers these genres, is the mysterious death of Prince George, the Duke of Kent, killed in an air crash on 25 August 1942.

As a former Senior Investigating Officer, with thirty years police service, I investigated the deaths of hundreds of people. Their deaths ranged from murder and manslaughter to accidental deaths, suicides, work-related deaths, car crashes and deliberate and accidental drug overdoses, to name but a few of the causes.

I was trained at the world-renowned Metropolitan Police Detective Training School and told by my tutor that the most important case for a detective was the investigation of a person's death. That statement is logical, but he quickly added that it is a privilege to be entrusted with the investigation into someone's life and death.

Any good detective wants to investigate a death to the best of their own ability, to uncover the truth and the cause of that death. Failure to do so, I believe, is disrespectful to the deceased and their family and could even be regarded as neglectful.

The death of the Duke of Kent, his entourage and the crew of the Sunderland aircraft that was to convey him to Iceland, is one that I believe resonates with my tutor's comments all those years ago.

Over many years I have examined a good number of deaths which appeared to be non-suspicious, but after detailed investigation, they were found to be anything but normal.

I worked with forensic pathologists, scientists, crime scene examiners, photographers and many other experts in various scientific fields, in a bid to identify the cause of death. Ultimately, I attended many cases in HM Coroner's Courts and Crown Court trials.

In mid-1990s London, I worked on the first cold case murder review in Britain. Today, such enquiries and reviews are commonplace, but in the last decade of the twentieth century, they were a new addition to policing. For over a hundred years, the senior detective in a murder investigation had been placed on a pillar, but now they would be subjected to reviews and if required, re-investigation. As a Senior Investigating Officer, I also underwent numerous reviews.

In the final years of my police service, I was part of a Professional Standards Department, examining complaints and gross misconduct by police officers and civil staff. I would examine their processes and decision making, alongside dealing with deaths after contact with the police, liaising with the Independent Office for Police Conduct (previously known as the Independent Police Complaints Commission – IPCC). It is because of my professional experience, that I believe I have the credentials to review the death of Prince George, Duke of Kent.

The death of the Duke of Kent in 1942, is a case that has always been surrounded by mystery and conspiracy allegations. A number of books and articles have been written over recent decades about his death, many speculating that he was on a covert mission to collect the Deputy Reichs Fuhrer, Rudolf Hess, and transport him to Sweden for peace talks – all contrary to the will of the Prime Minister – Winston Churchill. Others have speculated that the duke and his colleagues were murdered, rather like his associate, Polish Premier, General Sikorski who died in another air crash off

Gibraltar in 1943. Both crashes it has been alleged, were the work of the British intelligence services, in a bid to silence both men after their involvement in a covert peace initiative with the earlier arrival of Rudolf Hess in May 1941.

Some commentators have speculated that the Duke of Kent was an embarrassment to the nation and the Royal Family, a man who was reportedly bi-sexual, had a number of affairs, some of them extra-marital and used what we now call Class 'A' drugs. This they have speculated may have led to his death.

While these are the more outlandish and spectacular alleged causes for the duke's untimely death, (not forgetting the unfortunate air crew and his personal entourage who also died) others have blamed the weather conditions, poor navigation, poor airmanship, instrument failure and the drinking of alcohol on board the flight; or any mixture of these.

The problem as we shall see in this book, is that the authorities (mostly the Royal Air Force and the Air Ministry in London), seemed in all haste to want to deal with the issue with an immediate Court of Inquiry.

Although it was wartime and fatal accidents were a regular feature, surely the Prime Minister Winston Churchill and the duke's brother – King George VI – would want an in-depth investigation into the crash?

The apparent impetuous manner in which the investigation and the subsequent Court of Inquiry was convened, is, over eight decades later, somewhat mystifying.

The authorities deemed it necessary to clear the wreckage from an uncontrolled and unpreserved crash scene as soon as possible, with apparently very little investigation. The Duke of Kent, who was said to have possessed an attaché case full of Icelandic Krona bank notes handcuffed to his wrist, was buried within a week of his death and before the Court of Inquiry had completed its investigation and released their findings.

In addition, the sole survivor from the crash, was allegedly made to sign a *document* of some sort in his hospital bed and not called upon to give oral evidence at the Court of Inquiry… although as we shall see, surviving records appear to contradict this and do not make this clear.

To exacerbate and fuel the various conspiracy theories, the original Court of Inquiry report, the relevant witness statements and any other documents have gone missing or allegedly been destroyed.

Many similar accident reports from the Second World War were apparently destroyed some years ago and it is said this report could have been one of those tossed into the dreaded shredded. The question is why the file on the second worst air crash in British history at that time, which included King George VI's youngest brother among the fatalities, was not saved from the shredder while others were preserved is a mystery.

In Britain today, enquiries with the United Kingdom's National Archives, the RAF Museum, the RAF Air Historical Branch, the Royal Archives at Windsor Castle, the Defence Accident Investigation Board (DAIB) and the Air Accident Investigation Board (AAIB), have all failed to locate any detailed evidence of the crash or the subsequent RAF Court of Inquiry. The only available documents in Britain, are squadron operations record books (ORBs) which do not mention the crash or the Form 1180 – a very basic record of the aircraft's loss and the names of the two main pilots (more on this later).

The only papers directly linked to the investigation now available, are those attached to the personal file of Pilot Officer Sydney Wood Smith in the Australian National Archives.

Pilot Officer Smith, an Australian by birth, died in the crash and a number of pages from the Court of Inquiry report were sent to Australia. Copies of twenty pages from the original *Proceedings of Court of Inquiry or Investigation file for a flying accident (Form 412)* and two more pages from the *Report on Flying Accident or Forced*

Landing – not attributable to enemy action (Form 765) are attached to his file and available for public examination. These papers were certified copies and did not bear any of the original signatures from witnesses or Inquiry members.

The Australian papers are all that remain (as far as we know) of the original case file. The original scene photographs, maps, plans, meteorological and flight plans, the Sunderland aircraft's Form 700, as well as aircraft technical and aircrew logbooks, have all long since disappeared from public scrutiny.

The original witness statements, medical reports (including possible post mortem reports) and the investigators' notes, have also disappeared and are unavailable for public examination. Consequently, conspiracy theorists have used this dearth of evidence to produce their own theories.

However, there is other evidence available in the form of media reports from August 1942 and some aerial photographs of the crash site, which are still in existence. There are also the death certificate entries of those killed and recorded in the National Records of Scotland, but no civil Fatal Accident Inquiry file is available. This would have been conducted on behalf of the Procurator Fiscal, if he/she wanted an additional inquiry alongside the RAF Court of Inquiry, but as we shall see this raises some questions.

The newspaper reports from 1942 and since, plus the recorded comments of witnesses over the following decades, provide some evidence.

Some of this evidence comes from the sole survivor of the crash – Flight Sergeant Andrew Jack – while other evidence is via third parties and according to English and Scottish law, therefore hearsay.

By gathering all of this evidence together and analysing it carefully, we can build a very good picture of what actually happened that day in August 1942 and the following weeks. Notwithstanding the fact this event took place in the middle of the Second World War and fatal non-combat air crashes were common place, it reveals some major procedural issues that would in my opinion, in modern day Britain, probably lead to a judicial review and questions in parliament.

In addition to my professional qualifications and experience, I have held a life-long interest in military aviation. I always wanted to be an RAF pilot and having passed the relevant aptitude tests, I was dismayed to be stopped from fulfilling my ambition, by a very minor medical condition. Despite this, I continued with my interest and had civil flying lessons, while keeping up to date with developments in military aviation.

After many years of reading the numerous books, newspapers and magazine articles on the death of the Duke of Kent, I decided to take a proper, evidential and as far as possible, forensic review of the case – a form of cold case review.

I obtained the surviving Court of Inquiry documents from the Australian Archives, I approached the UK National Archives for records relating to the incident, including records for No. 228 Squadron, the crash recovery teams, RAF Oban and Alness/Invergordon, as well as all manner of material regarding the fatal crash. I obtained copies of the death records, maps, photographs, newspaper articles, numerous books, magazines and any written comments left in university archives or elsewhere.

I also examined the backgrounds of the aircraft's crew, their passengers, as well as the often overlooked, members of the Court of Inquiry. I examined what the politicians said via Hansard, as well as the aircraft's own operational history.

I approached the Royal Archives at Windsor Castle, who were very helpful in locating an original file detailing preparations for the duke's flight to Iceland. Sadly, they did not know of a 1942 diary for the Duke of Kent and they did not know if he even kept one. If any material still exists, they believe it may be held by his immediate family and therefore remain private property.

I have carefully examined the available material, cross-checking it and asking questions that were either not asked in 1942 or should have been. I have carried out as full a review as possible, as I would have done as a police Senior Investigating Officer.

One of the main concerns is the actual crash investigation and the Court of Inquiry. Many people have suggested that air crash investigation was very basic and in its infancy in August 1942. They contend that there were so many fatal accidents across the United Kingdom, there was no time to speculate and ponder the causes of these crashes. It may have been in its infancy at the time, but as we shall see later in this book, crash investigation as a science was well underway in mid-1942 and a long way from its infancy.

In his book *Air Crash – the clues in the wreckage*, Fred Jones, an experienced air crash investigator, explains that in August 1941 he was completing his engineering apprenticeship at the Royal Aircraft Establishment in Farnborough when he was taken under the proverbial wing of Dr W.D. Douglas. Douglas was a specialist 'defect and accident investigator' who was, according to Jones, 'Always in demand by the official accident investigators of the day.' Douglas had developed the techniques for analysing and considering the evidence taken from the wreckage of crashed aircraft.

Fred Jones describes that in 1941 he was working on a Stirling bomber crash, problems with Spitfires and then Westland Whirlwinds in 1942. In late 1942 he also worked on the issue of structural failures in Hawker Typhoons and Hotspur troop-carrying gliders. By 1943 he had been involved in fourteen major investigations in a year. They even assisted the Americans with enquiries with a P-47 Thunderbolt crash. These men were the scientists, the forerunners of the modern-day Air Accident Investigation Board, but there were other air crash investigators...

A review of the Royal Air Force lists from July 1942, finds a whole department – *The RAF Accident Branch officer list – Air*

Crash Inspectors, in other words the air force's own air crash investigators.

While many researchers, writers and historians have either defended the crew of the Sunderland or gone to great lengths to find evidence of a conspiracy, I have kept to the hard facts that are available; whether they be from primary witnesses or second-hand from third parties who spoke directly with the now deceased witnesses. Although hearsay evidence is not permitted in UK law, due to the nature of this case and the time lapse of over eighty years, I have included it, but only if it came from a person who allegedly heard it directly from a primary witness.

In English Coroners' Courts, the level of proof is the 'balance of probabilities', i.e. something is more likely than not. This is the level of proof we shall use in this re-examination of the case.

I will look at the evidence and where necessary question it, I hope this will give a carefully considered and balanced review of the available evidence. I will touch on the conspiracy claims, but this review will concentrate on the available evidence.

I must thank a number of people for their assistance with this book. The first is George Bethune, who, for many, many decades, has sought the truth in this case.

George's father, Will Bethune, was a Special Constable in August 1942 and one of the first individuals to arrive at the scene of the fatal crash. George has spent decades trying to gather witness testimony and get to the bottom of the story. I am extremely grateful to George for his help, direction and allowing me to use the evidence he has uncovered over so many years of research. His efforts are a major part in assisting my own research for this book. I hope this book will meet his expectations!

I would like to thank Alan Hendry, a local Caithness journalist who has written a number of pieces about the crash and who assisted me in connecting with George Bethune, while allowing me to use some of his articles.

I would also like to thank Valarie Amin at the Highland Life Centre for assisting me with my research and searching the archives.

I would like to thank the staff at the Scottish Records Office for giving me so much of their valuable time and the Australian National Archives for their advice and assistance. I would also like to thank Highland Libraries for allowing me to use their image of the crash site.

Finally, I would like to thank Dr Alastair Noble and the staff at the RAF Air Historical Branch at Northolt, who kindly answered a number of questions for me.

This book, I hope, will go some way to finally resolving the cause of the crash which killed His Royal Highness, Prince George, the Duke of Kent and so many of his colleagues in August 1942; while dismissing some of the main conspiracy theories that surround this case.

Chapter One

25 August 1942

On the morning of Tuesday, 25 August 1942, a pristine Short Sunderland Mk III flying boat, bearing the squadron letters DQ-M and the serial number W4026, sat tethered to its mooring buoy on the calm waters of the Cromarty Firth. The adjacent shore base was RAF Alness near Invergordon, some fourteen miles north of Inverness in Scotland.

The large four engine, high-winged flying boat had been recently re-painted in a new colour scheme, its undersides and fuselage a gleaming white, while the upper surfaces were camouflaged in a dark sea grey and dark green pattern, the standard upper wing pattern of the time.

The Short Sunderland was a large aircraft, the workhorse of Coastal Command with a standard crew of about ten, but it could carry a number of passengers. In service with RAF Coastal Command for a number of years, by 1942 its long endurance allowed it to undertake convoy protection and anti-submarine patrols over the North Atlantic Ocean. It could carry anti-submarine bombs or depth charges, as well as over a dozen .303 Browning machine guns. Although it was a relatively slow, lumbering machine, it could certainly defend itself and became known as the flying porcupine to Luftwaffe air crews.

Sunderland 'M' for Mother was a relatively new aircraft in August 1942, equipped to carry VIP passengers, it even had curtains on its hull windows, allowing some privacy and comfort. The aircraft was also equipped to carry out operational duties with No. 228 Squadron, part of No. 15 Group, Coastal Command and was based at RAF Oban on the west coast of Scotland.

The crew had flown the aircraft over from their base at Oban on 24 August, for a 'special flight'. They knew they would be taking someone of importance to an as yet undisclosed location, utilising the aircrafts VIP interior and its renowned endurance, but only the unit's senior officers knew the identity of their passenger.

Having stayed at RAF Alness overnight, the next morning the crew, which had a wide mixture of experience, checked their aircraft, while their captain, Flight Lieutenant Frank Goyen, the co-pilot and the navigator, completed their briefings which included a thorough meteorological presentation. The weather forecast for the first part of the flight would be poor with low cloud, however, this was expected to clear later over the far north of Scotland.

Also present for the briefing and going along on the trip, was their squadron commander – Wing Commander Thomas Lawton Moseley. He was also a pilot and navigation expert, meaning the crew for the coming flight would comprise of three pilots, a separate navigator and seven other wireless operators and air gunners.

The aircraft would be armed with its usual number of Browning .303 machine guns for self-defence, but it would also carry eight depth charges – just in case they spotted a surfaced U-boat between Scotland and Iceland. Although this was a special VIP flight, it was also an operational flight.

After their morning briefings, the Sunderland crew were tendered across the flat calm waters to the waiting aircraft. They clambered aboard through the hatches and started to make their individual pre-flight checks.

The Sunderland crew realised the conditions were not great for a take-off. Contrary to common perception, flying boats like the Sunderland, preferred small waves on the surface of the water, as this assisted in allowing the large hull to free itself from the *suction* of the sea.

The flight plan dictated that once the Sunderland had taken off, it would head out over the length of the Cromarty Firth towards Tarbat Ness lighthouse, where a navigational fix would be obtained. The aircraft would then almost instantly enter the low cloud base, before heading northwards on a pre-determined navigational bearing towards Clyth Ness to the north of Dunbeath.

As the crew readied themselves, another tender approached the Sunderland, this one ferrying HRH Prince George, the Duke of Kent and his entourage of three. They entered the aircraft via the usual access hatch and started to make themselves as comfortable as possible in the bottom of the hull, an area often called the crew rest area or the wardroom.

The No. 228 Squadron Commander, Thomas Moseley, was quick to ensure his royal guest and party were comfortable and welcomed them on board, undoubtedly explaining a number of interesting points to the duke.

As we shall see from later evidence, it appears he also invited the duke to climb the vertical ladder to the raised flight deck, to view the cockpit and its excellent vantage point. The duke, an avid aviator and pilot himself, managed to climb up the ladder, despite being incumbered by an attaché case handcuffed to his right wrist. What was in it was anyone's guess, but it didn't surprise the crew that a dignitary should carry such an attaché case attached to his arm.

Once on the flight deck, the duke stood between the Squadron Commander and the aircrafts captain, as they sat in the two pilots' seats. The third pilot, the young Australian named Pilot Officer Sydney Wood Smith, was not required and probably sat in the crew rest area having been temporarily evicted from his seat on the flight deck by his Commanding Officer. Also on the flight deck was the navigator Pilot Officer George Saunders, Sergeant Leonard Sweett the flight engineer and a wireless operator sergeant.

After a brief discussion, the crew went through their start-up procedure and the four Bristol Pegasus XVIII engines sprang into life, shaking the airframe as the mooring rope was finally released by the air gunner in the nose with the assistance of a tender's crew. After releasing the tether, the gunner ducked back down inside and under the front gun turret which was then slid forward to cover the mooring hatch.

The captain spoke with the watch tower who gave him permission to taxi to the end of the aquatic runway, an area marked by a long series of floating markers on the Cromarty Firth. One final check with the crew and the instruments told the captain they were ready to depart. With a glance at his fellow pilot and the overcast sky, the pilot opened the throttles to the four engines and they increased in volume, shaking the airframe to the point an uninitiated passenger would have been concerned for the aircraft and their personal safety.

The Sunderland, slowly at first, started to move along the seaborne runway, gradually accelerating in speed. The distance until it finally released itself from its watery bonds was over three quarters of a mile, but eventually the heavily laden flying boat clawed itself into the air. The last remnants of salt water dripped away from the pristine hull as the Sunderland passed through 300 feet and towards the low cloud base. The crew knew they had to fly over water to the north of Scotland before changing course and heading off towards Iceland. With the aircraft's altimeter set with the local barometric pressure, they would be safe, flying over the sea until they encountered better weather near Wick in the far north of Scotland.

The aircraft turned northwards and the positional fix was made at Tarbat Ness lighthouse, as they climbed slowly into the cloud layer and the crew continued with their regular tasks.

The rear gunner, a man with the loneliest place on board the Sunderland, headed off to his position under the towering tail of the aircraft. Flight Sergeant Andrew Jack entered the rear gun turret, closing the doors behind him before plugging in his intercom lead and checking his four Browning machine guns.

The Sunderland would fly up the coastline of Caithness before changing course. On the ground and along the coast, local people could hear the drone of the Sunderland's four Bristol Pegasus engines. They were used to the sound of flying boats and other aircraft patrolling up and down the coastline, but they could not see this machine due to the low cloud base.

The nearby land mass was not the most hospitable, with rapidly rising ground giving way to heather and bracken covered rocky crags and peat moorland. Few trees could grow on this high ground, so adverse were the elements in this part of Scotland.

After about half an hour of flight, a number of people on the ground between Ousdale, Berriedale and Braemore were perplexed to hear the sound of aircraft engines heading inland, towards the higher ground. While aircraft had previously flown inland, the local populace had experienced ears, tuned to the engines of passing aircraft. They knew the different tones, the likely direction of flight and even the probable altitude; and those who heard the Sunderland overhead that afternoon, knew something was not right with this particular flight.

Near Braemore and in the Berriedale Water (river) valley, people heard the aircraft overhead and knew instinctively there was likely to be a crash, as the ground rose sharply towards Eagles Rock in the thick low cloud.

Eventually, their worst fears were confirmed with a sudden hollow, crunching metallic sound, quickly followed by the crump of an explosion. The engine noise stopped abruptly and although they could see nothing due to the low cloud, their sense of smell confirmed what their ears had told them, as the unmistakable smell of burning aviation fuel pervaded the air.

A number of local people were quick to react and set out for the crash site, while calls were sent for assistance and a local doctor to attend. After a lengthy period of time, the first witnesses came upon the crash site, a scene of utter devastation still shrouded in thick low cloud.

The aircraft type was indistinguishable, having smashed itself into a billion pieces. Some of the debris was still burning and the peat and bracken was smoldering, almost the full fuel load had burst into flames as the Sunderland disintegrated on the hillside. Some larger pieces of wreckage were identifiable, even to the uninitiated, as parts of the engines and the wing floats remained relatively intact. The tail section comprising of the massive tail fin, rudder and the rear gun turret, was also identifiable, having been thrown into the distance by the impact.

Although it was a scene of devastation, the witnesses' eyes were quickly drawn to the scattered bodies of the crew and their passengers. Bodies lay either in what remained of the wreckage or a short distance from it. Some of the bodies were mangled, others were burnt, but it was clear they had all died from catastrophic and instantaneous injuries.

The body of the Duke of Kent was located a short distance from the main area of debris with a severe head injury, apparently thrown from the wreckage. He was identified from his personal identification and covered with a parachute, as were the other bodies. The attaché case attached to his wrist had burst open and witnesses found foreign bank notes scattered over the hillside.

As time passed, further assistance arrived and eventually the military authorities would take control of the crash site.

Why the Sunderland had flown inland and struck the high ground with such fatal consequences was a mystery. It had clearly changed course away from its planned flightpath and flown inland. The question was why?

The news the King's brother had been killed was quickly sent to London via the Air Ministry and on to the Prime Minister, Winston Churchill. In time, later that evening, King George VI and Queen Elizabeth would be informed of the deaths at Balmoral Castle. The duke's wife Princess Marina, the mother of his young children, would also be informed of the loss of her beloved husband.

The Royal Air Force and the Air Ministry were quick to arrange a Court of Inquiry, the aircraft's logbooks, servicing records, as well as those of the air crew were impounded. The personal effects were taken from the bodies and witnesses were located and evidence gathered. The crash scene was photographed and within a few days, the Court of Inquiry was convened.

It was assumed the entire crew and all their passengers had been killed – a total of fifteen men – but on the morning of 26 August, the injured rear gunner, Flight Sergeant Andrew Jack staggered into a crofter's cottage. Suffering from shock and burns, he was a terrible sight and gave the crofter's wife quite a shock. He had been missed by the initial rescuers, staggering off from his detached gun turret in the tail section before their arrival. With no idea where he was and suffering from his injuries, he spent the night curled up in the bracken, before waking and carrying on, following a stream downhill to the crofter's home.

Flight Sergeant Jack was taken to a local school converted for the war into the Bignold Hospital in Lybster near Dunbeath. There he was treated for his burns, cuts, bruises and shock. (The Bignold hospital had been based in Wick since 1930, but after being damaged by enemy air action, it moved to the school house in Lybster.)

Initially, Flight Sergeant Jack spoke freely about the flight, the crash and their Royal passenger, but on 29 August that stopped when he was visited by two senior officers of the Royal Navy and the Royal

Air Force. After their visit he became silent and would not discuss the incident with hospital staff, other patients, or even his own family when they visited him the same day.

The British and free worlds media were in a state of shock. The following day they reported the death of the duke and in total, fifteen men on board the stricken Sunderland. The *Daily Mirror* reported, *'Duke of Kent dies in crash flying to Iceland'*, while the *Daily Telegraph*'s headline proclaimed, *'Duke of Kent killed in air disaster'*. The *Daily Mail* ran a similar headline adding that all those on board had lost their lives.

Over the next few days, the newspapers ran a number of reports, some more detailed than others. The local Caithness newspapers were especially dedicated and managed to locate a number of those who had attended the crash site. Many of the national newspapers followed the local papers lead and published accounts of the crash and when the sole survivor, Andrew Jack, was found, his story was recounted in detail.

The Duke of Kent's funeral took place on the same day the rear gunner was visited in Bignold hospital by the senior military officers. The Court of Inquiry was quickly concluded and the matter was resolved. Somewhat oddly, the cause of the crash was deemed to be the very experienced captain (Flight Lieutenant Goyan) altering and changing his course for unknown reasons. The crew and their passengers were killed in a terrible accident.

The deceased were buried with full military honours at various locations around the nation and the Court of Inquiry's verdict was given a stamp of approval by the Chief Inspector of Accidents (RAF). The findings were reported to the King, the Prime Minister and to Parliament. The matter was now officially closed.

Over the following decades, conspiracy theories started to flourish. The most contentious theory surrounded the Deputy Führer, Rudolf Hess.

Hess had flown to Scotland in May 1941 and according to conspiracy theorists, he was being held prisoner in Scotland in August 1942. The conspiracy theorists claimed the Duke of Kent was to collect Hess from a location in Caithness and transport him to freedom, not in Iceland, but to neutral Sweden, all part of an attempted peace initiative.

Other conspiracy theorists believed the duke was murdered because he had been party to the arrival of Hess in May 1941. They believed the duke was involved in a long-term plan to make peace with Nazi Germany, together with the Duke of Hamilton and the exiled Polish Premier, General Wladyslaw Sikorski. They pointed to the death of General Sikorski in another suspicious plane crash off Gibraltar in 1943, as further evidence of a plot to remove these 'conspirators'. Some would go even further. It is known that Churchill and Free French leader Charles De Gaulle did not agree on a lot of plans and some claim an attempt to kill De Gaulle in another air crash in 1943 is evidence of British Intelligence Service involvement in assassinating such senior figures. (The aircraft's controls had been tampered with and the matter was later blamed on German Intelligence.)

Another conspiracy theory concerned the duke's unusual life before he married Princess Marina and became a respectable prince of the realm. Allegations of bisexuality, cross-dressing, drug taking, extra marital affairs and even an illegitimate child, meant Prince George was a *wild card* and to some in the establishment an embarrassment. However, that was all in the past and by 1942 he was a well-respected family man, doing his best for the war effort and his country. Would someone really harbour a grudge for so long and want to kill him?

The number of bodies reportedly found at the crash site also sprouted into another conspiracy theory, giving some credence to the belief that Rudolf Hess, or another unidentified person, had been on board the aircraft. There were claims of a mysterious extra passenger and one witness even claimed this was a woman.

When fifteen bodies were reportedly found, the rear gunner, Flight Sergeant Andrew Jack, had not yet stumbled into the crofter's cottage. Later, once he was reported to have survived, the newspapers continued reporting that fifteen bodies had been found at the crash site. This seemed to corroborate the conspiracy theories that Rudolf Hess or another unknown individual had been on board the aircraft and perished with the others.

In 1948, six years after the incident, local Caithness journalist Norman M. Glass published his book – *Caithness and the war 1939-1945*. In his text, he was still reflecting on the fact that all fifteen of the Sunderland's occupants were killed!

As time passed, the conspiracy theories grew in intensity with a number making a pretty compelling case for their own allegations, backed up by many hours of investigation and linking various documents and reports; but they always needed the proverbial smoking gun to complete their case, something they could never produce.

Other items, as we shall see in the evidence, pointed to stranger issues surrounding the duke and his royal entourage.

It is against this backdrop that I decided to re-examine this case. To do this we must first look at the conspiracy theories and determine whether they could be correct and what they are based upon, before looking at the main body of evidence...

Chapter Two

Prince George, Duke of Kent and his entourage

Prince George was born on 20 December 1902, at York Cottage on the Sandringham estate in Norfolk. His great-grandmother was Queen Victoria, his grandfather Edward VII and his father the future King George V. He was christened George Edward Alexander Edmund and at the time of his birth, he was fifth in line to the throne after his father and three elder brothers; Edward, Albert and Henry, two of whom would become King Edward VIII and King George VI.

After his secluded childhood within the royal household, the young Prince George went to a preparatory school in Broadstairs, Kent. He then followed his brothers into naval college, first at Osborne and then at Dartmouth (the current Royal Naval College).

The young Prince George missed seeing action during the First World War, but he served during the 1920s on HMS *Iron Duke* and HMS *Nelson*. In 1928 he served on board HMS *Durban* in the West Indies, before leaving the Royal Navy after a bout of illness. Unusually for a member of the royal family, he then joined the civil service, holding posts at the Foreign Office and the Home Office, but he remained a reserve naval officer.

In 1928 Prince George joined the Freemasons and by 1939, he was the Grand Master of the United Grand Lodge of England. His position in the Freemasons has always been one seen to be at odds with his alleged support, no matter how tacit, with the politics of the Nazi regime in Germany; especially as the fascist doctrine detested Freemasonry and sent many of its continental members to the concentration camps.

Prince George developed a keen interest in aviation and gained his flying (pilots) certificate in 1929. He regularly flew aircraft to engagements and was the first royal to fly across the Atlantic Ocean.

In the 1920s, Prince George is said to have had an affair with Kiki Preston, a New York socialite. Preston had many alleged affairs, including Rudolph Valentino and the Argentinian Jorge Ferrara. She is also alleged to have shared a three-way relationship with Prince George and another Argentine male, the bisexual Jose Uriburu.

Kiki Preston was known in society circles as 'the girl with the silver syringe', due to her drug taking habit (allegedly heroin) and there have long been claims she introduced Prince George to cocaine and morphine. This relationship was so concerning for the prince's family and the British authorities, his brother Edward (at the time prince of Wales) is said to have implored his brother to break off the relationship for his own good. The relationship eventually came to an end, but that did not conclude the repeated allegations of drug misuse against the prince.

There were also claims that Prince George had fathered an illegitimate child, which had been adopted by a family in the United States. Some believe there may even have been a second child, but this cannot be confirmed.

There were also claims which I cannot substantiate, that Prince George was arrested one night in the West End of London with playwright and actor Noel Coward, with whom he had a long-time friendship. The two men were alleged to have been arrested wandering around, while dressed in women's clothing. It is claimed the arrests were covered-up and unlike the tabloid media of today, the Fleet Street editors did not report such salacious gossip to protect the British Royal Family.

In 1985, the author Michael Thornton published a book called *Royal Feud*. In it, he alleged there had been a sexual relationship between Noel Coward and Prince George. Coward, who would attend the Duke of Kent's 1942 funeral, was later denied a knighthood and the newspaper magnate Lord Beaverbrook was alleged to have arranged the theft of intimate letters between Prince George and the actor.

In an article in the *Daily Mail* on 9 November 2007, Michael Thornton stated that Beaverbrook's daughter, Janet Kidd, had told him that she had seen the Duke of Kent's love letters in her father's safe after the war. However, they disappeared when her father died in 1964 and they have never been seen publicly.

Noel Coward was a close associate of Prince George for approximately nineteen years. It has also been alleged there was a relationship between Prince George and Coward's long-term partner Graham Payn, but this has always been denied.

In early 1931, Prince George escorted his brother, the Prince of Wales, on a three-month tour of South America. The tour was officially deemed a great success, but there were concerns at home, with the two brothers regularly photographed enjoying themselves at a series of parties and receptions, often surrounded by a number of beautiful young women.

In the 1930s Prince George was one of the most eligible bachelors in the world, although he was surrounded by some controversy.

In 1934, George married Princess Marina of Greece and Denmark at Westminster Abbey and King George V bestowed upon his son, the title of Duke of Kent. Within two years the happy couple had two children, Prince Edward, the current Duke of Kent (since 2023) and his sister Princess Alexandra.

Despite the happy family on show to the public, there were continuing rumours of extra marital affairs. One such alleged liaison being with the actress and musical star Jessie Matthews, as well as another with Margaret Whigham. Margaret Whigham would later marry Ian Douglas Campbell, the 11th Duke of Argyll and become embroiled in her own sexual allegations after the war.

Prince George was always close to his brother, the new King Edward VIII and in June 1936, he was appointed his aide-de-camp.

Edward VIII has been well-documented as being an associate and in many ways a supporter of the fledgling Nazi regime in 1930s Germany; and his brother Prince George, Duke of Kent may well have had similar thoughts.

The British Royal Family were still reeling from the murder in 1918 of their relations, Tzar Nicholas and his family at the hands of the Bolsheviks. Like many aristocratic families across Europe, they feared the spread of communism. The Nazi party were vociferously anti-communist and to the royal families of Europe, must have seemed a perfect bastion against the advances of the Bolshevik hoards.

Baron William de Ropp had fought as a Royal Flying Corps pilot in the First World War. In the 1920s, he worked for the Bristol Aircraft Company and went to Germany, where he met with ardent Nazi, Alfred Rosenberg. Rosenberg sought to cultivate contacts in Britain, especially those within the upper echelons of society, so he was overjoyed to hear that William De Ropp had been introduced to Prince George, the Duke of Kent, as well as others in the aristocratic establishment who favoured appeasement with Germany.

These new contacts led to De Ropp becoming an adviser to Adolf Hitler and Rudolf Hess. However, Baron William de Ropp was an MI6 agent and sending information back to London, while the Nazis believed he was assisting them. There is no doubt he would have reported back to London any apparent interest in Berlin regarding the Duke of Kent and his extended aristocratic circle.

In early 1935, William de Ropp was sent to London by Alfred Rosenberg for a meeting with King George V, however the monarch sent his adviser to the meeting – reportedly the Duke of Kent. The two men chatted for three hours and Rosenberg is said to have later briefed Hitler about the duke's and therefore the King's views... whatever they were.

In the book *Mask of Treachery*, a book about Anthony Blunt the Royal Art Historian and Soviet agent; the author John Costello claims that the pre-war dialogue between King Edward VIII, the Duke of Kent and Hitler went through Prince Philip of Hesse – himself a Nazi, in an unofficial manner. Various letters went back and forth according to the author and at the end of the war in 1945, Anthony Blunt was dispatched on the directions of King George VI to recover the letters from the Hesse family before they fell into the wrong hands.

In his book, Costello also touches upon the possibility of a relationship between Prince George, the Duke of Kent, and Anthony Blunt. The pair shared a love of art and originally met at Trinity College, Cambridge University.

The links between Prince George and the Nazi regime appear to have been quite complicated, but with his brother Edward's close association via Wallis Simpson to Joachim von Ribbentrop, the German Ambassador to London. There were certainly plenty of avenues for the likes of Hess and Rosenberg to communicate with this upper echelon of British society.

In December 1936, King Edward VIII abdicated to marry the American divorcee, Wallis Simpson. Following his brother's abdication, Prince George, Duke of Kent, became aide-de-camp to his other brother, the newly crowned King George VI.

With a number of German relatives, the Duke of Kent remained in contact with some of them, especially with Prince Philip of Hesse and there are indications in Foreign Office files in the UK National Archives (references FO800/313 and FO800/316) that he was still in contact and wanting to visit Germany in the twelve months leading up to the start of the Second World War. He was reportedly involved in a bid to ensure peace as late as July 1939, with a plan whereby he would negotiate directly with Adolf Hitler. This was allegedly with the full support of his brother King George VI, who is said to have put the plan to Prime Minister Neville Chamberlain and Lord Halifax, the Secretary of State for Foreign Affairs.

In 1937, Prince George, Duke of Kent, was granted commissions in the Army (as a Colonel) and the Royal Air Force (as a Group Captain).

In 1938, the Duke of Kent was appointed a member of the Privy Council to King George VI. Other members of the council included the Duke of Norfolk, who was married to Lavinia Strutt, the sister of Prince George's equerry Pilot Officer Michael Strutt, (who would also die in the air crash in 1942). Another member of the Council was the Duke of Sutherland who owned Dunrobin House in Caithness, the location the duke's body would be taken after its recovery from the hillside.

Other Privy Council members who feature in this book include the Duke of Hamilton (Douglas Douglas-Hamilton), himself an RAF officer in Scotland and Harold Balfour, the 1st Baron Balfour of Inchyre.

Balfour was a former First World War fighter ace and holder of the Military Cross and bar; he would be the Under Secretary of State for Air under Sir Archibald Sinclair in August 1942. Sir Archibald Sinclair as we shall see, also plays a prominent part in this story.

The alleged pro-Nazi aristocratic leanings among those surrounding the Duke of Kent and the King can be further evidenced by two other members of the King's Privy Council – the Duke of Buccleuch (Walter Douglas Scott) and the Marquess of Lothian (Phillip Kerr).

The Duke of Buccleuch was compelled to resign as Steward to the King, after he had attended Adolf Hitler's 50th birthday party in 1939.

The Marquess of Lothian was a proponent of the view that Germany had been unfairly treated after the Treaty of Versailles. He had also met with Adolf Hitler, Rudolf Hess and Joachim von Ribbentrop in Germany in 1935. Lothian was sent to Washington DC as British Ambassador in 1939, probably to distance him from Europe, but he died after an illness in December 1940 aged fifty-eight years.

One associate of the Duke of Kent who was not a member of the Privy Council was Victor Cavendish-Bentinck, the Marquess of Titchfield, son of the Duke of Portland. Victor was Chair of the Joint Intelligence Committee of the Chiefs of Staff. His father's sister, Cecilia, was Queen Elizabeth's mother (mother-in-law of King George), making the marquess a relation to Prince George who was also the Queen's brother-in-law.

The Duke of Portland owned the land around the eventual crash site at Eagles Rock in Caithness, as well as Braemore Lodge and Langwell House near Berriedale and the Berriedale River. The marquess and these locations all feature in this story.

It is clear the British authorities were aware of the Duke of Windsor (Edward VIII) and the Duke of Kent's pro-German sympathies, but with a possible war looming, they needed to be removed from the political equation.

In 1937 the newly abdicated Edward, Duke of Windsor, toured Germany while living in France. He was photographed meeting Hitler and other high-ranking Nazi officials in Berlin, something that caused great unrest in Britain; especially as some believe photographs even showed him giving a Nazi salute.

In October 1938, the Duke of Kent was appointed Governor-General of Australia. He was due to take his position at Governor's House in November 1939, but with the advent of war, the appointment was postponed. Whether the appointment was a bid to send him well away from Germany is debatable.

In early 1940, Edward, Duke of Windsor, was sent to the Bahamas as Governor, effectively removing him from Europe and the Nazi sphere of influence.

It is strange, but were the two pro-German brothers to be sent well away from the German sphere of influence, while the Marquess of Lothian was sent to Washington DC?

The Duke of Kent had a passion for art and was a keen collector of paintings. In this capacity, he is said to have regularly met with and associated with the Finnish art historian Tancred Borenius, a man who advised him on his art collection and acquisitions (rather like Anthony Blunt). The men met throughout the late 1930s and into the wartime period. What the Duke of Kent may or may not have known, was that Tancred Borenius was an alleged MI6 agent (while Anthony Blunt was an MI5 officer and Soviet agent).

In June 1939, Prince George was promoted to the rank of Rear Admiral in the Royal Navy, Major General in the army and Air Vice-Marshal in the Royal Air Force.

When the Second World War started three months later, the duke served for a short time in Naval Intelligence, while his wife Princess Marina, became Commandant of the Women's Royal Naval Service – the Wrens.

In April 1940, King George agreed to the duke transferring to a role in the Royal Air Force as an Air Vice-Marshal, but the following month he reduced his rank to Group Captain to become a Staff Officer in RAF Training Command.

In June 1940, the duke was selected by the new Prime Minister Winston Churchill to fly to Portugal to visit Dr Antonio Salazar, the nation's premier in Lisbon. The official purpose of the visit was to celebrate the 800th Anniversary of the nation's independence, but in reality, it was a diplomatic visit for the duke to confirm the neutral government's preference for the Allies.

The Duke of Kent returned to Britain on 2 July 1940, just before the Battle of Britain. He remained in the country and appears to have kept a low profile while his country fought for its survival.

The duke continued to hanker for a role in which he could assist the war effort. He therefore joined the Welfare Section of the RAF Inspector General's Staff and was promoted to Air Commodore. Between late June 1941 and his death in August 1942, the duke toured numerous RAF bases checking on the welfare of airmen and WAAFs. He threw himself whole heartedly into his new role in welfare. He was often seen visiting RAF bases unannounced and with little fanfare, engaging all ranks in conversation and checking they were happy. The media were quick to identify his good work and sing his praises.

In the UK National Archives, there are two files (reference AIR 33/7 and AIR 2/5452) which give some details of his welfare visits. Some of the documents contained within those files indicate his concerns about NAAFI facilities, billet heating and even providing a carpet in the airmen's billets. His position and views clearly resonated among the hierarchy of the RAF, who did their utmost to respond in an expeditious manner.

In late August and September 1941, the Duke of Kent travelled to Canada and the United States to check on the Empire Flying Training programme which was training pilots and aircrew for the RAF. He was accompanied by Lieutenant John Lowther his private secretary, Wing Commander Sir Louis Greig and Inspector James Evans, his police protection officer. The media followed him around and numerous accounts and photographs appeared in the British, Canadian and American newspapers detailing his meetings with the US President Franklin D. Roosevelt in New York State and later in Washington DC.

On 4 July 1942, Prince George and Princess Marina were overjoyed to have a second son – Prince Michael of Kent. He was born at the family home at Coppins House, Iver in Buckinghamshire. The rest of the month of July appears to have been spent with the family and a christening took place in the private chapel of Windsor Castle, on 4 August. The proud new parents invited President Roosevelt and his wife to be godparents, but being unable to attend, King George VI stood as proxy for them.

On 13 August, Queen Mary, the new baby's grandmother, arrived at Coppins House and the renowned royal photographer Cecil Beaton took a series of images which were widely published in the national media.

Although he was at home with his young family, the duke was about to fly to Iceland on official business. In the Royal Archives at Windsor Castle there is a small file detailing the plans for what would become the fatal flight. (See Royal archives reference GDKH/PRIV/19.)

The first typed letter (unsigned) and marked confidential, is dated 31 July 1942. It states that during the previous July (1941), arrangements had been made for the Duke of Kent to go to Iceland, but this was cancelled at the last moment owing to some differences of opinion in the (British) cabinet. However, the visit was once again on the agenda and due to take place in August, with the King and Winston Churchill agreeing to it.

By this time in August 1942, British forces had all but withdrawn from Iceland and the American armed forces had taken over responsibility for the defence of Iceland and its facilities. This followed the entry into the war of the United States following the attack on Pearl Harbor nine months before.

Another letter in the Royal Archives file, this time dated 11 August 1942, was sent to Colonel T. Edgeworth-Johnstone at the War Office in Whitehall, London. This included an outline of the planned visit which would include contact with what remained of British forces on the island. This would include members of the

Royal Navy, RAF and the Army. The letter informed the Colonel that a draft programme had been received from the US forces and it was noted this included British Army units as well as the Royal Navy and the RAF. For this reason, the Colonel was being informed of the duke's visit. The letter apologised for the late notice of the visit, indicating that as the involvement of a British Army unit was not initially anticipated, the Colonel had not been informed earlier. The letter concluded with an invite for a representative of the Colonel to attend a meeting at the Foreign Office to finalise the programme for the duke's visit to Iceland.

On 15 August, another typed letter was sent by the duke's private secretary (almost certainly Lieutenant John Lowther RNVR) to the Private Secretary to the Minister of War Transport in London. This letter detailed the travel arrangements for the Duke of Kent and his party of five, who would be travelling to Inverness on the 7:20 train from Euston Station (actually the 1920 hours sleeper train), on Monday, 24 August 1942.

The party of five appears to have included the Special Branch protection officer for the duke, but he is now known to have returned to London, as the duke would be the responsibility of the military once on board the RAF Sunderland.

On the same day, the duke's Private Secretary also wrote to a Mr T. Harrison, the Station Master at Euston Station. The letter outlined the travel arrangements, adding that the party needed sleeper arrangements on the train and asked the Station Master to see whether arrangements could be made for the train to run as near to time as possible, as the duke was to fly north from Inverness. It added, if the train was late, the duke could not reach his destination before dark and the whole visit would have to be postponed.

This letter I would suggest, appears to be something of a breach of security. It would not take much effort for German intelligence to work out that if the duke was flying north from Inverness, it had to be via flying boat or large transport aircraft. In addition, if he was travelling north and had to get there before dark, the likely destination was probably Norway, Northern Russia or Iceland. With Norway in German hands and the likelihood of a British royal travelling to communist Russia very unlikely, the only viable destination was Iceland.

On Wednesday, 19 August, a letter was sent to Mr J.W. Stafford at the Passport Office in Queen Anne's Gate, London, asking whether the royal party would require their passports and visas for a visit to Iceland.

Although no written reply is included in the Windsor archives file, it appears a reply was received requesting the passports of the royal party be sent to the Passport Office in preparation for the visit. This can be evidenced with another typed letter to Mr Stafford two days later on Friday, 21 August enclosing the four passports of the duke, his private secretary, his equerry and valet. The letter also confirmed they were leaving London on the evening of 24 August and needed the return of the passports as soon as possible before that date.

The final letter in the file is dated 22 August 1942, and was sent to Commander Harold Campbell RN, Equerry and Groom of the Robes to King George VI, who was at Balmoral Castle at the time. This letter again appears to have been written by the Duke of Kent's Private Secretary – Lieutenant John Lowther.

This letter stated the Duke of Kent would be flying back from Iceland on Tuesday, 1 September 1942 and should arrive at Invergordon mid-afternoon. An aircraft would then fly the duke to Dyce where a car would be waiting for him, to take him to Balmoral Castle. The duke would only be accompanied by his valet and the cars chauffeur upon his return to Scotland.

According to the letter, on Sunday, 5 September, the duke was planning to drive to Dalmeny. This, it is believed, was to visit

Dalmeny House, the home of the Earl of Rosebery and stepfather of his equerry Pilot Officer Michael Strutt.

These were the plans of the Duke of Kent for his trip to Iceland and the days following his return.

As an active member of the royal family, Prince George, Duke of Kent, had his personal attendants. On the 25 August 1942 flight, he was escorted by an entourage consisting of:

Lieutenant John Arthur Lowther MVO, aged thirty-one and the Private Secretary to the duke. He was a member of the Royal Naval Volunteer Reserve and he was married with one daughter. He was a Member of the Royal Victorian Order (MVO) which was bestowed upon him by King George VI.

John Lowther was the son of Christopher W. Lowther and grandson of James W. Lowther, the 1st Viscount of Ullswater, a former Speaker in the House of Commons. The family home was at Campsea Ashe in Suffolk.

Pilot Officer the Honourable C.V. Michael Strutt, service number 5/15062, was twenty-seven years of age and a member of the Royal Canadian Air Force. He was the duke's equerry and son of Lord Belper, Lord Lieutenant of Nottinghamshire and brother of Lavinia, the Duchess of Norfolk. Michael Strutt was single, his mother having re-married the 6th Earl of Rosebery, residing at Dalmeny House in Scotland. As already mentioned, it appears the Earl was due to be visited by the duke upon his return from Iceland, possibly because of his position as Regional Commissioner for Civil Defence in 1942.

Michael Strutt had enlisted as an air gunner at the start of the war and was quickly commissioned. He was only on the

Sunderland because the duke's regular equerry, Squadron Leader Peter J. Ferguson, was recovering from surgery to remove a cannon shell splinter from his back, a wound he sustained as a fighter pilot with 602 Squadron in August 1940. (The duke had his own personal surgeon operate on his equerry to remove the troublesome splinter.)

Leading Aircraftsman John Walter Hales service number 927117, was twenty-five years of age and came from Norfolk. He was married and his wife lived in Littlethorpe, Yorkshire. He was valet to the duke on this trip, only being appointed a short time before the flight.

Another equerry, Sir Sidney Herbert (later the 16th Earl of Pembroke), was also missing from this trip, although the reasons for his absence are unknown. After the duke's death, Herbert became the Private Secretary to the Duchess of Kent.

As we have seen, over the decades conspiracy theorists have sought to claim the Duke of Kent was not attending Iceland in August 1942, but undertaking some nefarious activity possibly linked to Sweden and Rudolf Hess. The fact he clearly had some German sympathies has been utilised in a bid to corroborate the allegations regarding Rudolf Hess, but the documents contained in the Royal Archives file at Windsor Castle, clearly show a detailed plan for the Icelandic trip and even the duke's post visit plans, when he arrived back in Scotland.

Although many have suspected the Duke of Kent was engaged in repatriating Rudolf Hess or a peace initiative, surely these documents disprove those theories, although many a die-hard conspiracy theorist would undoubtedly claim they could be forgeries!

The Duke of Kent, in the years leading up to the Second World War, was apparently engaged in a bid to avert another major conflict. Under Neville Chamberlain that aim may have been applauded and supported, but many historians believe Winston Churchill did not take too kindly to these actions and may have disliked the Duke of Kent's activities. However, if the Duke of Kent's new position as Governor of Australia in 1938 was meant to remove him from the continent of Europe, it was decided by the Chamberlain government and not by Winston Churchill. The same can also be said about the early 1940 move to send the Duke of Windsor to the Bahamas. Chamberlain had been replaced by Churchill on 10 May 1940; could it be the meddling of the two royal princes was bothersome to both Chamberlain and Churchill?

The behaviour and allegations against the Duke of Kent were very unusual. The claims vary from party animal to cross-dresser, an alleged bisexual who took hard drugs and allegedly fathered at least one illegitimate child, not to forget his pro-German sympathies and contacts. His actions for approximately fifteen years prior to his death, were a dream for anyone looking for a motive in a conspiracy theory.

In the next chapter, we shall examine the Rudolf Hess theory in more detail. This is a conspiracy that has gained notoriety in recent decades, with numerous books and documentaries proclaiming evidence for the duke's involvement, which they believe led to his ultimate death; possibly with Rudolf Hess being the missing body at the crash scene.

vi   The Death of Prince George, Duke of Kent, 1942

Gibraltar in 1943. Both plots, it has been alleged, were the work
of the British intelligence services, but taken alongside the mysterious
circumstances surrounding the capture and subsequent death
of Rudolf Hess in May 1941.

Some commentators have speculated that the Duke of Kent was
an embarrassment to the nation and the Royal Family, a man who
was reportedly bisexual, had a number of affairs, some of which

Chapter Three

The Rudolf Hess conspiracy

D espite the allegations of drug taking, extra-marital affairs
and gay relationships, the one conspiracy theory that has
gained momentum in recent decades, is that involving the
Deputy Führer Rudolf Hess.

The amount of material available regarding this conspiracy theory is
endless, and various books, newspapers and television documentaries
have claimed Rudolf Hess came to Britain in an attempt to broker a
peace deal in May 1941. This claim alone is spectacular, but some now
include the Duke of Kent in that plan, while others have claimed it to
be linked to the duke's ultimate fatal demise.

We must understand these claims before we look in detail at the
crash of the duke's Short Sunderland in August 1942. Over the next
few pages, I shall outline these allegations.

On the late evening of 10 May 1941, a single twin engine
Messerschmitt 110 was detected by the RDF chain (radar)
approaching the Northumbrian coastline. The aircraft flying at very
low level, flew inland near Alnwick Castle, the seat of the Duke of
Northumberland and on towards southern Scotland. Two Spitfires
from No. 72 Squadron, based at RAF Acklington near Alnwick,
were vectored towards the lone raider, but neither made contact with
the fast-moving Messerschmitt in the dim light of dusk.

The Messerschmitt dropped to an even lower altitude, some
reports suggesting just fifty feet, as it sped across the border
countryside, before being positively identified by a member of the
Observer Corps as a Messerschmitt 110. It continued onwards in a

north-west and westerly direction in the gathering darkness. Its flight path perplexed the RAF fighter controllers who knew the enemy heavy fighter was near, if not beyond the limits of its endurance and fuel capacity. Where could it be going?

The enemy machine was continually tracked as it headed towards Ayr on the west coast of Scotland and then seemed to turn around. A Boulton-Paul Defiant of No. 141 Squadron was scrambled and the crew vectored towards the Messerschmitt, but not before the enemy aircraft crashed about twelve miles from Dungavel House, the home of the Duke of Hamilton.

The pilot of the Messerschmitt – Rudolf Hess – parachuted to earth at Floors Farm, Waterfoot, Eaglesham, where he was detained by a farmer named David McLean. Hess did not try to escape, but calmly introduced himself as Hauptmann Alfred Horn, before saying he had an important message for the Duke of Hamilton. Hess repeatedly told his captors that his name was Alfred Horn and that he needed to speak with the Duke of Hamilton. He was conveyed by the local Home Guard to a scout hall, before being passed on to the regular Army and conveyed to Mayhill barracks in Glasgow. After his arrival Hess continued to demand an audience with the Duke of Hamilton.

The Duke of Hamilton was the duty Wing Commander at RAF Turnhouse near Edinburgh and was aware of this unusual flight and the subsequent crash near his home. The fact there was no rear gunner on the aircraft was also a bit of a mystery for intelligence officers (the Messerschmitt normally having a two-man crew).

The Duke of Hamilton was said to have been surprised when he heard the German pilot – Hauptmann Alfred Horn – was demanding to see him. The duke travelled the next morning to Mayhill Barracks in Glasgow and spoke alone with the German pilot.

When the duke met with the pilot, Rudolf Hess finally revealed his true identity, announcing that he was on a mission of humanity and that Hitler wanted to end the war. Very little was recorded of what passed between the two men that morning and whatever was recorded, it is still under lock and key or even shredded.

The Duke of Hamilton left the barracks and travelled to examine the wreckage of the Messerschmitt 110 with an RAF Intelligence Officer, he then made arrangements to meet with Winston Churchill as soon as possible.

The Duke of Hamilton met Winston Churchill at Ditchley Park in Oxfordshire, a location he used as a weekend retreat. The duke briefed the premier about the arrival of Hess and the two men moved immediately on to London, where they met and briefed senior members of the Cabinet. There is no doubt the arrival of Rudolf Hess caught the British authorities completely off guard – or did it?

After the Cabinet meeting, the Duke of Hamilton was sent with Ivone Kirkpatrick, an expert in foreign affairs who had previously met with the Deputy Führer, to positively identify their German visitor.

Hess told the two men that Hitler had expansionist plans, but wanted to allow Britain to keep its Empire. He would allow the Empire to continue if the British gave him a free hand in Europe. These comments echoed those made by Hitler before the Battle of Britain, when he had previously sought peace.

Rudolf Hess claimed to know the Duke of Hamilton from an earlier meeting, but the duke would always deny ever having previously met with the Deputy Führer in pre-war Germany, especially during a visit he made in the 1930s.

The British were apparently completely confused by Rudolf Hess and did not know what to do with him, but it was clear, Winston Churchill was in no mood for a peaceful solution.

In Germany, the national radio network broadcast news of the flight to Britain and it claimed Hess was suffering a mental illness. Back in Britain, Hess was moved around from location to location, even staying under guard for a short time in the Tower of London.

He is alleged to have even been held at various locations in Wales and Scotland.

While the British and German people were given the above accounts, they were unaware of some previous alleged acts.

The Duke of Hamilton has been identified by some as being a member of the Anglo-German Fellowship, an organization which wanted better relations and trade between the two old foes before the war. His family have always denied this, but the duke had been to Germany pre-war when he was still the Marquess of Clydesdale.

An avid aviator like Prince George, the marquess had attended the Berlin Olympics in 1936 and met a number of senior Nazis including Hermann Goring the head of the Luftwaffe. He attended a dinner hosted by Joachim von Ribbentrop, the German Ambassador to London, at which he was introduced to Adolf Hitler and probably Henrich Himmler. However, the Duke of Hamilton would always deny ever meeting Deputy Führer Rudolf Hess at the function.

Hermann Goring, as head of the new embryonic Luftwaffe, invited Hamilton to inspect his new air force. This it is said, was due to the duke's professional interest in aviation, but he would later claim he was interested and wanted to gain information, which he later passed on to the British authorities upon his return.

Whilst in Germany, the Duke of Hamilton is said to have met with the student Albrecht Haushofer. His father, Professor Karl Haushofer, a former army general, had studied geopolitics with Rudolf Hess at university in Munich and when his associate rose to become Deputy Führer of Nazi Germany, the academic became his personal foreign affairs advisor.

It is claimed that on 31 August 1940, at the height of the Battle of Britain, Rudolf Hess met with Karl Haushofer, the father of Albrecht. Karl Haushofer allegedly told Hess that he believed King George VI wanted peace and was very much opposed to Winston Churchill, who many in the British establishment saw as a war monger. Karl

Haushofer told Hess that he believed he could make contact with the King, via the Duke of Hamilton who had met his son Albrecht before the war.

Hess of course knew of the views of the abdicated King Edward VIII and his brother the Duke of Kent via Rosenberg and De Ropp. This new information now included the Duke of Hamilton and King George VI.

Rudolf Hess agreed to an approach being made, and in September 1940 Haushofer wrote to the Duke of Hamilton via an intermediary in Lisbon, Portugal, and a woman in Cambridge, England. The letter however was intercepted by the British security services and the Duke of Hamilton did not see its contents or allegedly know of it, until March 1941, when he was finally approached by the intelligence services. (It must be assumed during that period of time MI5 had been checking the duke's associates and his own personal political views.)

There have long been allegations the Duke of Hamilton was sympathetic to pre-war German policy and aims, but at the same time there have been some claims he was engaged with MI6, in a bid to lure Rudolf Hess to Britain under the false impression the nation was seeking peace. Whatever the truth, Rudolf Hess thought he would receive a warm reception and flew the specially adapted Messerschmitt 110 to Scotland. Some historians also claim this flight was made with the authority and knowledge of Adolf Hitler and possibly Hermann Goring, as the aircraft had extra fuel tanks for the flight, although many historians doubt these claims.

Prince George, the Duke of Kent, becomes embroiled in this conspiracy theory via a number of different avenues. The first is his friendship with the Duke of Hamilton and his connections via De Ropp and Rosenberg.

The Duke of Hamilton was a distant relation of Prince George and had been the commanding officer of No. 602 (City of Glasgow) Squadron, Royal Auxiliary Air Force from 1931 to 1936. After departing, he always maintained a close relationship with the unit and the Duke of Kent's equerry, Squadron Leader Peter John Ferguson, had also served with the unit before being injured in combat in 1940.

The next alleged link concerns the Finnish art historian Tancred Borenius, an MI6 agent who is claimed by some to have been involved in luring Hess to Britain.

John Harris and his co-author, Richard Wimbourn, have written a number of books about the Hess affair, linking the Duke of Kent to the peace plan and directly to Tancred Borenius, who assisted the Duke of Kent with his art collection. (See: *Rudolf Hess Treachery & Deception, Rudolf Hess a new technical analysis of the Hess flight, May 1941* and *Rudolf Hess: the British illusion of peace.*)

Polish Premier General Wladyslaw Sikorski is another name thrown into the Hess conspiracy with links to the Duke of Kent. After his arrival in England, General Sikorski took up residence at Inver Lodge, literally next door to the Duke of Kent's home at The Coppins in Buckinghamshire. Without doubt the two men knew one another and met from time to time, and in recent decades there have been claims that Sikorski even offered the Duke of Kent the throne of Poland in a bid to avert post war Soviet domination of his homeland.

Sikorski set about managing the Free Polish forces, many of whom were based at a new headquarters at the Bridge of Earn, Perthshire and at Eastend House in Lanarkshire. Historians and researchers like John Harris and Richard Wimbourn have claimed there were links between Sikorski and the Duke of Kent. Another interesting point is that after Rudolf Hess arrived in Scotland on 10 May 1941, Sikorski flew into nearby Prestwick airport the following morning, a distance of about twenty-five miles from the German's landing site.

What is even more mysterious is the fact the Polish Consul, Roman Battaglia, was the first official to speak with Hess in the Busby Scout Hall, where he was initially detained by the Home

Guard. How did he know Hess was there and who informed him of his arrival? Who gave permission for him to speak to Hess?

General Sikorski would later die in a B-24 Liberator crash, just after take-off from Gibraltar airport in July 1943. Only the pilot, a Czechoslovakian airman, survived as the bomber sank to the sea floor. Many have long contended this was an act of sabotage, while others believe it was a simple tragic accident. Those who contend this was a deliberate act, cite the possible connection with Rudolf Hess, while others point to the politics with Churchill regarding plans for the general's homeland after the conclusion of the war. Whatever the cause, some have drawn parallels between the fatal crash of Sikorski and that of the Duke of Kent the year before, pointing out their friendship and the joint allegations surrounding Rudolf Hess.

In their book, *Double Standards: The Rudolf Hess cover-up*, the authors Picknett, Prince and Prior repeated many of these claims, but with some astounding additions.

Robert Brydon the authors' researcher states in the book, that in 1975 during a conversation with Elizabeth Byrd at her home in East Lothian, the former secretary to Lord Malcolm, brother of the Duke of Hamilton, said Lord Malcolm had: 'Implied his brother (the Duke of Hamilton) had taken the flak for the whole Hess affair in order to protect others higher up the social scale. He strongly hinted that the cover-up was necessary to protect the reputations of members of the Royal Family.'

Lord Malcolm Douglas-Hamilton was also an RAF officer during the war, reaching a similar rank to his brother, commanding and flying De Havilland Mosquitos with No. 540 Squadron, with whom he was awarded a Distinguished Flying Cross. However, recent research indicates that in the 1930s he may have had links to Franco's Nationalists in Spain and flew a De Havilland Rapide aircraft to them in 1936. General Franco was a fascist and friend of Adolf Hitler who supported him in the Spanish Civil War.

Elizabeth Byrd later introduced Robert Brydon to another elderly lady who did not want to be identified in the forthcoming book. She was therefore given the pseudonym of Mrs Abbot. She claimed to have been stationed in May 1941 at Dungavel House. She added the house had its own airstrip which was often used as a relief landing ground for RAF pilots from nearby airfields. It had temporary runway lights which could be switched on and off from a switch in the house.

Mrs Abbot then claimed that on the night of 10 May 1941, as they were leaving the house, she was surprised to see the landing lights illuminated, but a few minutes later, they were extinguished.

Mrs Abbot later enquired why the runway lights had been switched on and said she was told this was as a result of a phone call from Bowhill, the home of the Duke of Buccleuch (the member of the Privy Council who had to resign his post in 1939 for attending Adolf Hitler's birthday party). She also claimed they were quickly turned off by a group of strangers who had entered Dungavel House that night.

Robert Brydon and the authors tried to obtain some corroboration for this account and located another woman who was said to have worked at the house, but she also wished to remain anonymous and they assigned her the pseudonym Mrs Baker.

Mrs Baker confirmed in conversation with author Stephen Prior in 1996, that the runway lights had been illuminated on the night of 10 May 1941. She also claimed an unknown aircraft had passed overhead – the inference clearly being this could have been Hess in his Messerschmitt 110. Mrs Baker then casually added two significant pieces of information according to Prior: She first stated that in 1941, two packing cases bearing the marks of the Messerschmitt aircraft factory had been delivered to Dungavel House and stored in the hangar. She was told, but could not confirm this, that they contained 'petrol tanks.' This was an astounding allegation and one that is somewhat hard to believe, but her final comment was even more astounding...

Mrs Baker claimed, 'The Duke and his people were in the kennels,' adding that this group included a number of Polish personnel. (The kennels was a small cottage next to the airstrip.) Researchers have confirmed the Duke of Hamilton was actually at RAF Turnhouse that night and this was pointed out to Mrs Baker by Stephen Prior. To his surprise she retorted, 'Not the Duke of Hamilton, the Duke of Kent.'

Was Prince George, the Duke of Kent really part of the peace plan reception committee at Dungavel House, the night Hess arrived in May 1941? Historians and researchers have always been unable to pin down exactly where the Duke of Kent was on the evening of 10 May 1941.

No diaries are available for the Duke of Kent and when I asked the Royal Archives, they told me they did not hold any diaries for the duke and if they did exist, they must have remained with his family.

However, in his article for *After the Battle* magazine, published in 1982, David J. Smith states that the Duke of Kent was at RAF Sumburgh on the Shetlands on Friday, 9 May 1941 and at RAF Wick in Caithness on Monday, 12 May. (This was also previously stated by Norman N. Glass, a local journalist, in his 1948 book: *Caithness and the war 1939-1945*.) We also know from photographic evidence, that the duke visited No. 8 Air Gunnery School at RAF Evanton, coincidentally just a mile or two along the coast from RAF Alness and the Cromarty Firth, on Tuesday, 13 May 1941.

The interesting fact is that none of these RAF stations Operations Record Books, state they received a visit from the Duke of Kent around this time. This seems odd, but we must remember, the duke liked to carry out these visits with little fanfare or announcement. It therefore appears very likely Prince George, the Duke of Kent was staying in Scotland over the weekend when Rudolf Hess arrived.

To try and confirm this assertion, I made a Freedom of Information Act application to the Metropolitan Police, asking if they could inform me where the duke and his police protection officer (Inspector James Evans) where between the 5 and 11 May 1941. If I could locate his protection officer, it was likely the duke would be close-by. I was informed by them that despite checking a number of indices and records, they could not find any of the information I requested, although to be fair it related to an event over eighty years ago.

The conspiracy theorists have always pointed to the fact Rudolf Hess flew over Alnwick Castle in Northumberland, the ancestral home of the Duke of Northumberland. Northumberland was married to the disgraced Duke of Buccleuch's daughter Lady Elizabeth.

After Hess flew over Alnwick, a phone call was said to have been received at Dungavel House from the Duke of Buccleuch's other residence at Bowhill, directing them to switch on the airstrip runway lights. Throw into this mix the high probability the Duke of Kent was in Scotland at the time and the Duke of Buccleuch's sister Alice – Alice was married to the Duke of Kent's brother, the Duke of Gloucester – and this conspiracy theory starts to gather some degree of plausibility.

This is just a summary of the claims surrounding the arrival of Rudolf Hess in May 1941, his links to the Duke of Hamilton and other members of the British aristocracy, the involvement of Tancred Borenius, General Sikorski and more importantly for our story, the Duke of Kent.

The problem with the accounts of the two elderly ladies, employees of Dungavel House, is we do not know who they are. Both women were given pseudonyms by the authors of the book and both are now believed to be deceased. Can we really believe their accounts?

In 1996 when Stephen Prior spoke to Mrs Baker it was fifty-five years after the event, was she so fearful of a reprisal for talking, so long after the alleged event? She was likely to have been in her late

70s or older in 1996, an age when many elderly people are happy to finally give up their secrets.

The alleged links between Rudolf Hess and the Duke of Kent do not end at this point, for in the book *Double Standards*, the authors claim that on the day the Duke of Kent died, Hess was actually in Scotland. He was alleged to have been housed at either Braemore Lodge on the Duke of Portland's estate in Caithness, or in a cottage next to Loch More, about halfway between Dunbeath and Thurso in Caithness. This latter location was on the estate of the Secretary of State for Air, Sir Archibald Sinclair, a man who would also become embroiled in the inquiry into the loss of the Sunderland. Sinclair had served in the army during the First World War and as Winston Churchill's second in command in early 1916.

Archibald Sinclair went into politics like his friend and army commander, becoming a Liberal MP. In 1939, he was offered a place in Neville Chamberlain's government, but declined it. When Winston Churchill took the country's reins, Archibald Sinclair became Secretary of State for Air.

Both Braemore Lodge and Loch More are a short distance from the crash site of the Sunderland in August 1942, Braemore Lodge being less than three miles up the Berriedale Water from the crash site on Eagles Rock.

It is because of these facts and the previous allegations from May 1941, that many conspiracy theorists believe the Short Sunderland 'M' for Mother crashed while assisting in the attempted repatriation of Rudolf Hess and a peace deal with Germany. They claim the Duke of Kent, as a member of the peace initiative, was on board to escort Hess back home, but unfortunately the aircraft crashed and all bar one crew member were killed instantly.

The body of Rudolf Hess was never found at the crash site, but conspiracy theorists believe his body was hidden from the public. Evidence for this allegation comes from the press reports that there were fifteen bodies found at the crash site and all those on board had been killed. Reports stating there had been fifteen fatalities continued, even after Flight Sergeant Andrew Jack was found to be alive.

The conspiracy claims, however, go further with allegations a doppelganger replaced Hess, by now the allegedly deceased Deputy Führer. This man was jailed at the Nuremburg trials and spent the rest of his life in Spandau Prison in Berlin. Many people believe Hess spent the rest of his life incarcerated while others were released, to prevent him telling the truth. He would die in August 1987 as an infirm and frail 93-year-old, but some people have suggested, outlandishly, that he was murdered to ensure he kept his secret.

While the allegations around the arrival of Hess in 1941 could to a point be factual, the allegations around the repatriation and death of Rudolf Hess and the Duke of Kent do seem more like Hollywood fictional scripts.

While conspiracy theorists have given some compelling evidence at times, there are others who have fought back against these claims.

One such man is James Douglas-Hamilton, the son of the Duke of Hamilton. He has written a number of books about the Hess affair, denying his father's involvement in any conspiracy.

In his book *The Truth About Rudolf Hess*, you will not find one mention of the Duke of Kent or General Sikorski. This is particularly interesting, because although the text is a bid to counter the conspiracy theorists, you would expect the alleged involvement of the Duke of Kent and the crash in 1942 to have been considered and rebutted.

These claims lead to a final conspiracy question. If the British authorities wanted to kill Rudolf Hess and the Duke of Kent, why kill so many innocent airmen and the royal entourage? And why over land when they could have brought the aircraft down with a bomb over the sea?

This is the background to the conspiracy theories surrounding the Duke of Kent's death in August 1942. As we have seen, there is little doubt the aristocracy and some of the British Royal Family wanted peace with Germany, but we should not forget many common people across Britain and its Empire were also desperate for peace.

The British Royal Family, through its own blood lines, had German DNA in their bodies and the Duke of Kent was visiting relatives in Germany right up to the start of the war in September 1939.

There is also an arguable case that even Adolf Hitler wanted peace with Britain, his real target being the communist Soviet Union, a nation full of despised Bolsheviks, enemies of European royalty, the aristocracy and now Poland (in the case of Sikorski's involvement in this alleged affair).

The night-time Blitz which had rained bombs down upon British cities for many months in 1940–41, ended when Rudolf Hess arrived in Scotland. Some have argued this was because of the lighter nights which prevented night time raiders venturing too far over Britain, while others believe Hitler was preparing to invade Russia. The delayed invasion of Russia (Operation Barbarossa) started on 22 May 1941, just twelve days after the end of the Blitz and the arrival of Rudolf Hess.

Many historians have argued over the reasons for the delay in the launch of Barbarossa, some claiming it was due to the ongoing fighting in Greece and the Balkans; but there are some who believe the delay may have been linked to the arrival of Hess in Scotland and one last effort to broker a peace deal with Britain.

To consider the loss of the Duke of Kent in August 1942 and all the possible reasons and causes, we have to understand the Hess affair and the duke's own private life. While many claim the crash was an accident, the allegations will not go away and continue to swirl around the incident.

I hope this summary has given you a good understanding of the history surrounding the Duke of Kent as we now examine the Sunderland 'M' for Mother and its crew in August 1942…

Chapter Four

The Royal Party, their arrival and the crew of Sunderland 'M' for Mother

On Saturday, 22 August 1942, Jean Jack and her mother travelled to Oban to visit Jean's brother Andrew Jack, a Flight Sergeant and air gunner in the Royal Air Force. Andrew Jack was serving with No. 228 Squadron, a unit equipped with Short Sunderland aircraft for anti-submarine work and convoy escorts.

RAF Oban was a major flying boat base with two squadrons operating from the bay. Most of the nearby town of Oban supported the operations, with various properties being requisitioned for military use, including Dungallan House, which became the station headquarters. The main RAF base with its slipways and hangars was on the small island of Kerrera on the opposite side of Oban Bay.

In a 1985 interview with Robin MacWhirter for a BBC Scotland radio programme titled *The Crash of W4026*, Jean Jack recalled her brother, Flight Sergeant Andrew Jack, pointing out *his* Sunderland floating at its moorings in Oban Bay. He told his sister and mother he could not show them around the aircraft, as it had been, 'Done up to take high hied yins somewhere.'

Jean recalled in the interview that the aircraft looked like a big white bird having been newly painted.

The aircraft in question was 'M' for Mother, serial number W4026. The aircraft was a relatively new machine, having only been delivered to No. 228 Squadron on 14 May that year. It was flown from the depot back to the squadron by a man who would almost exclusively fly it until its final flight. That man was Australian Flight Lieutenant Frank McKenzie Goyen.

Built as part of an order for twenty-seven aircraft by Shorts at Rochester, Kent, W4026 was a Mark III and fitted with all the latest instruments and navigational aids. This included the relatively new Distant Reading gyro-magnetic compass and the Air-to-Surface Vessel (ASV) Mk II radar.

In addition, as Andrew Jack pointed out to his relatives, the aircraft had been equipped to undertake VIP transport duties, as well as its normal operational use. The rest area in the lower hull was equipped with more comfortable seating and curtains on the porthole-like windows.

'M' for Mother had made a number of short flights with Frank Goyen at the controls, transporting senior Royal Navy officers to bases and establishments in north-western Scotland.

The Sunderland was powered by four powerful Bristol Pegasus XVIII engines, each capable of 1,065hp, giving a top speed of 210 mph and a cruising speed of 178 mph. The aircraft had an endurance of up to thirteen hours and a maximum ceiling of just over 17,000 feet; although it usually patrolled at a much lower altitude looking for submarines above the trans-Atlantic convoys.

The four engines on this particular aircraft, by the time of the fatal crash, had only been run for between 160 and 166 hours. They were in effect, still brand-new engines. The airframe had a total of only 157.10 flying hours, the remaining engine running times being incurred through trials and tests while on the slipways or water.

Prior to the fatal flight on 25 August 1942, the aircraft was serviced and the special equipment (i.e. the radar and the new compass) was checked on 23 August. The aircraft was to all intents and purpose in perfect condition.

The aircraft was painted with Flight Lieutenant Frank Goyen's own personal emblem under the cockpit, a cartoon Kangaroo with a joey in its pouch. To emphasis the offensive capabilities of the Sunderland, the kangaroo wore boxing gloves.

As Flight Sergeant Andrew Jack had told his relatives, the crew were expecting to transport someone important over the next few days, but they did not know who their illustrious passenger would be.

The crew were soon told they were to reposition their aircraft by flying it to RAF Alness on the Cromarty Firth near Invergordon, to await their passenger. On Sunday, 23 August, the Sunderland took off from Oban at 3:35pm for the fifty-five minutes flight via Loch Linnhe, Fort William, Loch Lochy, Loch Oich and along the Great Glen and Loch Ness to Invergordon before landing at Alness. The aircraft followed this route, as there was a long-standing Air Ministry directive that all flying boats should fly over water in case of an emergency landing. They should only venture over land for other emergency reasons.

The crew of the Sunderland consisted of:

Flight Lieutenant Frank McKenzie Goyen, service number 42057, was a 25-year-old Australian pilot from Shepparton, Victoria. He joined the Royal Air Force and qualified as a pilot in October 1939 and had a long record flying the Sunderland. In fact, Frank Goyan was said to have been probably the most experienced Sunderland pilot in the RAF at the time of the crash. He had served at Gibraltar, Alexandria and Kalafrana in Malta for most of his service, but he was coming to the end of his tour with No. 228 Squadron.

In 1941, while based on Malta with the squadron, Goyen had a lucky escape when his Sunderland, which had just landed, was wrecked by strafing Messerschmitt 109s.

After the squadron returned to the UK, Goyan had been based at Oban and as previously mentioned, he had in the weeks leading up to the fatal flight, flown a number of high-ranking naval officers to bases around the Isles of Scotland. Goyan was not only an experienced Sunderland pilot, he was also used to flying VIPs around, and in 1941 he had conveyed the British Ambassador Sir Stafford Cripps to Moscow. Goyan was therefore the natural choice to pilot the Duke of Kent's transfer flight to Iceland.

According to the official records, Frank Goyen had over a thousand flying hours in his logbook. According to both the Court of Inquiry report (Form 412) and the Aircraft Accident Card (Form 1180), he had 906 or 907.20 hours flying time on the Sunderland. 264.50 of those hours had been flown in the six months prior to the fatal crash, making him not only an experienced pilot, but one who was a regular pilot and captain of his aircraft.

The strange thing is that on the final flight, the Sunderland crew would be captained by Goyen, but unusually, he would not be the 1st Pilot.

Wing Commander Thomas Lawton Moseley, service number 33064, was the Commanding Officer of No. 228 Squadron. He took command of the unit on 30 April 1942, having just completed a flying refresher course.

While a refresher course was nothing new for an officer who had been posted to a ground role for some time, Moseley had been working in a mainly ground based environment and non-flying duties for some time.

Thomas Moseley had joined the RAF in 1930, qualifying as a pilot. He flew flying boats and seaplanes from Kalafrana in Malta, but the exact details of his flying record are something of a mystery. The later Court of Inquiry report stated that he had flown twenty-eight different types totalling 1,146.00 flying hours, but only eighty-one hours were on the Short Sunderland, making him a comparative novice on the type compared to Frank Goyan.

In 1937, Thomas Moseley attended a Specialist Navigation Course at RAF Manston in Kent, where he was top of his class. He was therefore held back as a navigation instructor, before moving on to RAF St Athan in South Wales, where he again worked as a navigation instructor. Although some flying was likely, most of his role was ground based, but he was promoted to the rank of Squadron Leader.

In 1940, Moseley moved to Squires Gate airport, Blackpool, where he opened the School of General Reconnaissance before he was promoted to Wing Commander. Another posting, this time on the Deputy Director of Training's Staff at the Air Ministry soon followed in 1941, but again there was little opportunity to fly.

There is no doubt Wing Commander Moseley was an expert navigator and an experienced pilot, but most of his flying time was before 1937 and not on the Short Sunderland.

Since his arrival on No. 228 Squadron, Thomas Moseley had flown (according to the Squadron's Operations Record Book) on just fourteen flights, which included the repositioning flight to Alness on 23 August. These flights amounted to a total of just over seventy-two flying hours, but at no time had he captained an aircraft during this period.

In fact, on only four flights totalling about twenty-nine of those hours did he fly as 2nd Pilot (co-pilot), on the remainder he was just a spare pilot. It is likely when he flew as a spare on these flights, he may have handled the aircraft for a short period of time, but the fact is, he may have only had his hands on the controls of a Sunderland for a fraction of the seventy-two hours noted in the squadron record book.

Concerns about the current status of Moseley's flying hours in August 1942 can be further evidenced by the fact he did not fly at all between 26 July and 16 August 1942. In the month between 27 July and the fatal flight, he flew just seven hours and seven minutes as a 2nd Pilot. Prior to that, since 13 June, he had only flown thirty-one hours and twenty-two minutes as a spare pilot.

Why he went on the flight has long been debated, but it was most likely he went along to escort and engage with his royal guest.

The third pilot on the fatal flight was Pilot Officer Sydney Wood Smith, service number 403961, the man whose file in the Australian National Archives contains the sole surviving copies of the Court of Inquiry report.

Smith was married, aged twenty-four, and came from South Yarra, Melbourne, Australia. He joined the Royal Australian Air Force in 1941 and was trained in Canada under the Empire Training Scheme, where he gained his wings on 20 November

1941. After basic training he had flown the light, twin engine Avro Anson before converting to the Sunderland and joining No. 228 Squadron at Oban on 30 June 1942.

Although Smith had been with his first operational squadron since the end of June, he only started flying with his new unit on 19 July, just over five weeks before the fatal crash. He was taken under the proverbial wing of Frank Goyen and flew on twelve flights before the re-positioning flight to Alness on 24 August. Together with Goyen, Smith flew a total of thirty-seven hours, including a number of the VIP flights. After the fatal crash, the Court of Inquiry report would show him to have just a total of seventy-eight flying hours on Sunderland aircraft.

The navigator for the flight was Pilot Officer George Robert Saunders, service number 126975. He was thirty-one years of age and came from Sheffield in South Yorkshire, although he was married and his wife lived in Cheltenham.

George Saunders had been a member of the RAF Volunteer Reserve and was a relatively new navigator, having joined No. 228 Squadron in late July 1942. He was therefore, like Smith, inexperienced and by 25 August, had only flown three operational flights, two of them with a tutor navigator (Pilot Officer Arnold W. Dowsett RAAF). All three operational flights had been with Frank Goyen, but he also undertook a small number of VIP transit flights with his new captain. By the time of the fatal crash, Saunders had only flown thirty-three hours and thirty-nine minutes on the squadron.

It is clear that Frank Goyan was the only current and vastly experienced member of the four commissioned crew members. Wing

Commander Thomas Moseley, while being an experienced pilot, was short on experience in recent years, while Wood and Saunders were fresh out of the proverbial training box.

In the March 1992 edition of the *Aeroplane Monthly* magazine, author Roy Nesbit stated that the Secretary of the No. 228 Squadron Association – Eric Harrison – had received a letter from Archie Brember.

Archie Brember was the No. 228 Squadron navigation officer in August 1942 and stated that he was detailed to fly as navigator on the Duke of Kent's fatal flight. He told Mr Harrison that the other navigators on the unit protested so vociferously, that eventually, permission was given (presumably by Wing Commander Moseley) for lots to be drawn and the navigator for the flight to be selected. The navigator who won was the inexperienced Pilot Officer George Saunders.

As an expert navigator and instructor, one of the reasons Wing Commander Thomas Lawton Moseley joined the flight could have been to mentor and monitor the inexperienced George Saunders and not just to escort the Duke of Kent.

The rest of the Sunderland crew were:

Flight Sergeant Andrew Simpson Jack, service number 970168, aged twenty-one, from Grangemouth, Scotland. A keen sportsman, he had intended going into further education when the war started. He was a trained wireless operator/air gunner from the RAF Volunteer Reserve.

Sergeant Edward Francis Blacklock, service number 405467, a member of the Royal New Zealand Air Force and aged thirty. He was a wireless operator/air gunner and had joined the air force just after the outbreak of war. He was unmarried and came from Dunedin, Otago.

Sergeant Arthur Rowland Catt, service number 1252994, was aged twenty-four and was a pre-war airman who volunteered for aircrew duties. He trained as a wireless operator/air gunner. He came from Enfield, North London and was married.

Flight Sergeant William Royston Jones, service number 523047, was aged twenty-eight and came from Port Talbot in South Wales. He was an aircraft fitter, but also trained as an air gunner. He was single.

Flight Sergeant Charles Norman Lewis, service number 517386, was aged twenty-seven and came from Pembrokeshire in South Wales. He was an air mechanic and according to some records, a trained air gunner. He was single.

Flight Sergeant Edward James Hewerdine, service number 566884, was aged twenty-four and a wireless electrical mechanic, he was also a qualified air gunner. He came from Grantham in Lincolnshire and was married, his wife living in the town.

Sergeant Leonard Edward Sweett, service number 570678, was twenty-two and came from Looe in Cornwall. He was an electrical air fitter by trade. He was married and his wife and parents lived in Looe.

The non-commissioned men on board the Sunderland had a wide variety of experience, but Frank Goyen the captain knew them well.

We know Andrew Jack was the aircraft's tail gunner, but who was manning the wireless operator's position on the flight deck is unclear, as are the positions of the other members of the crew.

According to the plans we have already seen, the Duke of Kent and his small entourage are believed to have caught the 1920 hours train from London Euston to Inverness on the evening of 24 August 1942. Although they had originally planned for five berths on the sleeper train, only four were taken with the Duke of Kent, his Equerry, Private Secretary and Valet all travelling to Scotland.

The fifth place on the train was to have been taken by the duke's Royalty Protection Officer Peter Giles (although some say it could have been Inspector James Evans who had been with the duke in 1941). However, as this was to be a visit under military protection, the duke told his protection officer he was not required and he was granted a period of leave.

The Duke of Kent's train arrived at Inverness station the next morning, where he was met by Group Captain Geoffrey Francis, the Commanding Officer of No. 4 Operational Training Unit (4 OTU) based at Alness/Invergordon. He escorted the royal party by car to the air base a few miles away.

While undertaking research into this story, I spoke with George Bethune in Dunbeath, Scotland. His father was one of the Special Constables first on scene at the crash in 1942. George has spent a considerable amount of time gathering information and eye witness statements from those involved in and around the incident and he has provided me with a great deal of information for this book.

One such piece of information he gave me, concerned two women named Sandra Young and a Mrs Mitford. They were driving along the old A9 between Inverness and Alness on the morning of Monday, 24 August 1942, when they saw near the turn-off for Kirkhill, a large car, possibly a Rolls Royce or a Bentley. They also noticed a man nearby relieving himself at the side of the road. As they passed the man, both women said simultaneously to one another, 'My goodness, isn't that the Duke of Kent?'

The issue with this story is the duke, according to the official records, was still in London at that time and the ladies may be confused about the actual date. It is possible it was the twenty-fifth and he had just got off the sleeper at Inverness station when he was caught short and needed to relieve himself en route with his party to RAF Alness near Invergordon. (Alness was situated just off the A9 before the road continues on into Invergordon.)

The Duke of Kent and his party arrived at RAF Alness late morning, when he was introduced by Group Captain Geoffrey Francis to Wing Commander Moseley and Flight Lieutenant Goyan. The royal party then had lunch in the Officers' Mess.

The rest of the Sunderland crew were informed by their captain – Frank Goyan – who their distinguished passenger would be and where they would be going.

As the royal party took lunch in the Officers' Mess (clearly without the valet, Leading Aircraftsman Hales), Flight Lieutenant Goyen, Wing Commander Moseley, Pilot Officers Smith and Saunders went through their briefings, which included meteorological information, the latest intelligence and their route to Iceland. Group Captain Geoffrey Francis the base commander was also present during this briefing, such was the importance of the flight, or rather its passenger.

The Sunderland would be armed with its standard number of .303 Browning machine guns for self defence, as well as eight 250lb depth charges. These were stored on two racks on either side of the aircraft, (four on each side) inside the hull. They would be moved outside the hull via a pulley system if they were needed against any U-boat they sighted. (Some historians and researchers have claimed the aircraft actually carried six and not eight depth charges, but the number is immaterial.)

While the duke and his party concluded their lunch, the Sunderland crew headed to their moored aircraft in tenders. Once aboard the aircraft they started their pre-flight checks.

The air gunners usually rotated around the various different gun positions, but on this flight, no one wanted the solitary tail gunner's position. They all wanted to be near their royal guest. The gunners therefore tossed a coin to decide who would take the lonely rear gunner's seat. Flight Sergeant Andrew Jack lost the toss and was to take his position soon after take-off. Little did he know, but losing the toss would ultimately save his life.

In the *Caithness Courier* in August 2002, journalist Alan Hendry wrote an article: *Eagles Rock collision course*. In the article, re-produced here with his kind permission, he spoke with Dick Ross about his memory of 25 August 1942.

Dick was one of a number of school boys who enjoyed pottering about with makeshift rafts on the shoreline of the Cromarty Firth. On 25 August 1942, the arrival of a distinguished-looking party of air force and naval personnel – and, in particular, an unusually sleek motor vehicle – caught the attention of the carefree 14-year-old. Dick didn't realise it at the time, but this group included the Duke of Kent and his three-strong entourage.

Mr Ross, by now seventy-four and living in Alness near Invergordon (in 2002), recalled:

'Paddling in the shallows alongside the Ferry Slip, as it was called, I could not help noticing a line of cars and other military vehicles which parked in single file near to the head of the adjoining RAF pier, and this engaged my curiosity to the extent that I hurried up the beach and walked along the line of now empty vehicles, wondering at their unusual significance. One car in particular impressed me more than the other half-dozen or so. It was a Rolls Royce or Bentley, no less…

'I watched the group of men mainly togged in flying suits and helmets, together with others in RAF and Royal Navy uniforms. They all seemed in good humour and most of them boarded the RAF tender taking them to the flying boat moored across the firth.'

There was an 'Unusually ostentatious display of Royal Navy gold braid', according to Mr Ross (clearly Lieutenant John Lowther's dress uniform).

In the book *Royal Air Force Station Oban 1929-45* by Neil Owen, there is a description by one of the ground crew at Alness that day...

'Three airmen from the Marine Craft Section had been sought out by the Beaching Officer and directed to don shirt and tie instead of the habitual roll-neck jersey. George Campbell from Dumbarton was one of the crew of the tender, accompanied by airmen Murphy and Flynn. They were briefed to take the duke's party out to the aircraft.

'Campbell recalled subsequently, with absolute certainty, that both the aircraft's crew and the duke's entourage were in good spirits when taken out to the Sunderland and, despite subsequent rumours, they were all sober.'

George Campbell held his tender steady as all the passengers entered the Sunderland. He also noted that there were no other special passengers other than the Duke of Kent and his personal entourage. Campbell would retain the crew list in his pocket until it was later demanded, with some haste he said, by the Beaching Officer.

The Sunderland crew, having completed their pre-flight checks, started the engines and at about 1300 hours, the flying boat started to taxi to the take-off point. Inside the aircraft the royal party made themselves comfortable in the rest area.

At 1312 hours, the Sunderland took-off and headed out on its planned route. The Sunderland was loaded with 2,542 gallons of fuel and up to 2,000lbs of depth charges. Although we cannot be certain of its actual take-off weight, it must have been very close to its maximum of 58,000lbs.

The Sunderland clawed its way into the overcast sky after a lengthy take-off run over the flat calm waters of the firth. Once airborne, it completed a circuit over Alness and headed off in a north-easterly direction towards its first waypoint, the lighthouse at Tarbat Ness. From there the planned route would take them along the coastline towards Wick, turning for Thurso and westwards towards the Butt of Lewis. At this final waypoint they would check their position, before setting course for Iceland. It was a simple enough flight, especially for someone as experienced as Flight Lieutenant Frank Goyen.

As the Sunderland climbed away, it quickly disappeared into the low cloud and this was the last time anyone would see it in one piece.

Inside the aircraft, the crew went about their duties while the duke's party made themselves as comfortable as possible. We know Flight Sergeant Andrew Jack went off to his place in the rear turret and we can safely assume the other gunners and wireless operators took their own positions. The navigator, Pilot Officer Saunders, must have been at his navigation table behind the two pilots, but who was in the first pilot and the second pilot's seats? And where was the Duke of Kent? These questions would be very important to the Court of Inquiry.

It has long been said that high-ranking officers and other important passengers would often join the captain, and in this case the commanding officer, on the flight deck/cockpit area. The cockpit area of a Sunderland was relatively spacious compared to most aircraft (see image contained within the plate section of this book) and this would allow a passenger to observe the take-off and initial stages of the flight.

About thirty minutes after take-off, the Sunderland, flying in thick low cloud and probably at its cruise speed of about 120 knots, ploughed into Eagles Rock near Dunbeath. It flipped over in a forward somersault, catapulting Flight Sergeant Andrew Jack and his detached rear turret like a slingshot many yards from the main debris field. The aircraft disintegrated upon impact and burst into flames, killing everyone else on board instantly.

The final stages of the flight had been heard, but not seen by a number of people on the ground and these people would hurry to give assistance and become witnesses to the unfolding drama. The question was why was the Sunderland over land and flying in such low cloud?

In the next chapter, we shall examine what those people observed, although many would never be approached to give evidence in the subsequent Court of Inquiry, their vital evidence never being heard by the panel of officers designated to examine the crash.

Chapter Five

The witnesses to the crash

Sunderland 'M' for Mother had climbed and set course for Tarbat Ness lighthouse soon after take-off and it was soon enveloped by thick cloud. What actually took place inside the aircraft after take-off is a matter of speculation, as little is known apart from the later disjointed comments of Flight Sergeant Andrew Jack, the aircraft's rear gunner.

What we can assume is the two pilots set course and started to climb to their cruising altitude, at an efficient and economical rate. Behind them in the cockpit area, the navigator, Pilot Officer Saunders, laid out his maps and various instruments with a plotted course marked on them. Next to him sat one of the wireless operators (which one is unknown), listening to his R1155/T1154 wireless set combination, although the flight was probably made under strict radio silence.

The other air gunners would have taken their places and the 3rd pilot, Pilot Officer Sydney Wood Smith, was probably down the crew access ladder in the hull area with the royal party. One of the crew probably offered the Duke of Kent and his entourage a warm drink from the aircraft's compact galley next to the wardroom.

The other possibility is that Flight Lieutenant Frank Goyen, as aircraft captain, piloted the Sunderland with Pilot Officer Smith, while Wing Commander Thomas Moseley entertained the royal party below.

In such poor weather with little to no visibility, the crew would have navigated by compass and timing. They would have set the compass to allow for the magnetic declination for that area of northern Scotland. This at the time was a variation of thirteen degrees to the west of true north.

The Sunderland Mk. III had two main compasses, one was the P4A, mounted horizontally by the first pilot's left knee in the cockpit. Like many similar compasses of the time, if the aircraft was manoeuvred vigorously, it would swing crazily until it settled down again with a continuation of stable flight. It was also affected by induced magnetic fields, such as those created by electric instruments, or even the aircraft's own engines.

To combat these issues, the Sunderland Mk III was also fitted with a distant-reading compass known as the DR Compass. This was a relatively new instrument for the Sunderland in August 1942 and it had only recently been installed in the squadron's aircraft. Although crews, and in particular navigators, would have received training in its use, their actual experience of using the device must have been quite limited by 25 August 1942.

The distant-reading, or DR compass as it was more readily known, was designed to overcome the issues normally experienced with the standard P4A compass and other similar devices. To avoid magnetic contamination, the DR compass was installed in the rear section of the aircraft's fuselage, near the tail and well away from the four Pegasus engines, the radio and ASV radar equipment.

The DR compass contained a magnetic needle and a gyroscope, as well as an electric motor. This allowed for better stability and a more accurate and sustained heading to be displayed. An electrical cable passed from the main DR compass at the rear of the aircraft's fuselage/hull, back to the navigator's position at the rear of the flight deck. Here, another device known as the variation setting corrector or VSC was positioned on the navigator's plotting table. This allowed the navigator to adjust the DR compasses reading to allow for the magnetic declination, depending on where they were in the world.

As previously stated, as this was a variation of thirteen degrees west in Northern Scotland, the navigator would turn the instruments dial to set this amount of deflection from true north. A repeater dial in the cockpit's main instrument panel displayed the heading according to the DR compass and the navigator's VSC adjustment for the magnetic declination to the two pilots. The 1st Pilot would also still have the standard magnetic P4A compass by his knee.

As 'M' for Mother was flying in thick low-cloud in close proximity to high-ground, it was imperative the setting of the DR compass and its variation setting corrector were correctly adjusted prior to take-off. The navigator would have been the crew member primarily responsible for carrying out these actions and on this flight, it was the inexperienced Pilot Officer George Saunders who bore that responsibility. As we have seen, as a relatively new navigator joining No. 228 Squadron in late July 1942, he had only flown three operational flights, two of them with a tutor navigator. All three operational flights had been with his captain Frank Goyen, but he had also undertaken a small number of VIP transit flights with his Australian captain.

The issue of navigation, and in particular the DR compass, and the variation setting corrector is possibly of major importance to the loss of the Sunderland, her crew and passengers. This will be examined in more detail later in this book.

The Sunderland was to take a pre-planned route along the coast before turning westwards and then north-west towards Iceland, but as we already know, it headed inland and ploughed into Eagle's Rock between Braemore and Dunbeath in Caithness.

It appears from what little evidence is still available, that the military authorities failed to gather sufficient evidence to plot the aircraft's actual course that afternoon. However, George Bethune, whose father was one of the first to attend the scene of the crash, has carried out many years of enquiries and found and documented the following evidence: Robert Sutherland and George Grant were local estate workers in 1942. On the afternoon of 25 August at about 1:30pm, they were stood talking over a garden gate at Ousdale, about six to seven miles south-west of Eagle's Rock and just inland from the coastline. As they chatted, they suddenly heard the unmistakable sound of an aircraft passing overhead in the thick cloud cover.

In 2002, George Bethune interviewed Robert Sutherland who told him:

> 'George and myself had just finished our dinner and were standing outside, one on each side of the gate, discussing work and other things when we heard the plane passing.'

George asked whether the aircraft was over the sea, but Robert Sutherland added, 'No, no, the plane was inland from the house, but we could not see it because there was thick fog. It must have been pretty near to Donald's Mount and it sounded very low.'

Donald's Mount, or to give it its correct name, Meall Dhonuill, was a peak of about 275 metres on the opposite side of the Berriedale Water (River) from Eagle's Rock; but more importantly, it was near Meall na Caorach which stood at 396 metres…. The aircraft was heading for high ground. (See map in plate section.)

Two more local men also heard the approach of the unseen Sunderland. David Morrison and his son Hugh were just down river from Braemore on the Berriedale Water. They were working on the Duke of Portland's estate rounding up sheep when they heard the sound of the aircraft engines, but could not see anything due to the low cloud. The aircraft passed overhead and they expected an imminent crash, which they soon heard, together with an explosion high-up on Eagles Rock.

Hugh Morrison immediately jumped on his motorcycle and went to fetch help in the hamlet of Berridale, some five miles downriver and the Duke of Portland's nearby shooting lodge.

Two days after the crash, David Morrison told the Aberdeen *Press and Journal* newspaper:

> 'My son Hugh and I suddenly heard the noise of a plane overhead. Seconds later, there was a tremendous crash. We both felt something terrible had happened. I immediately told Hugh to get his motor bicycle which was close at hand and hurry off and tell the police and to get a doctor. I myself went towards the spot where I thought the plane had crashed.'

It appears from the few records that have survived, that all four of these men were never approached by the authorities to give statements, despite David Morrison speaking with the local media.

The RAF Court of Inquiry did however, trace two other witnesses regarding the flight path of the Sunderland. The first was William Sutherland, a member of the Royal Observer Corps based at Lower Newport on the A9 road, just north of Berridale on the coastline.

William Sutherland, according to his statement given to the RAF Court of Inquiry and now part of the papers in the Australian National Archives stated:

> 'I am a member of the Royal Observer Corps. At approximately 13:30 on 25 August 1942, I was in the post at Lower Newport, Berriedale on duty. A plane was heard approaching from the south in cloud at an estimated height of 1000 to 2000 feet. After a short period, we lost the sound of the machine again. It was then disappearing in a north or north-westerly direction. This was the only aircraft going north within half an hour either side of 1330 hours.'

At the later Court of Inquiry, it appears he added that visibility was about 100 yards with cloud covering the hill tops, the wind was fresh from the south–east.

Lieutenant John Stanley Whitehead, Royal Navy, also gave a statement and evidence to the Court of Inquiry. He stated:

'I am watch-keeping officer at RNO Wick. At approximately 1330 hours on 25 August 1942, I was fishing at the falls on Berriedale River to the west of Eagle Rock. A few minutes after this I heard an aircraft approach from the sea. It was impossible to see the aircraft, but from the sound it appeared to be very low, so low in fact that I half expected it to crash.

'The sound of the engines appeared to be quite normal. Immediately after this I heard a dull thud and the sound of the engines ceased and I assumed that the aircraft had crashed. I immediately packed-up my tackle and proceeded towards Braemore. Owing to the thick mist it was not until 1610 hours that I came upon the scene of the accident. In this search I was accompanied by three shepherds. As it appeared that we were the first to find the crash a further search was made to see if there were any survivors in the immediate vicinity. None were found.'

Lieutenant Whitehead was then apparently asked by the Court of Inquiry about the weather conditions in the vicinity of Eagle Rock. He told them at 1330 hours it was raining heavily with visibility down to approximately 100 yards. The mist was right down to the ground.

The evidence of Lieutenant Whitehead is unusual and he may have made an error. In a discussion with George Bethune, I was told the waterfalls are not to the west of Eagles Rock, but to the south, further down the Berriedale Water towards Berridale and the Observer Corps post at Lower Newport.

Finally, Lieutenant Whitehead stated the aircraft engines appeared to be quite normal and it was approaching from the sea. If it was approaching from the sea, it would have been travelling in a north or north-westerly direction, but that would have meant the two men at Ousdale were wrong about it being inland. It is possible Lieutenant Whitehead was confused by the low cloud, the direction of travel and the fact the river in which he was fishing is set in a narrowing valley which could cause sound waves to reverberate and bounce around the hillsides.

The fact that he only mentions three shepherds and does not name them is also interesting. Did the Court of Inquiry not wish to speak to these witnesses? Could they have not provided differing or corroborative evidence?

What the evidence of all of the men who heard the Sunderland proves, is that it was heading inland on a course somewhere between Ousdale and Eagles Rock, passing within a mile of the falls on the Berridale Water and within a mile and a half of the Lower Newport Royal Observer Corps post. If a line is drawn between the Tarbat Ness lighthouse and the crash site, it passes very close to Ousdale, the falls and the Lower Newport Observer Corps post. It then narrowly misses Donald's Mount (Meall Dhonuill) and passes over the river to Eagles Rock.

This flight path would be about thirteen degrees west of the anticipated and pre-planned flightpath along the coastline of Caithness. The need to set the DR Compass and the VSC with the local magnetic declination, which just happens to be thirteen degrees west, clearly points to a possible compass and navigational issue or error, which will be examined in more detail later in the book.

All of the six men who heard the Sunderland pass by could give very valuable evidence, but only the man from the Royal Observer Corps and the Royal Navy officer were approached for evidence. This is despite David Morrison's own account appearing in the local newspapers just two days after the crash.

In later years, a letter appeared in the *Aeroplane Monthly* magazine (April 1990) from a Mr J.N.C. Richardson from Derbyshire. In his letter he stated that in August 1953, he was seventeen years of age and on holiday with his parents at Lake Como in Italy.

The family became friendly with a man called Mr I.F. Luckin. He told them in conversation that eleven years previously (in August 1942), he had been a radar operator and been on duty when he watched the Duke of Kent's Sunderland on his screen. To his horror, he watched as the aircraft turned to port to take a short cut one valley too early. He was unable to intervene and help, as the flight was being undertaken in complete radio silence. He watched in horror as the 'blip' on his screen went out.

In reply to the article, Roy Nesbit could not confirm the identity of Mr Luckin, but stated that other Sunderland pilots had assured him, they never cut this corner and remained over water as per orders.

I have searched the RAF Officer lists and identified a Flying Officer J.K. Luckin who was based on the Air Staff of No. 14 Group, Fighter Command, in July 1942. He was based at the Drummossie Hotel near Inverness. Although his initials are different, it could have been a typing error and the chances of there being more than one officer called Luckin being based in that area at that time, are quite small.

Whether he was the radar operator that day or he was relating an account from another person is unknown. However, if the Sunderland had taken the suggested thirteen degrees west track from Tarbat Ness, it would have passed close to the radar station at Helmsdale and crossed the coastline some five to six miles up the coast near Ousdale and the witnesses Robert Sutherland and George Grant.

Over the decades, a number of people have suggested the Sunderland actually flew inland along the course of the Berriedale Water. An examination of the local Ordnance Survey map, (sheet 17: Strath of Kildonan) identifies a problem with this hypothesis.

The Berriedale River winds around, and in a few places, especially those close to the crash site, the valley sides become quite steep and narrow. This is despite the valley being locally known as a strath, which means a wide and shallow valley. The river valley near the crash site has steeper sides when compared to those further down its course near the sea.

In addition, with thick cloud down to ground level, this would have been a suicidal flight path, especially for such a large lumbering aircraft. For this reason, I believe the thirteen degrees west flight path is much more realistic than a flight up the Berriedale Water/River. The question is why was it on that route and was it descending if it flew over and missed the higher ground around Donald's Mount?

In the next chapter, we shall examine the evidence from the witnesses who initially approached the crash site and what they found at a scene of utter devastation.

Chapter Six

Scene and aftermath witnesses

After the Sunderland ploughed into the hillside, a number of people started to make their way to the crash site – not that they could see it in the thick, low cloud cover. The explosion had been heard and now the surrounding area was enveloped by the smell of burning aviation fuel. In Braemore, two miles to the west of the crash site, even the local school children on their dinner break could smell the lingering acrid smoke.

David Morrison continued his climb up towards the perceived area of the crash, while his son (Hugh) went off to get assistance on his motorcycle.

A search party was soon gathered by the Marquess of Titchfield, the son of the Duke of Portland, who was on holiday on his father's estate at Braemore. Victor Cavendish-Bentinck, the Marquess of Titchfield as we have seen, was Chair of the Joint Intelligence Committee of the Chiefs of Staff and a good friend of the Duke of Kent. The question is whether he knew this was the duke's aircraft, but there is no record of him ever stating this or being approached with regard to his organisation of the search party.

The Marquess of Titchfield's search party would include Hugh Morrison, estate shepherd James Gunn and a local crofter named James Sutherland, as well as some military personnel who were stationed at Braemore at the time.

Whether the party also included Lieutenant Whitehead who had been fishing on the Berriedale Water falls is unclear, as he did not mention the Marquess or any of this search party by name in his evidence to the RAF Court of Inquiry, but he did say there were three shepherds in his party when he attended the crash site.

However, the *Daily Record* newspaper on 27 August 1942, stated, 'Morrison claimed it was James Sutherland, with James Gunn and a naval lieutenant who found the wreckage with him first.' So, it would appear that Lieutenant Whitehead was with this search party at the scene, but why did he not mention this in his testimony to the Court of Inquiry? Why did he not mention the fact the Marquess had organized the search party? And why did he not give an account in his evidence to the Court of Inquiry of what he found at the crash site? And why were statements apparently not taken from these other men, including the Marquess?

In addition, it appears there was further evidence the naval officer did not disclose to the Court of Inquiry. In his 1948 book: *Caithness and the war 1939-1945*, local author and journalist Norman M. Glass states, 'An angler plying his art three quarters of a mile away was first to gauge what had happened. He forsook his hobby and made for the home of Mr James MacEwan, a gamekeeper who communicated with police headquarters in Wick...'

This statement appears to possibly refer to Lieutenant Whitehead or another unidentified man, but it was never mentioned in Whitehead's statement to the Court of Inquiry. The gamekeeper, James MacEwan, also appears to have been overlooked by the investigation team.

The large search party headed up over the rough ground in the general direction of the crash site, but failing to locate it, they split into two separate search parties.

After about half an hour, one of these search parties found the crash site. This group contained David Morrison, Lieutenant Whitehead, James Sutherland and James Gunn. The Marquess of Titchfield and the other military personnel therefore do not appear to have attended the crash scene. David Morrison later said about his arrival at the crash site: 'The plane had caught fire when it crashed and one part was still burning when we arrived.'

David Morrison and his party looked around the scene of utter devastation. The aircraft had disintegrated, covering the hillside with many thousands if not millions of pieces of debris. Here and there, lay a few larger pieces such as the wing floats, the engines, sections of the wings, flaps and the hull, plus the detached large tail unit and the rear gun turret. This latter portion of the aircraft had been flung like a slingshot as the Sunderland tipped over in a forward somersault. Although they could not see from ground level, the hull, the leading edge of the wings and the two wing floats had left impressions in the soft earth before the aircraft disintegrated. This indicating that the aircraft was in level flight or gently decreasing in altitude when it struck the rising ground. Bodies lay all around and amongst the debris, some of which was still burning.

Finding no one alive, David Morrison's party headed back down towards Braemore. On the way, they encountered Special Constables Will Bethune (George Bethune's father) and James Sutherland, not to be confused with the crofter James Sutherland.

The two Special Police Constables, both local fishermen, had been at Dunbeath harbour when the alarm was raised. The housekeeper in the Lodge at Braemore had used the telephone (one of the few around at the time) to call Langwell House in Berriedale. Langwell House was also owned by the Duke of Portland, but it had been requisitioned in 1941 by the military. Upon receipt of the call, word was quickly sent to the local Post Office, where Minnie Gunn (a distant relation of James Gunn, a member of the Morrison search party) telephoned the police station in Dunbeath.

PC Kennedy, the local Dunbeath police constable, was away on leave in Glasgow at the time, so his daughter Betty Kennedy took the call. She knew exactly what to do and informed Police Headquarters in Wick, before running down to the small harbour to alert the two

Special Constables (Will Bethune and James Sutherland) who cycled up to the gravel pit on the Braemore Road and walked to the crash site.

George Bethune told me his father Will's story, a story he had told innumerable times since that day in August 1942. This was a story his father also related to Robin MacWhirter for his BBC Scotland radio programme in 1985. Will Bethune said:

> 'We proceeded to Braemore where we got the strong smell of burning. In thick fog we cut right out over the hill, following in the general direction the smell was coming from. On the way in, we met the crowd on their way back from the crash to Braemore. The crowd told us that we need not go any further. It was a waste of time as everyone was dead. But we had to go on, it was our duty.

> 'When we came to the crash, we went among the dead, examining each body for signs of life. When I came to the duke's body, I noticed right away the high-ranking insignia and shouted, "Jimag, here's a high-up man". I looked closer and said, "My God Jimag, It's the King"'.

This final comment was because King George and his brother Prince George, Duke of Kent looked very similar.

The two men checked the body for identification. Will Bethune continued:

> 'On the left wrist there was an identity disk. I will never forget what it said: HRH the Duke of Kent, The Coppins, Iver, Bucks, England.'

Will also related that fixed to the duke's right wrist via a bracelet (handcuff like device), was a briefcase with the Duke of Kent's monogram on the front of it. The briefcase had burst open and there were a large number of Icelandic Krona bank notes fluttering around in the bracken. (George Bethune was later at pains to say his father never actually said they had come out of this briefcase, but he implied he thought that was their origin.)

The Icelandic Krona bank notes in denominations of one hundred is interesting. Although we have no idea exactly how many notes there were, if we assume there were about a hundred 100 Kr notes laying among the debris, that would amount to 10,000 Kr or £58 in 1942. However, to put that amount into some context, in 2023 that amount would be worth about £3,500. Was this just the duke's spending money?

Will Bethune continued:

'I did not search the briefcase, as it was not my duty to do that. By the way, the duke had not been in the cockpit at the time of the crash. That was clear from the position of his body on the hill and the badly burnt and damaged bodies that were still in the vicinity of the cockpit. When we had established that everyone was dead, Jimmy and myself had a look around. We noted many pairs of white gloves and lots of pairs of ladies shoes, although I can confirm, absolutely, that there was no female body on the site. There was, however, one other thing we noted, or rather, smelled. Above the reek of the burning fuel, we got the strong smell of perfume. After all this, we sat down to await the arrival of the police and the military from Wick, who we knew would be on their way.'

I have been unable to ascertain where exactly the Duke of Kent's body was found on the hillside, but clearly, Will Bethune indicates it was not located in the main debris field with the other bodies. When the two memorials were placed at the site in 1946 the larger memorial and cross bearing the names of the deceased was placed in the area of the main debris field, but the smaller plinth marking the location of the duke's body is over the crest of the hill and out of sight from the main cross. Who decided this was the exact position of the duke's body is unclear, but both the plinth and Will Bethune's evidence indicate his body was some distance from the others.

If Andrew Jack in his rear gun turret was catapulted a considerable distance as the aircraft somersaulted, the cockpit area in a forward somersault motion would probably not have received the same degree of velocity. Therefore, the cockpit and the flight deck crew would have been gathered close to one another among the main area of debris. If the duke had been in the crew rest area in the lower hull of the Sunderland when it hit the hillside, the bottom of the hull/fuselage may have been ripped out before the aircraft somersaulted and with no structural barrier left to hinder any movement. The duke may have been thrown a distance from the wreckage, leading to his fatal head injury. However, this is all supposition based upon the known available facts.

George Bethune also stated that his father had recounted seeing a number of bottles of alcohol at the scene, but he did not state what type of liquid they contained or whether they were full or empty (although it is reasonable to assume that some or all of the bottles were broken). These comments would later be used in another conspiracy allegation, regarding the use of alcohol and the possibility the crew and their passengers were intoxicated. This will be examined later in this book.

After a period of time, James Gunn returned to the crash site with Dr John Kennedy from Dunbeath. The two Special Constables briefed the local doctor, who sadly, was no stranger to air crashes on the high-ground around Dunbeath. Dr Kennedy examined each of the casualties pronouncing each one to be deceased. He then suggested they cover the body of the Duke of Kent, but Special Constable James Sutherland said, 'We will cover them all up.'

In his statement to the Court of Inquiry on 29 August 1942, Dr Kennedy stated:

'I am a medical officer for the Western District of the Parish of Latheron. At about 1400 hours on 25 August 1942, I heard casually on the telephone that an aircraft had crashed somewhere in the vicinity of Braemore. I immediately proceeded to Braemore by car with a small search party which I had organized. We proceeded down Berriedale River for 2 ½ miles hoping to get in touch with the large search party under the command of Lord Titchfield. Owing to the thick fog and rain we were unable to contact this party.

'I sent three members of my search party ahead in a north-easterly direction where I thought the plane would be. They reached the plane which had been previously found by James Gunn, shepherd of Braemore. They returned to where I was waiting and informed me that the occupants were all dead. I went back with them to the crashed aircraft and found eleven bodies in and around the wreckage and three trapped under burning wreckage. I examined all the bodies accessible and found that death was due to burning and multiple injuries in most cases. In all cases death must have been instantaneous.'

The evidence of Dr Kennedy, like that of Lieutenant Whitehead from the Court of Inquiry file, indicates there were further unidentified persons who had attended the crash site. In the doctor's evidence contained within the Inquiry record, he does not name those individuals and it appears that whoever took his statement or deposition, did not see any need to delve deeper into who actually attended the crash site and what they found and saw. This begs the question whether more detailed statements were taken and if the evidence recorded on the Court of Inquiry Form 412, is in fact, only a small sample of the evidence obtained, when it should contain details of all the evidence.

Sergeant Bob Henderson of the local Home Guard was next to arrive at the crash site. He had climbed to the site from the Ramscraig area to the east, situated between Berriedale and Dunbeath on the A9 road. According to Will Bethune and later related to me by his son George, the Home Guard Sergeant found the Duke of Kent's wristwatch among the debris. He handed it to Dr Kennedy noting that it had stopped at 1:42pm (almost certainly the exact time of the crash).

Sergeant Henderson also told the others at the crash site that he thought he had heard someone shouting as he climbed towards the crash site. He suggested there may have been a survivor, but no one could hear any more shouts.

After a few minutes Dr John Kennedy and James Gunn left the crash site. On their way down the hillside, they encountered two Police Constables – brothers Edward and Tom Carter. They were accompanied by PC Johnstone and an RAF Police Sergeant called James Swanson from the airfield at Wick. James Gunn offered to show them the way to the crash site and they gratefully accepted his offer.

In the early 2000s James Swanson, living in Edinburgh, was interviewed by the Caithness.org website and recounted his story which can still be found on-line. He said:

'I was stationed in Wick, at the RAF Station, from September 1940 to June 1944 as an RAF Policeman. Our Sergeant in charge was posted and in August 1942, I was promoted Sergeant in command of Police.

'The 25 August 1942 was a very misty day at Wick, when our planes were grounded because of the weather. I heard that the

Civil Police had received a message of what was thought to be a plane crash in the hills near Dunbeath. As we had no aircraft flying and no knowledge of any, it was left to the Civil Police to investigate.

'I contacted them and asked if they were going if they would take me with them. They agreed and the Carter brothers and another younger constable (Johnstone, I think was his name) and I drove down to Dunbeath and up into the Duke of Portland's estate.

'We were given directions as to where they thought the crash was and on following the path we met the doctor. I am not sure of his name, but he was around eighty years old at the time, and two others coming down. They told us then, that they were all dead, and one was the Duke of Kent. We got a bit lost in the mist and one of the men who was returning up to the crash, took us to the scene.

'A constable and I stayed at the crash site while the others went away to make their reports and arrange for a guard to take over. The aircraft, a Sunderland flying boat, had taken off earlier that day from Invergordon, on its way to Iceland, but in the mist had cut across too soon and hit the hills. During a visit earlier this year to a visitors' centre near Lybster, I heard that there were rumours that there had been females on board and much booze. Having spent some seven or eight hours beside the wreckage and the dead, I can say there is no truth in such stories.

'The only mystery was that we were told there was thirteen on board and we had accounted for all thirteen and yet the next morning their air gunner was found some distance away, injured, but still alive. We had heard someone calling, but two locals who had come up, went out and searched around, saying when they came back, they had heard a call, but when shouting back had got no reply. It seems he had been lapsing into unconsciousness and been unable to reply.'

At the crash site, when the group of civil and RAF police arrived, Special Constable James Sutherland was sitting on an unexploded depth charge. One of the new arrivals, probably RAF Police Sergeant Swanson said, 'Do you know what you're sitting on?'

Jimmy Sutherland calmly replied, 'Yes, I'm sitting on a bomb,'

Sergeant Bob Henderson of the Home Guard again thought he heard a shout in the distance, but this was soon discounted as the cry of a bird.

The two Special Constables, Will Bethune and James Sutherland, gave their verbal reports to the regular constables who then dismissed them and they left for home in Dunbeath. In time, the two Carter brothers left the scene to report to Police Headquarters in Wick, leaving just PC Johnstone and RAF Police Sergeant James Swanson to guard the site.

In August 2023 I attempted, via a Freedom of Information Act request, to obtain copies of the reports and Police Occurrence Books from Wick and Dunbeath in August 1942, but Police Scotland said they do not hold this information.

I continued digging and in late 2023 I identified that the Nucleus, Nuclear and Caithness Archive, based at Wick airport, held the Caithness Police Report of Crimes & Other Occurrences (Landward) book 1929-1943 and the Occurrence Book 1941-1944 (references NC/1/10 & NC/1/20). I was told by the archives that both files had a 100 years restriction placed on them and I needed to obtain the permission of Police Scotland to access this information.

I duly made a further Freedom of Information Act request to Police Scotland, but on 6 February 2024, I was amazed by their reply:

'Police Scotland does not hold the information requested. By way of explanation, the occurrence books that you refer to were checked, for the months of August and September, for mention of the Sunderland air crash at Eagle's Rock on 25 Aug 1942 and also for any mention of the Duke of Kent, however, there is neither mention of the crash or the Duke of Kent in either volume.'

I have also been informed via an article in the *John O'Groats Journal* and *Caithness Courier*, dated 21 August 2022, that a manilla file held in the Nucleus Archive in Wick, which contains details of Caithness Constabulary reports of wartime air crashes in that area, does not contain any report regarding the Duke of Kent's fatal crash.

Although eighty years have now passed since the fatal crash, surely someone must have realised the significance of the event, one which not only would interest historians, but was possibly liable to further investigation. The question is what happened to those police reports from 1942 when so many others have survived?

Over the next few hours that evening, the covered bodies remained in their original positions surrounded by the wreckage. The debris was still smoldering, but this had decreased over time. Senior military officers started to arrive in the late evening and examined the wreckage, but who these men were is a mystery as no surviving records identify them.

Overnight, men from the RAF Regiment bases at Wick and Skitten maintained a guard over the crash site. They had originally arrived intending to immediately remove the bodies, but the gathering darkness made this unsafe and the evacuation was postponed until the next morning (26 August).

When the morning of the twenty-sixth arrived, Home Guard Sergeant Bob Henderson guided the RAF Regiment stretcher bearers as they removed the bodies from the crash site. The bodies were taken in a series of ambulances to RAF Wick, but the Duke of Kent's body was taken to the Duke of Sutherland's Dunrobin Castle, a stately home the duke had previously visited. Later he would be sent by train to London Euston, the terminus he had departed on a sleeper train, just two days before. Upon arrival in London the duke's flag draped coffin was taken to Windsor Castle to await burial.

What scene examination had taken place at the crash site is unknown as there is very little detail in the surviving documents. Photographs were apparently taken at the scene, as there are five exhibited images referred to as B, C, D, E & F in the Court of Inquiry report 'Exhibit A was an OS aeronautical map of Scotland, while G & H were the meteorological reports for 25 August 1942.' However, what these images displayed is unknown, as no comments in the final surviving report refer to their content. Could they have included some of the images contained within this book? It seems likely, especially as they show an aerial view taken from an RAF aircraft, guards in position at the site and the Maintenance Unit recovery team.

The identities of the senior officers attending the scene on the night of 25 August 1942 and the next day are unknown. What is known, however, is they used Dr John Kennedy's house in Dunbeath as a headquarters and rendezvous point.

There is nothing in the surviving records or the RAF Wick or RAF Alness Operations Record Books relating to who attended the scene. It is almost as if this important crash site, with its VIP passengers, occurred in another dimension. It is worth at this point remembering that this was the second worst air crash in

British history at that time and the King's own brother had just been killed.

The RAF Alness Operations Record Book (see reference AIR28/402 in the UK National Archives) narrative for 25 August 1942 just states:

Operational Flying:

Sunderland M/228 (W/Cdr. Moseley and F/Lt Goyen) airborne 13:12 en route to Iceland carrying Air Commodore HRH the Duke of Kent and three other passengers. The aircraft crashed into a hillside at Braemore near Dunbeath at approximately 1400 hours, all the passengers and crew with the exception of the tail gunner being killed.

Clearly this entry was completed either late on 26 August, or on a later date, as Flight Sergeant Andrew Jack was still believed to be deceased until late the following morning.

The narrative states the crash occurred at approximately 1400 hours, some forty-eight minutes after take-off. This has been used by some conspiracy theorists to evidence their view the Sunderland had been to Loch More and was returning with Rudolf Hess on board. However, in reality, the crash appears to have occurred at 1342 hours.

The RAF Alness narrative also noted the weather as:

Wind: Easterly 10/15 mph.
Weather: Cloudy with periods of rain.
Cloud: 8/10 to 10/10ths at 1500/3000 ft. with fragments below 200/800 ft at times.
Visibility: mainly poor.

The loss of Sunderland 'M' for Mother and its crew and passengers, was quickly communicated to the Air Ministry in London. On the evening of 25 August, King George VI was informed of the death of his youngest brother, and by lunch time on the twenty-sixth, the remainder of the Royal Family had been informed of their loss.

Telegrams were sent to the families of the deceased airmen and the passengers. These included telegrams dispatched to the families of the Australian and New Zealand crewmen via their respective air force departments down under. It appeared that everyone on board the Sunderland had been killed.

Just before midnight on the evening of 25 August 1942, the Air Ministry made the following official announcement:

'The Air Ministry deeply regrets to announce that the Air Commodore, the Duke of Kent was killed on active service this afternoon when a Sunderland flying boat crashed in the North of Scotland.

'His Royal Highness, who was attached to the Staff of the Inspector General of the Royal Air Force, was proceeding to Iceland on duty.

'All the crew of the flying boat lost their lives.'

One man had by some miracle survived. In the next chapter we shall look at the sole survivor Flight Sergeant Andrew Jack and how the authorities handled his reappearance, when they had initially proclaimed everyone to have died in the crash.

Chapter Seven

Flight Sergeant Andrew Jack

On the late morning of 26 August, Mrs Elsie Sutherland, a crofter's wife, was at home making herself busy in her cottage, 'Rinsary' at Ramscraig, about two miles from the crash site. Suddenly a dishevelled apparition opened the gate of the cottage and stumbled across the small garden towards the front door.

The apparition before her was Flight Sergeant Andrew Jack, the tail gunner from the wrecked Sunderland 'M' for Mother.

Andrew Jack would later tell people he was in the rear turret when the aircraft struck the hillside, flinging him and his turret many feet from the main debris field and the burning aviation fuel. He was knocked unconscious, but came to and extricated himself from the damaged gun turret and its adjacent tail unit.

Jack found the Sunderland to have largely disintegrated, the remains were laying in a field of debris measuring many square yards in dimension. He found his colleagues and their passengers lying scattered and lifeless around and among the smoldering wreckage and bracken. Some of the bodies had been burnt and some had major injuries. He would later say that upon checking the bodies he believed Sergeant Leonard Sweett aged twenty-two years was injured, but alive in the wreck of what had been the central hull of the Sunderland. Jack tried to move the wreckage to rescue his friend, but his hands and face were burnt and he was unable to assist him. The question is whether Andrew Jack received his burns trying to check and recover his colleagues and their passengers, or were the burns received while he was in his detached rear turret?

Jack, for some unknown reason, probably through shock, went against protocol and wandered away from the wreckage. (Standard procedure called for aircrews to remain with any wreckage and await assistance.) However, Jack wandered off into the thick low cloud, straying into the Strath of Berridale Water. Whether he shouted for help is unknown, but it would be the natural thing to do and his could have been the shouts the rescue party heard in the hour or so after the impact.

Having become hopelessly lost in the thick cloud and suffering from his injuries and shock, Andrew Jack eventually laid down in the bracken and fell fast asleep, possibly suffering from concussion as well as from his visible injuries.

He slept through the summer night and woke the next morning in daylight. Jack said he went to the river to take a drink, but he could not cup his burned hands to drink the water. He therefore waded into the water to lap the water into his mouth with just his tongue.

As well as having burned skin, his flying suit was burnt and his flying boot soles had partly melted. He therefore stripped off the suit and his boots, leaving him barefooted in his uniform trousers and white roll neck woollen sweater. He placed his flying suit and boots on a footbridge over Berriedale Water, possibly one below Donald's Mount and placed the loose change from his trouser pocket in a stack next to his clothing. He then, as he later told his mother (and which she repeated a number of times afterwards) said, 'I lay down to die. I'm not going to get help here.'

Just a short time later, Jack heard a car horn in the distance, possibly part of the team removing the bodies on the morning of the twenty-sixth. He scrambled up out of the valley and headed off towards the direction from which he believed he had heard the car horn. He then found the crofter's house of Elsie Sutherland and opened the latch on the garden gate. Due to his burnt hands, Jack had great difficulty opening the latch, so he used his elbow to move it. Stumbling across the small garden to the door, he found Elsie inside and managed to mutter that he was a crashed airman, before asking her for a drink.

Elsie asked him whether he was from the Duke of Kent's crash and he replied, 'I am the only survivor.'

Elsie took him inside and sat him down, before giving him a glass of milk. She then gave him first aid which included having to cut off his woollen pullover. She then contacted the home of Dr John Kennedy in Dunbeath. He immediately rushed to the crofter's cottage and treated the injured airman, before having him transported, first of all to Dunbeath Police Station and then to the Bignold Hospital in Lybster, further up the coast on the A9 road.

In his 1948 book, local journalist Norman M. Glass gives a slightly different account of what Jack had reportedly told Elsie Sutherland.

Although he could only speak with difficulty, Flight Sergeant Jack said to Mrs Sutherland – 'I am an airman and our plane has crashed. I am the sole survivor.' As Norman Glass points out in his book, could it be Andrew Jack received his burns trying to drag bodies from the blazing debris and not from the wreck of his gun turret, which from photographs, appears to lie outside the area of burnt hillside?

A few days later, a local shepherd found Andrew Jack's burnt flying clothing and returned his stack of coins to him in the hospital.

Andrew Jack was treated for his burns and George Bethune told me his wife Nan's grandfather (Nan was her name) was in the hospital bed next to Andrew Jack. Her grandfather always said Jack was initially only too happy to speak about the crash and his own survival and this was confirmed by several local people, including Alice Gunn the hospital Matron. (Sadly, Alice Gunn is no longer alive.) Andrew Jack was happy to discuss the fact the Sunderland's air gunners had tossed a coin to see who would take the lonely rear turret position, the toss of the coin therefore saving his life.

The Jack family received a telegram on the morning of 26 August, informing them of Andrew's death. His sister Jean, who had visited him in Oban only a few days before, received the dreaded telegram and was in a state of shock. In an interview with Robin MacWhirter for his BBC Scotland Radio programme in 1985, Jean explained that shock and horror were soon replaced by great joy, when after just a few minutes, a second telegram arrived cancelling the first and informing the family of her brother's survival.

On Saturday, 29 August, the Jack family travelled to the hospital in Lybster to visit Andrew. Jean, her sister Nancy (a WAAF) and brother Bobby (a non-commissioned officer in the Scots Guards), saw Andrew in a small ward. At the hospital they found their brother, but they were disturbed by two senior officers, one in RAF uniform and the other in Royal Navy uniform. They wheeled the bed away from the family, through a door to a quiet corner and when their brother was later returned, he never spoke again about the details of the crash.

His brother later said his brother told him he could not talk as he had signed the Official Secrets Act, and when he could not sign it with such burned hands, he replied, 'They held my hand.'

From that moment on, Andrew Jack did not discuss the crash with his family or the local people.

Jean was surprised by her brother's condition, he was so burned, he had difficulty speaking with his facial skin tightening. In fact, his hands and face were covered in gentian violet and his lips were cracked and crusted. Jean would always maintain that her brother had been sworn to secrecy that day.

On 12 September, Andrew Jack was transferred to a larger hospital between Edinburgh and Glasgow – closer to his family home and away from the local witnesses and population.

Upon reading the Court of Inquiry report, it would appear from the manner in which the report is written that Flight Sergeant Andrew

Jack gave 'live' evidence in person to the RAF Court of Inquiry. As we shall see later in this book, the inquiry opened on 28 August 1942, the day before the burned and injured Jack received his hospital visits.

In the few documents available in the Australian National Archives file for Pilot Officer Smith, there is a section detailing the evidence of thirteen witnesses. Witness number seven was Flight Sergeant Andrew Jack. His recorded evidence states:

'I am an Air Gunner with No. 228 Squadron. On Tuesday, 25 August 1942, I was a member of the crew of W4026 which was on a passage from Invergordon to Iceland. We were airborne at about 1300 hours and the height of the cloud was about 500 feet. The captain, Flight Lieutenant Goyan, who was flying the aircraft, told us there would be a lot of cloud around, but he did not think it would last long. This was over the intercom. I was in the rear turret.

'As we proceeded the cloud came down thicker. I felt the aircraft losing height after about twenty minutes. The pilot was apparently trying to get under the cloud base. I do not remember anything after this.'

This evidence is very short and lacking in detail. It fails to mention who was where in the aircraft, who was in the co-pilot's seat, what the royal party were doing and where they were situated. It also fails to cover anything post-crash and the position of the bodies and who was where in relation to the crash site. Neither does it mention any attempt by Jack to move the bodies or any injured parties.

There seems to be particular emphasis on the weather, the fact Flight Lieutenant Frank Goyan was flying the aircraft at the time of the crash and whether the pilot was trying to 'get under the cloud base'. The comment, 'I do not remember anything after this', seems contrived and illogical. Clearly Andrew Jack does remember a period after this, when he regained consciousness and searched through the debris and casualties. Surely this would have some evidential value to the Court of Inquiry?

The evidential record dates this evidence was given on 29 August 1942, the day his siblings and the senior officers visited his bedside in the hospital. If this is correct, how could Jack have given personal 'live' evidence to the Court of Inquiry, or is this just a regurgitation of his bedside statement, probably the document written and signed by Jack in the hospital on the twenty-ninth?

In the Court of Inquiry document, there are also a series of questions and answers. This gives the impression he was giving live evidence which was recorded contemporaneously by a clerk, something we now know could not have taken place at an Inquiry hearing. The other explanation is these were questions and answers the two officers asked him at the hospital and noted on his recorded statement. These questions and answers are:

'Do you know who was navigating the aircraft?'

Jack: 'I don't know.'

'Did you hear anything else over the intercom?'

Jack: 'No.'

'Do you remember who was in the 2nd Pilot's seat?'

Jack: 'No.'

'Did you think the aircraft climbed much before it started to come down again?'

Jack: 'No, not much.'

'Was the last thing you remember being in cloud?'

Jack: 'Yes.'

This line of questioning is one that any lawyer or police officer will recognise as being made of 'closed questions.' In effect, they expect a short answer with little explanation, hence the short answers seen in the record. Lawyers like to use these tactics in a court when trying to keep a witness on a particular track, however, police officers are trained to ask 'open questions', starting any questions with the words – why, what, when, how etc. This is in a bid to obtain ALL the facts and get the witness or suspect to talk freely. In this case, the line of questioning would appear to be trying to steer the witness and not obtain the full facts.

It appears they were very interested in the weather and Jack could remember details of this and that Goyan was the pilot and captain. However, Jack says he did not know who was co–pilot and who was navigating the Sunderland. Surely, Jack would have known who was the appointed navigator and who the other two pilots were on board the aircraft. This, in my humble opinion, is very strange and seems to be a possible case of selective amnesia.

As Norman M. Glass pointed out in his book, could it be Andrew Jack received his burns trying to drag bodies from the blazing debris? Is this why the Duke of Kent's body was found some distance from the main debris field and the other bodies? Had Jack tried to save the duke and was now too embarrassed to say anything, or had he been sworn to silence?

Flight Sergeant Andrew Jack returned to service the following year after recovering from his injuries, but some people did speak with him about the incident. Jack was later commissioned and remained in the Royal Air Force, retiring in the mid-1960s. Towards the end of his career he worked at RAF Prestwick near Glasgow. It is said he started to drink heavily and died in 1978 in Brighton hospital, Sussex.

On 18 May 1961, Andrew Jack spoke to the media. The article was not so much an interview, but a repeat of the official account of the crash, interspersed with some of Jack's own comments. (See: *The Day the Duke died – Now at last the lone survivor tells his story*, the *Scottish Daily Express* 18 May 1961.) This would be his only public statement on the incident nineteen years before. He said in relation to his actions after the crash:

> 'All along I had been trying to get help. I knew help was useless, they were all dead. But I felt someone ought to be told. I think that's why I walked away and went on wandering, though the best thing I could have done from my own point of view was stay with the wreckage.'

Jack said he had taken his position in the rear turret ten minutes into the flight. He said he tested the intercom to the cockpit before adding, 'I had no conversation with any other member of the crew or captain again.' This comment was added to in later years as we shall see later in the book.

Jack said they flew into low cloud about twenty minutes into the flight adding, 'I can't recall exactly – then feeling the plane descending...I didn't know any more until I woke up and found myself on the ground.'

In 1943, Jack was sent back to No. 228 Squadron and the unit transferred to RAF Aldergrove in Northern Ireland. Corporal Tim Wilson would later write a letter to author Roy Nesbit, which was published in his *Aeroplane Monthly* magazine article, *A travesty of the truth* in September 1996.

Jack had told Wilson that Wing Commander Thomas Moseley had been in the number 1 pilot's seat and Goyen was sat in the number 2 seat. The Duke of Kent had been stood between them. Andrew Jack had also said, 'I had no conversation with any other member of the crew or captain again.' (This, as we have seen, was repeated in the 1961, *Scottish Daily Express* article.) This has led some to believe that he may have been cryptically stating he had spoken to the duke or another member of his entourage, but nothing can be confirmed. However, it could easily refer to Wing Commander Moseley, who was not a member of the crew per se.

Corporal Tim Wilson added that Flight Sergeant Jack told him he had called the cockpit once more after dropping smoke floats, but it was Wing Commander Moseley who responded, not Flight Lieutenant Goyen. This therefore seems to corroborate the assertion Jack meant he only spoke to Moseley and not a member of the crew.

Smoke floats were often dropped by the rear gunner to measure the wind speed, this may not appear to be that important, but why was this not part of Jack's evidence to the Court of Inquiry? This would surely be a vital piece of information when considering the navigation of the doomed aircraft.

If this is correct, clearly Wing Commander Moseley was flying the Sunderland and Goyan was in the 2nd Pilot's seat as earlier stated by Andrew Jack.

Flight Sergeant Andrew Jack was said by those who knew him to have carried to his grave an anger that Frank Goyen was blamed for the crash and the loss of so many lives in August 1942. Was he sworn to secrecy and what did he really know? Had he been threatened with some form of punishment if he revealed all he knew?

There are major concerns with the evidence of Andrew Jack. Apart from facts being possibly omitted… why was his limited evidence to the Court of Inquiry recorded in a manner which appears to indicate it was given 'live' directly to a hearing, rather than via a statement taken in the hospital at Lybster, with a few closed questions added to it by the two unidentified military officers?

The Jack family have carried the stigma of the crash with them since 1942. In *The Times* newspaper on 24 March 1996, Elspeth Jack, Andrew's widow, claimed her husband confided in her that the Duke of Kent and many of the crew had been drinking champagne on board the Sunderland before the flight. He also told her that the Duke of Kent had urged the crew to take off in poor weather conditions and that he believed the duke was at the controls when it crashed, but he wasn't sure. She stated:

> 'For the rest of his life, Andy said it was a shame the pilot was blamed. He thought the Duke of Kent was at the controls, but he wasn't sure.'

His son Ian Jack, in the same *Times* newspaper article in 1996 said:

> 'My father did say that in no way was the pilot to blame, but there was nothing he could do about it because he was still in the RAF. He was very bitter about the way Goyen was treated.'

On 23 December 2003, Mrs Margaret Harris, niece of Andrew Jack, claimed the family had been burdened with the truth of what happened that fateful day in August 1942. The report stated:

> 'Mrs Harris claimed the Duke of Kent was piloting the ill-fated aircraft and a mysterious, unnamed person on board could have been the married royal's boyfriend…. He (Andrew Jack) actually pulled him (the duke) out of the pilot's position…. What got to him was his mates being blamed for an accident that wasn't their fault…. He was left in no doubt it was to remain a secret. He was in hospital and with burnt, bandaged

hands, he had to sign a paper, possibly the Official Secrets Act. He told my dad in confidence it became too much for him one night and he told him… a mysterious extra person was on board the plane. He never ever mentioned who the person was and he never went into detail whether it was a man or a woman.'

The account from Margaret Harris was given thirty-six years after the death of Andrew Jack. How much was heard first hand and how much was via a second party is unclear, as none of the report attributes the comments as coming directly from Andrew Jack to Margaret.

It is possible Margaret never heard these comments directly from Andrew Jack, she heard them via the family and others. Over time, she possibly read or heard the conspiracy theories and they were entwined with the family story. As a result, her account to the BBC is possibly partially true and partially conspiracy theories.

While other evidence points to the fact the Duke of Kent was not piloting the aircraft that day, there was certainly some confusion over who was flying the aircraft and in command at the time of the crash. In addition, there was confusion about the number of people on board the aircraft and the number of bodies found at the crash site.

Andrew Jack remained quiet for years, but there is no doubt he was frustrated and angered by the Court of Inquiry's conclusions, but was there another issue….

The tail section and the gun turret do not lie within the area burnt by the exploding aviation fuel, so how did Jack receive his burns and burnt flying kit? Andrew Jack reportedly told people he had tried to recover Sergeant Leonard Sweett from the debris, but he could not assist him. Did he recover and pull the Duke of Kent's body far away from the burning debris field, sustaining his burns in the process?

The Duke of Kent's body was reportedly found a good distance away from the main wreckage and the burnt area. Today a small tablet allegedly marks the spot where the duke's body was found, well away from the main memorial cross. This smaller memorial was placed there shortly after the war. The tablet lies beyond the position of the tail section and Jack's gun turret. Although no one can today confirm this is the correct spot where the duke was found, if it is even remotely correct, either the duke was thrown – like the gun turret – beyond the debris field, or it is possible he was moved there by Flight Sergeant Jack who received his burns in the process.

If Andrew Jack was sworn to secrecy, he could have been angered by the blame attached to his colleague Frank Goyan. He could also have been angered by the fact his actions in attempting to assist his colleagues and possibly the Duke of Kent, were ignored by the Court of Inquiry. This may be the case, especially when Dr Kennedy was later rewarded for his efforts at the crash site.

We shall look more closely at the Court of Inquiry in a future chapter, but it is clear that Flight Sergeant Andrew Jack probably knew more about the events leading up to the crash and those immediately after it, than he ever publicly admitted.

If Andrew Jack was sworn to secrecy, why did he remain quiet until 1961 and why then just repeat the same old story to the *Scottish Daily Express*, while allegedly telling others different accounts in private?

Chapter Eight

The following days

One man who appears to have never been called to give evidence or make a statement was Captain Ernest Fresson OBE. A Scottish aviation pioneer, he was very well respected, and in 1942 flew on a regular route between Kirkwall and Inverness. He knew the terrain and the weather in this part of the world like the proverbial back of his hand.

In the *Scotsman* newspaper on 7 September 1985, Richard, the son of Ernest Fresson, submitted a previously unpublished account of the Sunderland loss written by his late father.

In the account, Ernest Fresson said he was on the Inverness to Kirkwall run on 25 August 1942 and the meteorological office reported bad weather along the route as far as the Pentland Firth, where conditions were expected to improve.

Captain Fresson flew north above the cloud layer at 4,000 feet and found the Pentland Firth as forecast, to be bathed in sunshine. Later, they departed from Kirkwall around 1:00pm on the return trip and flew to Thurso in sunny weather. There was low cloud over Thurso and they turned on to a south-easterly course to bring them over Dunbeath, which they passed above clouds at 1:30pm.

At approximately the same time Fresson departed Kirkwall, the Sunderland flying boat had taken off from Alness. Ernest Fresson claimed he was later told there had been a last-minute change of captain on board the Sunderland which had delayed its departure. (Who told him this was not explained by Fresson or explored further by the reporting journalist.)

Ernest Fresson also claimed that for reasons unknown, having been airborne for barely ten minutes, the captain of the Sunderland was heard by the rear gunner (clearly Flight Sergeant Jack) over the intercom, to say, 'Let's go down and have a look.' Again, we do not know how Fresson knew this, but this is an interesting comment which does not appear to have ever been put to Andrew Jack for clarification or confirmation.

Knowing as the pilot must have done, that there was a very low cloud ceiling on the first part of the trip, Ernest Fresson never understood what possessed the Sunderland captain to take such an unnecessary risk.

If this comment, attributed to Andrew Jack, is to be believed, either Flight Lieutenant Goyan, or if the captaincy had changed – Moseley, at about 1320 hours said over the intercom, 'Let's go down and have a look.'

The problem with this statement is it comes via an unknown third party and was not heard directly by Fresson from Andrew Jack. The same applies to his comments about a change of captain on board the Sunderland before the flight took off. Goyan was always the captain for this flight, so what does this actually mean, did it mean Wing Commander Moseley was not only the 1st Pilot, but also the captain? Did this mean Goyan had been relegated to just the 2nd Pilot position with Moseley 1st Pilot and captain?

As we shall see later in the book, Jack does not appear to have mentioned this to the Court of Inquiry and did not mention going below the clouds between their take off and climb and the ultimate crash. As evidence, these comments attributed to Ernest Fresson, while worthy of note, are somewhat lacking in credibility because we do not know their provenance. However, there is other evidence from him which he could have given personally to the Court of Inquiry.

On the morning of 26 August, the day after the Sunderland crash, Ernest Fresson said he was informed by RAF Fighter Control at

Drumossie about the accident. As the whereabouts of the wreckage was not accurately known, he was asked to keep a look out on his next flight north.

He spotted the crash site in land, a few miles up the coast from Berriedale. As they flew over the top of the escarpment, they saw the ground strewn with debris. The aircraft had evidently caught fire, for the wreckage was still smoking as they flew over almost twenty-four hours after the crash. Fresson descended to 100 feet and flew around the crash site. The four Pegasus engines were scattered around the wreck and the only recognisable part of the flying boat was the rear gun turret, rudder and tail fin, which had broken away from the structure at the point of impact.

Fresson and his radio officer could distinguish three or four bodies lying amongst the debris. It was obvious that a considerable amount of fuel on board had caught fire and had melted much of the light alloy wreckage. The position of the crash was some eight miles south-west of the village of Dunbeath and the altitude was around eight to nine hundred feet above sea level.

After climbing to 2,000 feet, to obtain a better radio signal with Inverness, they sent a message telling them they had located the Sunderland and that as far as they could tell, there were no survivors.

This account is very interesting, as we know the wreck had already been located and everyone was believed to have been killed on the evening of 25 August, so why ask Fresson to undertake this flight? In addition, did he fly over before all the bodies had been retrieved on the morning of the twenty-sixth?

George Bethune told me that in the days following the crash, many local people ventured up to the crash site. Many of them over the following years in conversation with George, stated they were allowed to wander around quite freely. There had been a cursory guard at the site in the hours and days after the crash, but once the bodies had been removed, no one appeared to care about the scene. There was no physical cordon and no one bothered to stop the inquisitive local population from looking through the debris.

The phone box outside the Post Office in Dunbeath did have a guard for a few days, but the local population soon realized this was to discourage its use by journalists rather than the general public.

Most of the wreckage remained at the crash site for a number of days and into September. In the meantime, many locals would pick up souvenirs and take them home. George Bethune told me many of these artifacts still lie in local cupboards and on various mantlepieces to this day. It is therefore possible a small vital piece of evidence is still sitting in a Caithness cupboard in the mid-twenty-first century.

One young man (in 1942) who possessed such a souvenir, was eight years old John Angus Miller. Speaking to Alan Hendry from the *Caithness Courier* newspaper in August 2005 and to George Bethune before his death, John recalled as a young boy, how quick he was to visit the scene and pick up a small item that took his fancy. This was a small silver coloured object which he took home. His mother looked at the object and proclaimed, 'Look at the "stamp", it's silver and comes from an expensive scent bottle.'

This appears to have been a hall-marked silver cap from one of the bottles of scent the other witnesses remember seeing and smelling at the crash site. Another witness – Zena Sutherland – told George Bethune that she visited the site shortly after the crash and remembers the strong smell of perfume in the air.

Other visitors took possession of much more deadly items. David Sinclair, a member of the local Home Guard, who were always short of supplies, removed belts of .303 ammunition from the aircraft's various machine guns. The .303 ammunition was later used for target practice by the Dunbeath Home Guard.

The aptly named Bert Gunn also helped himself to parts of the rear turret's guns. He proudly carried these down to the Bignold

Hospital in Lybster, where he is said to have presented part of his find to Flight Sergeant Andrew Jack in his hospital bed.

Other parts of the wrecked Sunderland soon disappeared, including the flying boat's anchor chain, which was soon put to good use on a local water cart.

In the days that followed the crash, No. 63 Maintenance Unit from Carluke near Glasgow, attended the site to remove the wreckage. They were commanded by Squadron Leader D.A. Harrison and by sheer chance, they had also been employed in recovering the wreckage of Rudolf Hess's Messerschmitt 110 in May the previous year. The unit were assisted by two squadrons of men from the RAF Regiment based at Wick and nearby Skitten.

Squadron Leader Harrison does not appear to have made a report to the inquiry or his statement no longer exists, as neither he or his comments are mentioned in the surviving papers in the Australian National Archive.

In the *Mail on Sunday* newspaper, on 10 July 2021, Christopher Wilson wrote an article about the death of Prince George, the Duke of Kent.

In his article he recalled speaking with a Leading Aircraftsman Arthur Baker (service number 1505244) a few years previously. Having met the retired airman at his home in Mablethorpe in Lincolnshire, the pensioner recalled the fact he had been based at RAF Skitten as a member of 'B' Flight, 2847 Squadron, RAF Regiment in August 1942. The airman produced his medals and memorabilia to prove he had been a member and stationed at Skitten, before stating he was one of a number of men sent to the Sunderland crash site in lorries. They were told to find the bodies and bring them back to the vehicles.

Arthur Baker recalled the site being a terrible mess, the aircraft having totally disintegrated. One body had been thrown well away from the debris, a good fifty yards away he recalled. This was a man lying on his back in the heather. Arthur stated, 'He didn't seem very damaged, but for a major injury to his eyes. In his left hand was a fan of playing cards – Lexicon I believe.'

Arthur then realised this body was Prince George, the Duke of Kent, in his flying suit. Lexicon was a card game which rose to prominence in the 1930s, but the cards had letters on them and players tried to make words from the cards they were dealt, rather like the modern board game *Scrabble*.

Arthur Baker did not mention any attaché case or the Krona currency, but the head injury correlates with the severe injury the duke was said to have sustained. Despite this statement from Arthur Baker, no other witnesses are known to have mentioned the Lexicon playing cards, but it is possible they did not think this was important?

Arthur Baker recalled carrying the Duke of Kent back to the debris field on a large piece of metal wreckage. They then continued the search for the other bodies and he recalled a strong smell of scent in the air.

Arthur then made an extraordinary claim. He said he saw ladies clothing lying about and a jewellery case. Then he saw a body with a partially severed leg. He identified the body as that of a woman and opened the clothing to confirm the deceased person had female breasts. Arthur shouted out to his sergeant, but his supervisor told him to cover the female up and to get away from her. The sergeant was then said to have ordered, 'What you've seen here, you speak about to nobody.'

What are we to make of these comments? This information does perhaps corroborate the claims of Andrew Jack's niece, Mrs Harris, when she claims Jack said there had been another mysterious passenger on the Sunderland.

In later years, another man known only as D.G. Jubb from Norton near Doncaster contacted the Caithness.org website. He had also served in the RAF Regiment at Skitten in August 1942. He recalled being sent to the crash site and finding the debris, but he did not make such spectacular comments about what they found and saw. In fact, he would later send two items back to Caithness, a piece of burnt parachute and a piece of debris (probably burnt aluminum).

Will Bethune repeatedly said, until his death, there had been no female bodies at the crash site, so what was this witness talking about?

Will's son George later spoke with a local shepherd in Braemore named Addie Gunn before his death. He witnessed the operation to recover the wreckage stating:

> 'Two long ropes were attached to a substantial piece of the wreckage with smaller pieces heaped on and securely tied. Then fifty to one hundred men would pull the load like a sledge, all the way to the Gravel Pit on the Dunbeath to Braemore road from where army low loaders took it all away.'

This appears to have been a distance of about two miles, back breaking work for the men of the RAF Regiment, but a tracked vehicle was also used according to Addie Gunn, to remove some of what he called important parts of the debris. Exactly what these parts were is unknown, but it is likely to have been the four engines and the tail section.

Despite this mammoth effort, not all of the wreckage was removed from the crash site. The aircraft's depth charges were not removed from the site, but detonated in a controlled explosion, as it was deemed safer to do this at the scene. A few days after the crash, they were detonated all at once. This created a huge crater and a blast that was felt many miles away in Braemore, Dunbeath and Berridale. A second smaller explosion soon followed, possibly one depth charge having failed to detonate with the others. The local population had been given no warning of the explosion and the blast gave them a shock.

Two witnesses to the detonations at the crash site were John MacDonald and his son Iain, as well as their dog. Years later, they informed George Bethune they were told:

'Lie on your stomachs, close your eyes, put your hands over your ears and open your mouths…. When the explosion came, the blast lifted the metal covering us right up in to the air and then it thudded down on top again, leaving us breathless and the dog howled.'

The metal sheet they referred to was possibly part of the aircraft. The debris that was not removed from the crash site was pushed or thrown into the large crater the blast created and covered over. In recent years, walkers and visitors to the site have reported the peaty ground giving up its secret wreckage. Various items, including a brass fire extinguisher, as well as other unidentifiable pieces of debris have been handed in to the Dunbeath Heritage Museum where they can be seen on display.

A number of the deceased's family members attended the crash site in the weeks following the crash and the father of the Duke of Kent's equerry, Michael Strutt, attended and reportedly removed 'certain items' from the scene, although what he took is unknown.

On 14 September, just under three weeks after the crash, King George VI visited the location, escorted by the Duke of Sutherland, the Caithness Chief Constable William Cormack and a number of RAF officers; whether this included Air Vice-Marshal David Colyer and Wing Commander Arthur Warren Kay from the Court of Inquiry is unknown.

In his personal diary, King George noted that, 'The ground at the scene had been scored and scorched, over an area about 200 yards long and 100 yards wide by its trail and by flame.'

The King was guided to the crash site by James MacEwan, one of the Duke of Portland's gamekeepers who had allegedly been contacted by Lieutenant Whitehead shortly after the crash. He also met with Dr John Kennedy, as well as David and Hugh Morrison.

Hugh Morrison would later recall that 'His Majesty already knew something about the crash site' as by coincidence, his brother Donald Morrison was at that time working at Buckingham Palace.

George Bethune, during his enquiries, spoke with the Morrisons' sister Chrissie and she confirmed that soon after the crash, Donald Morrison had attended Braemore and prepared a detailed report, including a description of the crash site for King George.

On 16 September 1942, the site clearance was deemed to be complete and all service personnel left the area.

In 1946, Marina, Duchess of Kent visited the crash site and sat alone on the spot, deep in thought for some time. She would return to it again before her own death on 27 August 1967, almost twenty-five years to the day her husband was killed.

We shall now look at the management of the crash scene, the handling of the deceased and the Court of Inquiry.

Chapter Nine

The scene management & crash investigation

Within hours of the fatal crash being reported, a formal investigation was started to identify the cause.

Air Vice-Marshal David Colyer CB DFC, Air Officer Commanding No. 15 Group, Coastal Command, undoubtedly after consulting with the Air Ministry, ordered a Court of Inquiry. This opened on Friday, 28 August 1942, three days after the incident. According to the only papers now available in the Australian National Archives, it was held at Invergordon (believed to have actually been RAF Alness).

The typed copy of Form 412, Proceedings of Court of Inquiry or Investigation, held in the Australian National Archive files for Pilot Officer Sydney Wood Smith, gives the names of the three members of the Court of Inquiry, these were: Wing Commander A.W. Kay from Headquarters Coastal Command, Squadron Leader W.J. D'Amboise Stacey of No. 15 Group, Coastal Command and Flight Lieutenant D.S. Stacey, a pilot from the recently formed No. 423 Squadron which was based at RAF Oban with Short Sunderland aircraft.

Air Vice-Marshal David Colyer joined the Royal Flying Corps in 1916, flying RE8 aircraft over Palestine where he was awarded the Distinguished Flying Cross. Between 1919 and 1932, he held various ground and academic roles, with a year as a flying instructor in 1923. He was also part of the engineering staff in Iraq between 1925 and 1927.

In 1930 he was Air Attaché to Latvia before joining No. 32 Squadron and flying Hinaldi and Virginia aircraft.

In 1936 he became Air Attaché to Paris, but in July 1940, he became Senior Air Staff Officer No. 61 Group in Northern Ireland. Later in the year, he became Director of Personnel Services RAF and by April 1942, he was Air Officer Commanding No. 15 Group, Coastal Command. His credentials as far as piloting and operating flying boats were concerned, were therefore somewhat limited.

After the Duke of Kent's death and the Court of Inquiry, David Colyer was posted to be Director General of Personnel Services in late 1942 and he was Assistant Chief of the Air Staff by August 1943.

In January 1945, he was sent to Washington DC as Chief of Air Mission and retired in 1947. He then returned to the British Embassy in Paris as the Civil Attaché.

It would appear David Colyer did not suffer any career limitations after the death of the Duke of Kent and the Court of Inquiry, but it is worth pointing out that he is one of only two Second World War Air Marshals not to have been knighted. Colyer had already been made a Companion of the Order of the Bath (CB) in June 1942, (two months before the crash); and in June 1958, he was made Companion of the Order of St Michael and St George (CMG), but he never received the higher-grade knighthood.

Air Vice-Marshal Colyer appointed the President of the Court of Inquiry, designating Wing Commander Arthur Warren Kay, a trained pilot and member of the Coastal Command Headquarters staff. Although Kay is shown on the Form 412, Proceedings of Court of Inquiry or Investigation, as a Wing Commander, this was only an acting rank and he was, in effect, still a Squadron Leader. This was a low rank to be president of a Court of Inquiry and certainly one of such magnitude.

According to documents in the UK National Archives (ref: ADM273/9/275 & AIR 76/268/160), Kay was born on 15 November 1897 and joined the Royal Naval Air Service (RNAS) in July 1916. After attending Cranwell, he trained as a pilot and was sent to serve with the famous No. 1 Squadron, Royal Naval Air Service at Furnes, Belgium, in May 1917.

Arthur Kay served under the famous ace Raymond Collishaw, flying Sopwith Tri-planes, but after less than a month, he was deemed unfit for high altitude flying and sent to Eastchurch on the Isle of Sheppey as a flying instructor.

After the conclusion of the war, Captain Kay left the recently formed Royal Air Force in April 1919. Later he joined 908 County of Essex Barrage Balloon Squadron in September 1938, but what he did between 1919 and 1938 is unknown.

After rejoining the service, Kay was recommissioned as a Flying Officer and became officer commanding 'C' Flight in February 1939. The unit was mobilised on 23 August 1939 with Kay now a Flight Lieutenant. A few weeks later, he joined Headquarters No. 30 Group on temporary operations duties.

RAF Officer Lists for that time show Flight Lieutenant Arthur Kay as still serving with the Balloon Branch in August 1940 during the Battle of Britain, but he was made temporary Squadron Leader in June 1941.

On 8 June 1942, less than three months before the fatal crash, he was made a substantive Squadron Leader on administrative duties at Coastal Command Headquarters.

In effect, Kay had moved on from being a Flight Lieutenant with the Barrage Balloon Command in the summer of 1940, and two years later, he was a temporary Wing Commander and Court of Inquiry President for the death of the King's brother and the second worst air crash in British history up to that time.

For an inquiry of such importance and magnitude, these do not look like the credentials required for such a post, with no apparent personal experience of flying boats or their specialist navigational requirements.

It is possible that Warren had flown civil flying boats between 1919 and 1938, but no record of this can be found and it seems unlikely considering his medical issues during his time in the service.

In December 1943, Warren was still at HQ Coastal Command, but now assigned to accident investigation work. What training he had received to undertake this new role is unknown. He remained with Coastal Command until 1945, having been promoted to the substantive rank of Wing Commander.

The second officer on the Court of Inquiry was Squadron Leader William John D'Amboise Stacey, from No. 15 Group, Coastal Command. Born in 1907, Stacey had joined the Royal Air Force in the 1920s and trained as a pilot, before joining Imperial Airways in the 1930s with whom he gained experience of flying boats. While with the RAF he had flown a number of different transport aircraft, but also the Rangoon flying boat.

Stacey left the RAF and joined the reserve list in January 1934, but he joined the RAFO (Reserve of Air Force Officers) in September 1937 and was commissioned as a Pilot Officer. Stacey became a flying instructor and was promoted to Flight Lieutenant (presumably after having already become a Flying Officer) in September 1940.

In 1942, Stacey was posted as a temporary Squadron Leader (still RAFO) to No. 15 Group, Coastal Command. After serving on this Court of Inquiry, he remained with No. 15 Group and was made substantive Squadron Leader in 1943. He remained in the RAF post war and featured in the *London Gazette* on 21 September 1954, when he was a Squadron Leader with the RAF Reserve.

The third and final member of the Court of Inquiry, was Flight Lieutenant Douglas Stuart Lindsay DFC, an Australian pilot attached to the newly forming No. 423 Squadron at RAF Oban (also flying the Short Sunderland).

Lindsay had joined the Royal Air Force in 1938 and been commissioned. He initially served with 201 Squadron flying the Sunderland in 1941, being awarded the Distinguished Flying Cross. He was promoted to Flight Lieutenant in August 1941 and joined 423 Squadron when it was formed at Oban.

Lindsay was made temporary Squadron Leader in July 1943 and Squadron Leader in September 1945. Post war he stayed in the RAF, becoming a Wing Commander and serving in the 1950s at HQ Coastal Command until 1959. He was promoted to Group Captain and in November 1969, he joined the Air Staff of HQ Southern Maritime Region before becoming commanding officer at RAF St Mawgan in Cornwall. In 1965, he became Senior Air Staff Officer to Air Staff HQ Malta, before finally retiring in 1970.

Lindsay, although relatively inexperienced for a role on the Court of Inquiry in 1942, was at least an operational Sunderland pilot who in time would reach high command in the Coastal Command arena.

Kay was, on this evidence, clearly inexperienced in flying boat and Sunderland operations. He was also a Squadron Leader and not a substantive Wing Commander.

Stacey was also relatively inexperienced for the role on the inquiry and although it cannot be confirmed, it would be unlikely either he or Warren had experience of sitting on such a panel – and certainly not one of such magnitude. Remember, this was the second worst air crash in British history at that time and one which also featured the King's own brother.

As we shall see in a later chapter, for such a major incident, the ranks, experience and roles of these three men appear to have been unsuitable, especially when compared to other crash Courts of Inquiry. Just over a year before this Court of Inquiry was convened, two of the panel had been Flight Lieutenants and the third a Flying Officer.

We also know from the witnesses that there was no official cordon in place and numerous members of the public were free to wander around the crash site once the bodies had been removed, picking up artifacts, some of which they took home.

Exactly where the bodies were found in relation to the debris is unrecorded in the surviving records, but most importantly, who was found in what was left of the cockpit and the hull rest area where the royal party would have been sat is also unclear. No known site plans, sketch maps or notes appear to still exist giving such detail. This leads to a number of possible conclusions:

1. No maps, sketches or scene notes were made at the time or shortly afterwards.
2. They were not included in the Court of Inquiry papers OR
3. They were destroyed or lost.

Any of these three conclusions is a serious matter and undermines the veracity of the Court of Inquiry's findings. Although the Australian copy of the papers states there were exhibited photographs and meteorological papers, there is no mention of plans or sketch maps of the scene layout. If a subsequent review was ever undertaken, whether that be judicial or otherwise, the lack of such documents would be extremely detrimental to the Inquiry.

We know as previously mentioned, that the Court of Inquiry papers held in the Australian National Archives list an aeronautical Ordnance Survey map and five photographic images. However, what these images depict is not stated in the surviving documents. It would have been evidentially very valuable to have had a note attached to each one, explaining where and when they were taken, as well as what the image featured.

As well as having no evidence from the crash scene concerning where the bodies were located, there is very little, if anything, in the way of details of their injuries, medical examination and identification. Neither is there any evidence of what type of wreckage lay on the hillside. There was no explanation or description of what items had survived and if so where they were located. There is also no detailed evidence of the wreckage being examined by a technical expert or engineer.

Any police officer attending the scene of a fatal accident or incident will not only make a sketch plan of the scene, but note what they did, who was where and what they found – especially any injuries and items they believe may be relevant to the investigation. They would also seek to identify the individual casualties and any witnesses wherever possible.

While it would be wrong to assume this scene was not evidenced in more detail, on the face of it, the information available today appears to show very little was obtained. The question is whether more detailed evidence was ever obtained? If it was, why is there no mention of it in the surviving papers in Australia?

This, in conjunction with the inexperience of the Court of Inquiry board members, leads to speculation this may have been an insufficient investigation by untrained, inexperienced individuals.

In addition to the possible failings in crash scene management and evidence preservation, there is no evidence that anyone ever tried to locate any witnesses outside those listed in the record. There is no evidence of appeals in the media, or otherwise, for witnesses (even though it is accepted this was wartime and air crashes occurred with some regularity). As we have already seen, there were quite a number of witnesses who were apparently never approached to make a statement or be interviewed. A number of witnesses, like the Morrisons, gave statements to the media, but apparently not to the Court of Inquiry.

Then we have the actual assessment and examination of the crash site itself. With a fatal crash of this magnitude, even in wartime surely we could expect a proper and thorough investigation by trained experts?

Many people have suggested that there was no formal crash investigation in 1942, and too many aircraft were involved in fatal accidents for them all to be investigated. However, to reiterate my point – this was the second worst British air crash up to that date in terms of fatalities and the King's youngest brother was killed.

We have already seen that there was a form of scientific investigations unit at the Royal Aircraft Establishment at Farnborough. In addition, in the July 1942 RAF Officers List, there is a section called *Accidents Branch*. This had an establishment of twenty accident inspectors under the leadership of Vernon Sydney Brown OBE MA AFRAeS,

Vernon Sydney Brown held the role as an honorary group captain and later air commodore. He had served as a pilot in the Royal Flying Corps, being later utilised in a number of experimental flights and trials. He had attended Caius College, Cambridge and was renowned as someone who questioned the mechanics and science of flight. He remained in the RAF throughout the 1920s, becoming an Engineering Instructor before joining the Air Staff's Directorate of Training in April 1934.

In November 1937, Brown resigned his commission and joined the Civil Service as Chief Inspector of Air Accidents. When the war started in 1939, he was granted his honorary rank of group captain in the RAF Volunteer Reserve.

Together with his team of Air Accident Inspectors, Brown resolved a number of major cases. He would remain in the role until his retirement in 1952, but his work laid the foundations for an effective air crash investigation unit, which in time morphed into the current world-renowned Air Accident Investigation Board (AAIB) at Farnborough.

With a crash of this magnitude, one would have expected Vernon Sydney Brown and his team of accident inspectors to be involved in the investigation, and the media were quick to report their involvement. *The Scotsman* newspaper on 27 August 1942 reporting on page 5: 'It is understood the Chief Inspector of Accidents of the Royal Air Force left for the spot.'

While the *Birmingham Daily Post* the same day reported: 'It is understood the Chief Inspector of Accidents visited the scene yesterday.'

The *Bradford Observer*, the *Daily Herald* and the *Liverpool Daily Post* all reported on the same day: 'It is understood the Chief Inspector of Accidents of the Royal Air Force has left for the scene.'

Clearly the message although somewhat confused in terms of a time frame, was that Vernon Sydney Brown was attending the crash scene.

Who was sent to examine the wreckage and make a thorough assessment is unstated, but in time, Sir Archibald Sinclair the Secretary of State for Air would tell parliament of the Court of Inquiry's findings; adding that the Chief Inspector of Accidents (Vernon Sydney Brown) was in agreement with the findings of the Court of Inquiry.

However, some years ago, George Bethune spoke with Rob Wilson (now deceased) during his own enquiries into the crash and its aftermath.

Rob Wilson was an honorary Flight Lieutenant and senior inspector in August 1942, part of Vernon Sydney Brown's team of Air Accident Inspectors (he was later promoted to Squadron Leader). In conversation with George Bethune, he recalled being in the unit's main office not long after the Duke of Kent's crash, when he was suddenly summoned upstairs to Brown's office. He was apparently summoned to overhear a telephone conversation between Brown and the Deputy Secretary of State for Air, Sir Arthur Balfour.

The Deputy Secretary of State, a member of the King's Privy Council, wanted the Accident Branch to conduct an investigation into the crash of the Sunderland, but Brown, Rob Wilson recalled, refused stating: 'I will not investigate a Sunderland flying into a hillside in fog no matter who was on board.'

Rob Wilson recalled his senior officer – Vernon Sydney Brown – telling Balfour that they had between eighty and ninety planes a day crashing and only four or five warranted investigation by his team of inspectors. The call was discontinued. Balfour called again almost immediately, but he still failed to convince Brown and there was no input from the Air Accidents Branch, despite media reports to the contrary and Sir Archibald Sinclair's later comments in parliament.

Later in March 2024 I spoke with *Northern Times* journalist Jonathan Brett Young. In 1992, Jonathan wrote an article about the crash with the assistance of his editor Jim Henderson, a man who had worked for the *Scottish Daily Express* and previously tried unsuccessfully to interview the sole survivor, Andrew Jack.

The article stated that Rob Wilson vividly recalled the day in question and a signal arriving which requested Accident Investigation Branch assistance. Just as they were about to start enquiries, Wilson says Balfour telephoned Vernon Sydney Brown. Wilson said he was summoned to the office while Brown was on the telephone, because he had personal knowledge of the area of the crash site, but he was somewhat disappointed when his commander made an offer of Accident Investigation Branch assistance should nothing emerge from the initial RAF Group investigation.

Rob Wilson recalled there being good reasons for this decision as it looked like a 'stuffed cloud accident', i.e. one where the aircraft was hindered by cloud and hit the ground. Secondly, the Accidents Branch had trained a number of officers from RAF Groups to carry out preliminary crash investigations. Wilson added that Accidents Branch were very busy at the time and the fact a VIP was on board should make no difference.

The two accounts conflict somewhat, but the full facts may be deduced from joining the two together. It is possible the signal arrived and was followed up by a call from Balfour. The head of the Accidents Branch was busy and did not want to send a team, especially as they had already given training for preliminary investigators at Group level. Therefore, they agreed that the Air Accidents Branch would only become involved if nothing was deduced locally by the Group's investigation officer.

The problem is, there is no apparent evidence listed from a specially trained investigator at Group level. The only possibility is that one of the three board members had undertaken this training, but there is no mention of this in the report or the witness evidence. However, in July 1943, Arthur Warren Kay went to serve on another famous crash Court of Inquiry (more details later). The question is whether he was already trained by Vernon Sydney Brown's team prior to the Duke of Kent's crash in August 1942, or was he subsequently trained after this event? I contacted the RAF Air Historical Branch and they informed me that there are no surviving Second World War training records, so we cannot confirm if and when he was trained as a preliminary investigator.

It is worth remembering at this point that Harold Balfour, the Deputy Secretary of State for Air was a member of the King's Privy Council. The question is whether Balfour made the call to Brown on the request or direction of King George VI, rather than Archibald Sinclair or Churchill?

If the directive or request had come from Winston Churchill or Sir Archibald Sinclair, they could have ordered Vernon Sydney Brown to undertake a full air crash investigation. This leads to the ultimate question of why Sir Archibald Sinclair reported to parliament that Brown had agreed with the Court of Inquiry's findings when he knew they had not been involved?

It appears Vernon Sydney Brown was aware that the Duke of Kent had been on board the aircraft from his comment, 'No matter who was on board,' and he probably knew the number of men killed, making this a very significant case, so why did he refuse to assist? Was it just because his team was busy, or did he honestly believe a local preliminary investigator and a local investigation was sufficient?

The weather at the time of the crash was a vital factor in this investigation. On the evening of the crash, Sir Charles Portal, Chief of the Air Staff, informed the Prime Minister, Winston Churchill (see UK National Archives file: PREM 4/8/2A), that the aircraft had crashed with twelve people on board (clearly incorrect) and the pilot was Wing Commander Moseley, who he described as, 'An expert navigator and considered to be the best pilot in the squadron he commanded.' This latter comment is arguable considering his flying history.

In addition, Portal stated that weather conditions over the first part of the journey were: Cloud 1,000 feet, visibility three miles. There was however, a bad patch off Wick where clouds were at 300 feet. North of the north coast of Scotland, the weather improved; clouds were 4-8/10ths at 2,000 feet and still further improvement would have been experienced further north and west.

Sir Charles Portal also told the premier the Sunderland had hit high ground at about 2,300 feet (which was incorrect – it was about 690 feet above sea level) and to the west of Dunbeath.

Interestingly, in his last comment to Churchill, Sir Charles Portal added: 'Pending a full enquiry, the cause of the accident can only be surmised, it seems probable the pilot decided, in view of the bad patch round Wick, to climb through the cloud, he presumably drifted further to the west than he intended, and hit the hill when he thought he was over the sea.'

Portal's report was somewhat inaccurate in terms of some of the detail and he was clearly working on the sketchy information he had been given by his staff.

While this summary of the weather is similar to that in the RAF Alness narrative (Operations Record Book) for that day, the documents in the Australian National Archives state that the inquiry file contained two weather reports/forecasts for that day: one for the planned route and the other for RAF Alness. Like the scene photographs, the details of these two weather reports are now unrecorded and unavailable. Even the two meteorological officer witnesses do not go into much detail in their evidence as we shall see when we examine the witness evidence to the Court of Inquiry.

Air Vice-Marshal David Colyer's private papers are held for the nation at the Imperial War Museum in London. In October 2023, I visited the location and examined these documents.

The documents cover his time in the Royal Flying Corps during the First World War, as well as his time as Air Attaché to Paris before the next war. Letters from his wife, various newspapers cuttings and other official letters and documents are contained within the file. Even his commission papers and his dog-tags and identity cards are in the box file. The final document covers his retirement in 1962.

There is one letter from June 1940 to Sir Archibald Sinclair, the Secretary of State for Air from Leo Amery the Secretary of State for India. He drew Sinclair's attention to the good work David Colyer had undertaken as Air Attaché in Paris, in ensuring the return of Sir Francis Wylie to Britain from India. Clearly this placed him on Archibald Sinclair's radar just two years before the crash and it is likely the two men had spoken about this incident.

Various other newspaper cuttings from Britain and the United States covered Colyer's air force career throughout the Second World War. However, there is not one document or press cutting relating

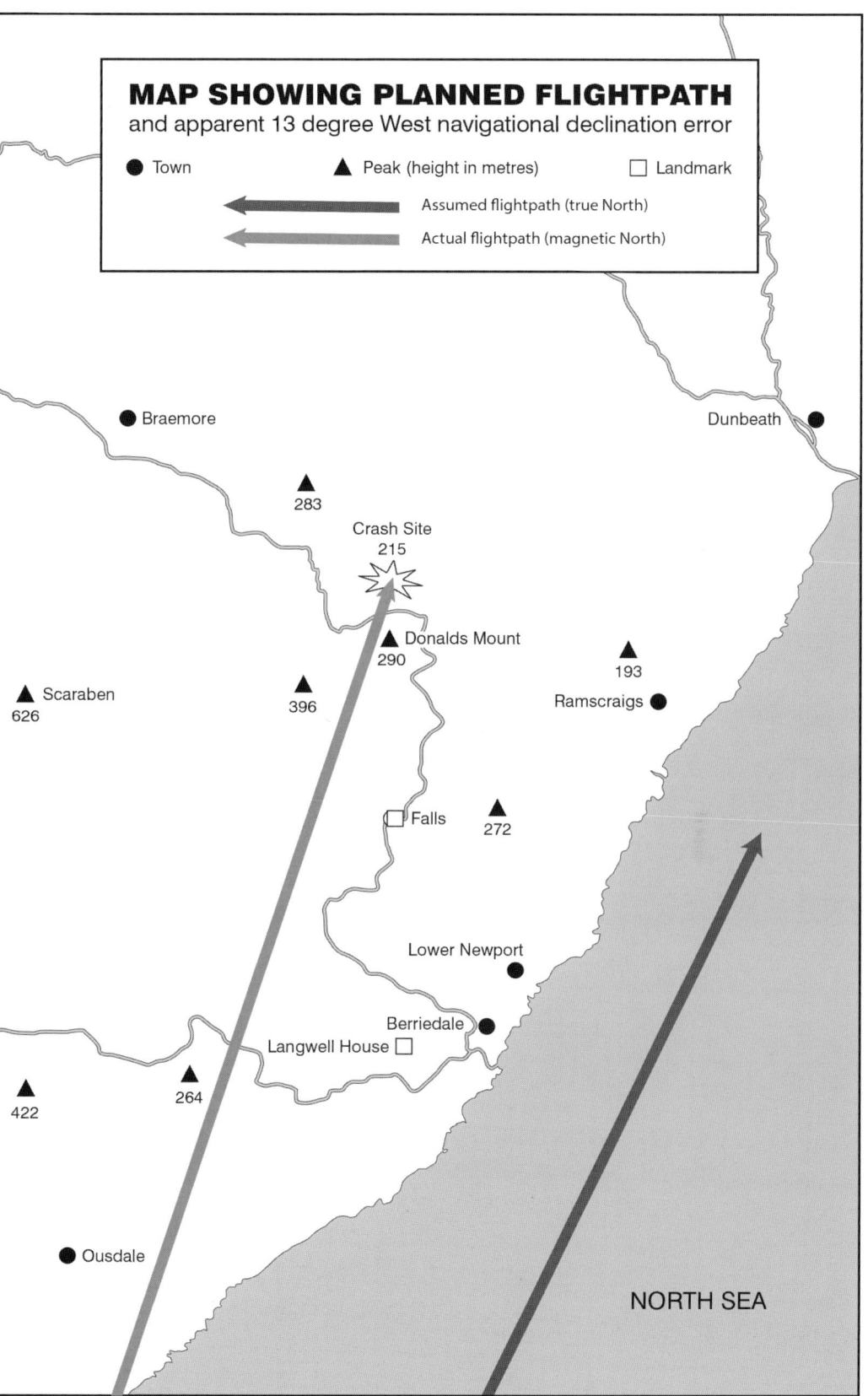

MAP SHOWING PLANNED FLIGHTPATH
and apparent 13 degree West navigational declination error

● Town   ▲ Peak (height in metres)   ☐ Landmark

Assumed flightpath (true North)

Actual flightpath (magnetic North)

● Braemore

Dunbeath ●

▲
283

Crash Site
215

▲ Donalds Mount
290

▲ Scaraben
626

▲
396

▲
193

Ramscraigs ●

☐ Falls

▲
272

Lower Newport
●

Berriedale ●

Langwell House ☐

▲
422

▲
264

● Ousdale

NORTH SEA

HRH Prince George, the Duke of Kent and Marina, Duchess of Kent. (*Authors collection*)

The only remaining evidence of flying boat operations at RAF Alness on Cromarty Firth – the old slipway from the workshop and hangar area into the Firth taken March 2024. (*Author*)

Left: The RAF
Alness site is now a
business park with
this memorial to RAF
Alness at the main
entrance. (*Author*)

Below: Unidentified
Sunderlands
undergoing servicing
at an unknown base.
(*Historic Military
Press*)

An aircraft in a similar paint scheme to the Duke of Kent's aircraft at its moorings. (*Historic Military Press*)

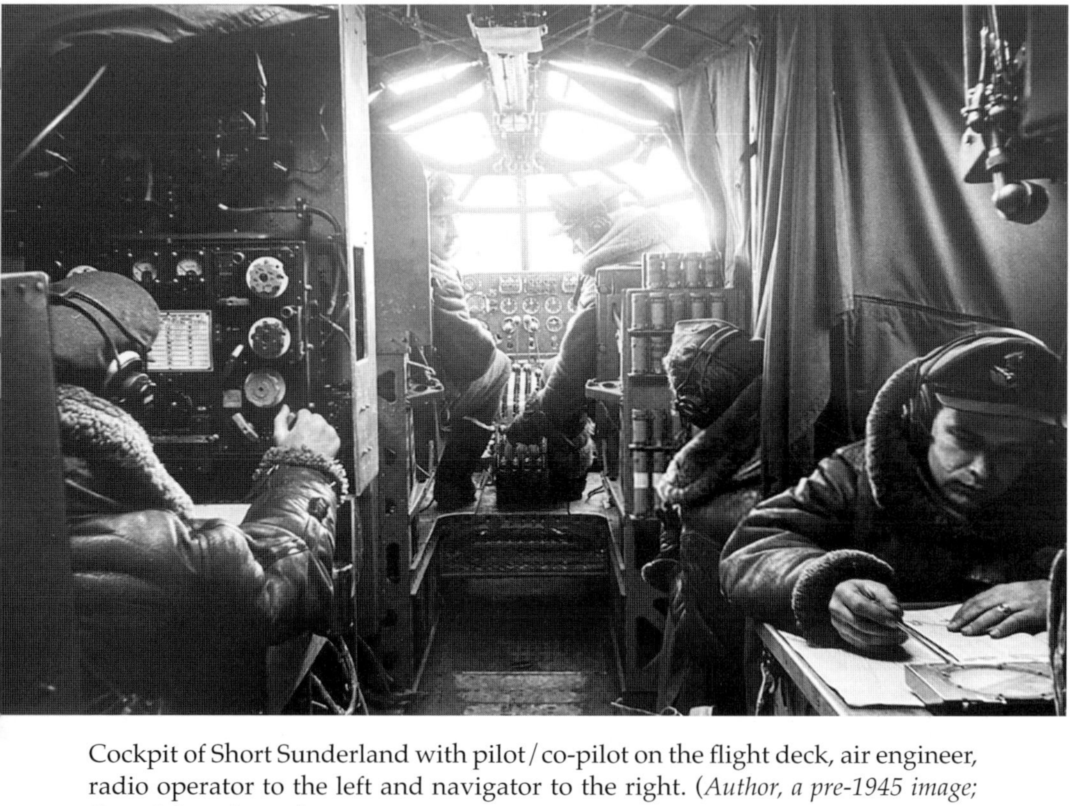

Cockpit of Short Sunderland with pilot/co-pilot on the flight deck, air engineer, radio operator to the left and navigator to the right. (*Author, a pre-1945 image; Copyright unknown*)

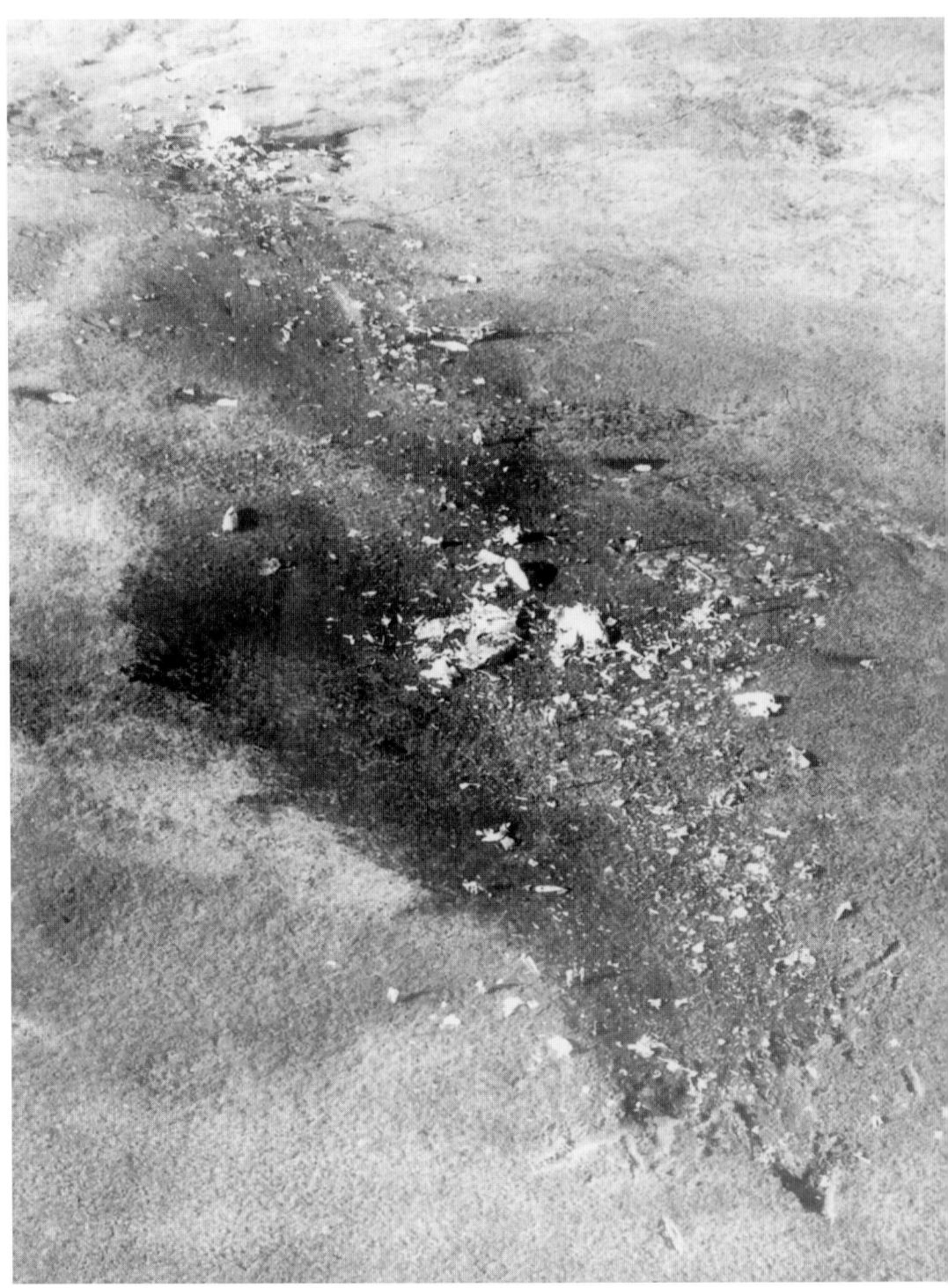

The debris field looking NNE. It appears the hull and wing floats (lower right corner) struck the soft earth and the aircraft bounced once before digging in and somersaulting forwards, leaving an impression of the wings leading edge, the main debris, including engines and wing floats, is in the central area, with tail and rear gun turret top centre. Note the scorched area from the burning fuel. (*Highland Libraries*)

Close up sections from the last image, showing the impression in the ground and main central area of debris. (*Highland Libraries*)

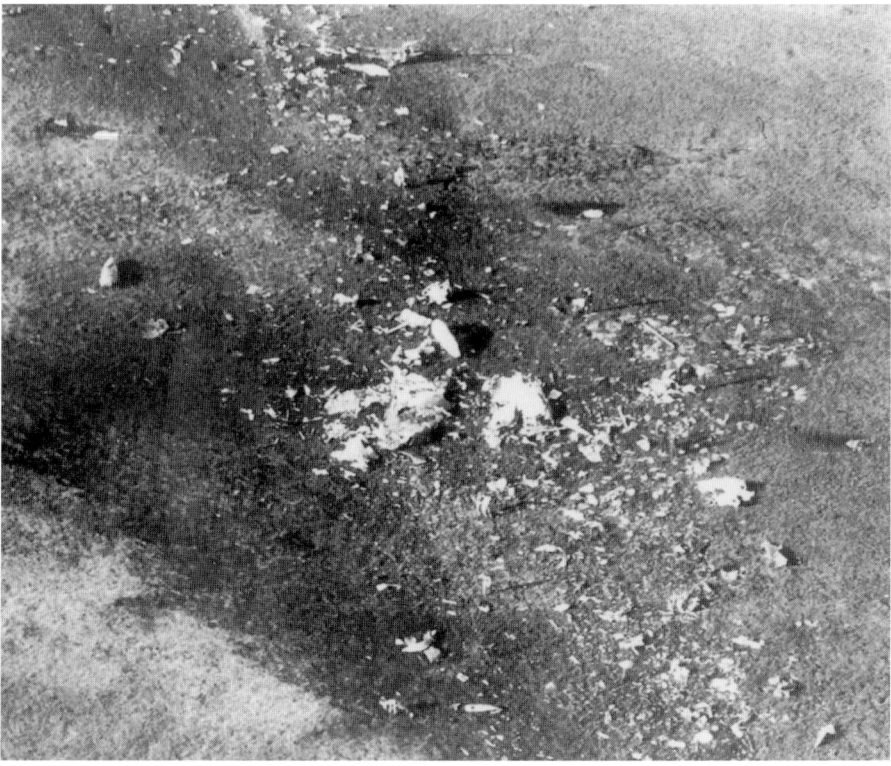

A close-up of the remains of the tail and rear gun turret from the top of the first image. (*Highland Libraries*)

Another close-up of the remains of the tail and rear gun turret from the top of the first image. (*Highland Libraries*)

The RAF Recovery team at what appears to be the main debris field. (*Getty Images*)

An RAF image taken from a photographic aircraft looking north-west. The remains of the rear turret and tail are to the right, main debris, engines and wing floats to left. (*IWM image*)

The RAF Regiment stand guard next to a wing float and engine. The camera is looking in a southerly direction with Donald's Mount/Meall Dhonuill in the distance. This appears to have been roughly the direction from which the aircraft struck the ground. (*Getty Images*)

Above: A grainy photographic image of the crash site. (*Courtesy of George Bethune*)

Left: Special Constable William Bethune. (*Courtesy of George Bethune*)

The position of the main DR compass in the rear fuselage of the Sunderland at the RAF Museum Hendon (black cylindrical object left-hand side). The lonely rear turret is in the distance down the narrow walkway. Although the museum aircraft is a later model, the DR compass is in the same position. (*Author*)

The huge tail and rear turret on the museum's Sunderland. (*Author*)

Depth charges under the starboard wing of the aircraft. (*Author*)

Above and below: The crash site memorial today, Donald's Mount is to the right of the cross and Berriedale Water can be seen in the distant valley. (*Author*)

IN MEMORY OF
AIR CDRE. H.R.H. THE DUKE OF KENT
K.G., K.T., G.C.M.G., G.C.V.O.
AND HIS COMPANIONS
WHO LOST THEIR LIVES ON ACTIVE SERVICE
DURING A FLIGHT TO ICELAND ON A SPECIAL MISSION
THE 25TH OF AUGUST 1942.

"MAY THEY REST IN PEACE."

The graves of Thomas Moseley and Frank Goyan in Pennyfuir cemetery, Oban. (*R. Morgan*)

Right: George Bethune in 2024. (*Author*)

Below: An oil can and a brass fire extinguisher recovered by walkers from the crash site and preserved in Dunbeath Heritage Centre.

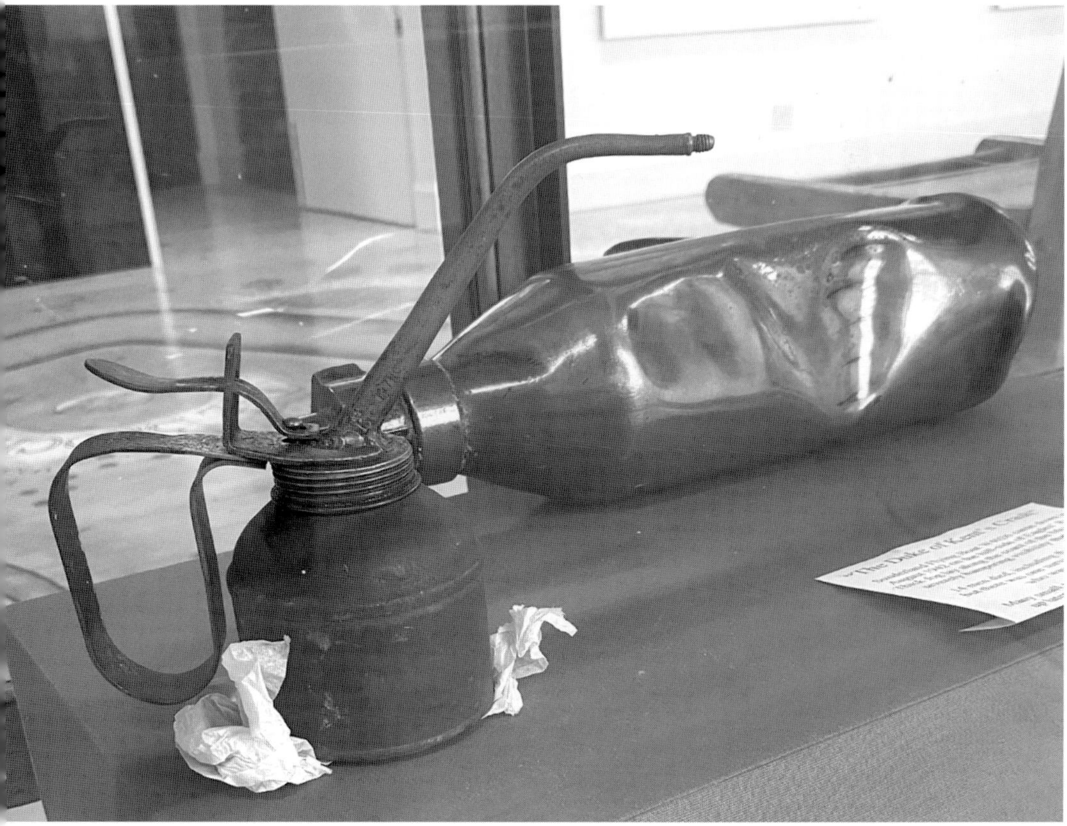

Among the various tools and aircraft parts recovered from the crash site was this broken early 1940s Chesebrough Vaseline jar from New York. (*Author*)

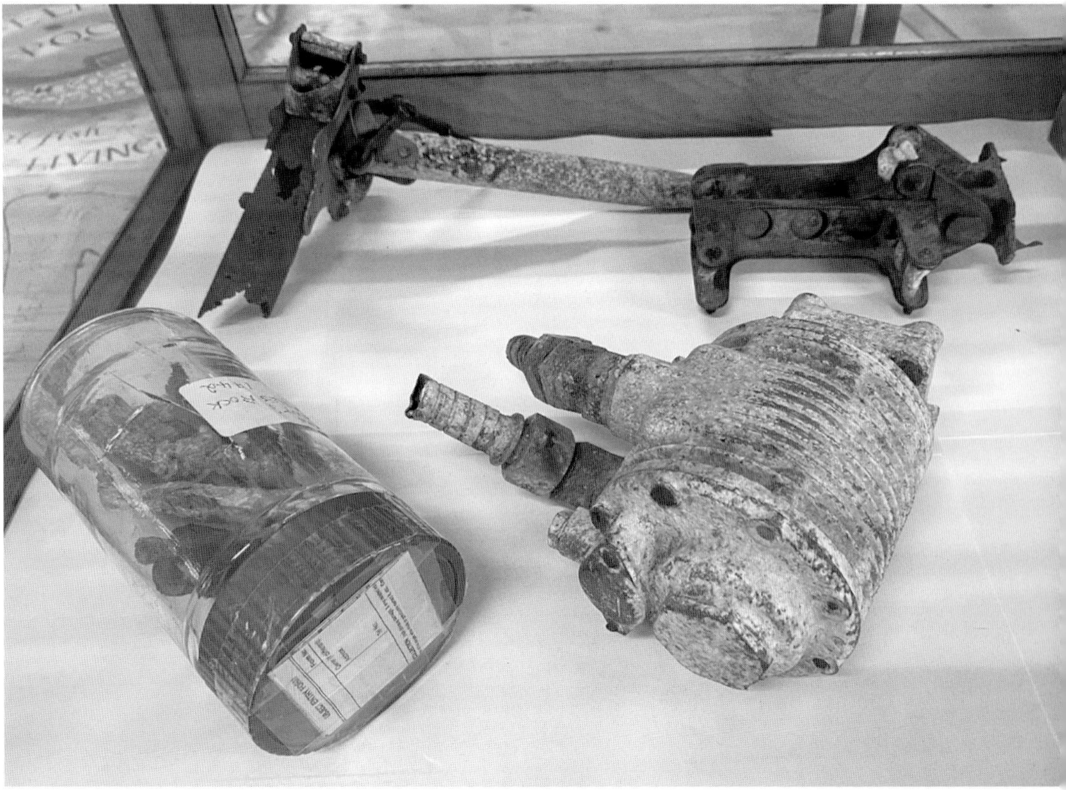

Various other parts. (*Author*)

to the fatal crash and the Court of Inquiry for the Duke of Kent in August 1942, which seems very odd.

In the Imperial War Museum, we have a box detailing the career of a very senior RAF man through two world wars, with his commission papers, his promotions, letters, transfers, documents and newspaper cuttings, but probably the most important and dramatic incident in his service career is nowhere to be found – not even one cutting from the hundreds of newspaper articles from across the world. Have they been redacted and purged by officials or was he just the ultimate, loyal professional who did not want to collect such material?

The only document touching on his time as Air Officer Commanding No. 15 Group, Coastal Command, is a copy of a signal he made to the command on 15 November 1942, three months after the Court of Inquiry. That was the date he left his position and moved on to another appointment on the Air Staff.

In the next chapter we shall examine the only known surviving documents relating to the Court of Inquiry, the Australian Archives copy of the Form 412, Proceedings of the Court of Inquiry or Investigation, its attached witness evidence and any questions and answers, as well as the Form 745, Report on flying accident or forced landing not attributable to enemy action.

Chapter Ten

The Board of Inquiry

As we have seen, the Court of Inquiry was established at Invergordon (RAF Alness) on 28 August, three days after the crash by order of Air Vice-Marshal David Colyer.

All Courts of Inquiry are governed by a strict set of protocols set out in King's Regulations.

According to the regulations, a Court of Inquiry may consist of any number of officers, its composition being determined by the convening officer (in this case Air Vice-Marshal David Colyer), according to the circumstances under which it is assembled. Three members, the senior acting as the inquiry president, will, in most ordinary cases, be sufficient.

The officer convening a Court of Inquiry will appoint the president by name, or failing to make such an appointment, the senior member on the inquiry panel will preside. Once the convening officer has appointed a president, no officer senior in rank to the president, will be appointed to serve as a member of the court of inquiry panel or board.

These instructions in 1942 were very clear and even those less experienced in handling such inquiries had the requirements set out for them on page two of the Form 412 – Proceedings of a Court of Inquiry or Investigation.

I will not repeat the entire instructions here as they can be read on the images of the form contained in the photographic section of this book, but some of the notes of guidance were very clear and impacted upon this investigation.

I have highlighted with bold print, those I believe were especially important in this case:

Section 2 states: **It must be borne in mind that the findings (including an opinion as to the cause of the accident and the degree of responsibility and any recommendations for the future), must be based upon and supported entirely by the recorded evidence of the witnesses or by additional facts ascertained by the Court themselves** which are to be recorded in sections 8 and 9 of the findings.

Section 3 states: **The Court or Investigating Officer will therefore not omit to see that the necessary witnesses are called and that their evidence on all material points is ascertained and recorded.** If the Court or Investigating Officer have not considered it necessary or feasible to visit the scene of the accident or to examine the logbooks, they will state these facts in items 8 and 9 of the findings.

Section 4 states: **Any special cause for the particular injuries of any member of the crew should be brought out in evidence and recorded.**

Section 5 states: **Investigation should be made to determine whether the failure of any part of the engine or aircraft, or the inefficient working of any accessory was a contributory cause of the accident,** and an opinion recorded under item 9 of the findings.

Section 7 states: Where the injuries to any person involved in the accident are such as to preclude his evidence being available when the Court or Investigation is held, it will be so stated.

Section 8 states: **The evidence of every witness may be recorded by hand or type-written. This will be done on ordinary fool-scrap sheets. Both sides of the sheet will be used; the use of a fresh page for each witness is unnecessary. The pages of these sheets (after being signed as described below) must be consecutively numbered and securely fastened.** (Author's note: There is no mention of a witness taking an oath on this form or in King's regulations).

Section 9 states: Each witness must sign each page of the evidence upon which his own evidence is recorded, but the signature of the President or Investigating Officer is not necessary in addition.

Section 10 states: The questions put to witnesses should be as simple as possible, and the Court of Investigating Officer should see that the recorded evidence of each witness is free from ambiguity, although it may not agree with the evidence of another.

Section 11 states: When it appears that the inquiry affects the character or professional reputation of an officer or airman, compliance with the provisions of paragraph 1318 of King's Regulations and Air Council Instructions is to be ensured.

(Author's note: Paragraph 1318 of King's Regulations ensures that an officer or airman has the right to defend their reputation and can question witnesses who may be relevant to the matter affecting their reputation. They can also offer their own evidence and defend their own reputation.)

The instructions were very clear, the Court of Inquiry should ensure all witnesses and all material points are covered and examined, nothing should be omitted. This included particular injuries with any special causes, as well as an investigation into the workings of the engines and the aircraft in general. It should also determine whether there was any 'inefficient working of any accessory' which was a contributory cause of the accident.

In effect, the instruction was basically telling the investigators that they should examine all relevant witnesses and record their evidence, attend the crash scene, examine (or get a specialist to examine) the engines, instruments and airframe for possible faults or incorrect use etc. No stone should be left unturned!

Examination of the Form 412 held in the Australian National Archives finds it to bear no signatures of any of the Inquiry panel or the witnesses. This is because it is a typed certified copy of the original Form 412 which has now disappeared. The witness testimony is also typed rather than contemporaneously handwritten as was normally the case in an inquiry. Each page of witness testimony has written at the top of the page: *Certified True Copy* and *(Signed) ??? F/O Adjutant.*

The Form 412, which was completed once the inquiry was concluded, states that the four Bristol Pegasus engines were seriously damaged, noting the Air Ministry and manufacturer's serial numbers, as well as a list of the Sunderland's crew.

Page 1 of the form clearly lists Wing Commander Thomas Lawton Moseley as the 1st Pilot, Flight Lieutenant Frank McKenzie Goyan as the aircraft Captain and Pilot Officer Smith as 2nd Pilot. The navigator was Pilot Officer George Saunders and the flight engineer was Sergeant Leonard Sweett.

It is worth remembering this form was completed after the Court of Inquiry had been concluded, as was the Form 1180 (accident card) which also listed the three pilots in this order.

If these records are correct, Wing Commander Thomas Moseley appears to have been 1st Pilot of the Sunderland, possibly for the first time in his career and certainly for the first time on No. 228 Squadron.

Pages 2 and 3 detail the flying hours and experience of both Moseley and Goyan, while page 3 also states that the aircraft was on a 'Transit flight to Iceland, No special Instructions.' On the same page, the section which should include the time of the crash was left blank, something that many conspiracy theorists have been keen to point out, often claiming this was a deliberate omission to cover the collection of Rudolf Hess from Loch More.

The aircraft was noted as having taken-off at 1311 hours, with the wind 10 mph from the east, visibility 2,200-4,400 yards, cloud 10/10ths at 1,000 feet with fragments as low as 200 feet.

In the section giving details of how the aircraft was controlled at the time, there is a confusing jumble of names with the 1st Pilot now shown as Flight Lieutenant Goyan and the 2nd Pilot as Wing Commander Moseley, completely contradicting the entries on page one of the form. Was this indicative that the Inquiry panel were undecided about who the pilot was that day?

On page 4 the report states the engine logbooks, airframe logbooks including the Form 700, pilots' logbooks and the Special Equipment maintenance form had all been checked and were correct.

The Form 700 has for many years been a maintenance and engineering logbook, which even has technical faults or issues entered into it; e.g. the port outer engine boost dial in cockpit instrument panel is giving an incorrect reading. The aircraft captain would sign this form before the flight, effectively assuming control of the Sunderland, so whoever signed the form was the captain as far as the Court of Inquiry was concerned.

Section 9 on Page 4 then states unequivocally: 'We (I) have visited the scene of the accident before aircraft was removed and found the following material facts: 1. The engines were under power at the time of the crash, 2. Parachutes were not used.'

The form is signed by Kay, Stacey and Lindsay, so we must assume as stated, that all three men attended the crash scene. However, there is no evidence in the surviving record/evidence to say when exactly that occurred, something a police senior investigating officer and any air crash investigator today would record in their own notes or logs.

The copy of the report from the Court of Inquiry held in the Australian National Archives, gives details and a list of thirteen witnesses, their evidence and questions and answers for each of them. As already stated in the case of Flight Sergeant Andrew Jack, this appears to have been a copy of each witness's original handwritten contemporaneous notes, written by investigators and signed by the witness. Each witness is indicated to have signed the original papers together with the date they provided the evidence.

The first witness was Flying Officer Ronald Albyn McCallum, service number 63977. He was Duty Controller at RAF Invergordon on 25 August 1942. He gave his evidence on 30 August according to the record and answered a number of additional questions from the Court of Inquiry. He states, according to the papers attached to the Form 412:

'I am a controller at RAF Station Invergordon. At approximately 1000 hours on 25 August 1942, I briefed the captain Flight Lieutenant Goyen and the 1st Pilot Wing Commander Moseley of Sunderland 'M' of No. 228 Squadron. I routed them via Tarbat Ness, Clyth Ness, Thurso, Cape Wrath and Butt of Lewis to Iceland. The aircraft was airborne at 1312 hours.'

Q. 'Was the Captain given any height at which to fly?'

A. 'No.'

Q. 'Did he express any intention of flying at any particular height in view of the prevailing weather conditions?'

A. 'No.'

Q. 'Why in view of the low cloud, was the aircraft routed over the land?'

A. 'Because this is the normal route given in any weather conditions.'

Q. 'Did the Captain or his 1st Pilot query or pass any comment with regards to this overland route?'

A. 'No.'

The witness must have seen and exhibited the meteorological reports introduced to the Court of Inquiry and listed as exhibits on the form 412. However, their evidence gives no mention of what the weather forecast was, or what those exhibits actually contained.

It would appear from this evidence, that the crew were briefed to fly overland between Clyth Ness and Thurso – something as we have seen, standing orders from Coastal Command directed flying boat pilots to avoid, except in an emergency.

Although the overland flightpath is not specifically stated in the evidence, why was the first navigational waypoint after Tarbat Ness, the lighthouse at Clyth Ness near Dunbeath and the next one Thurso? If they were to avoid flying overland, surely the next waypoint after Clyth Ness would have been Wick or John O'Groats on the north tip of Caithness? This appears to indicate without actually stating it, that the route was across the low land to Thurso and in breach of the directive.

The question is, did everyone concerned from the witnesses to the Court of Inquiry panel, know this was the case and something that was in contravention of an official directive?

If this issue and the planned routing was ignored, it was an important omission, when to most people it was clear there was a possible navigation or airmanship cause for the crash.

It is interesting to note that the witness Flying Officer McCallum, clearly states that Wing Commander Moseley was the 1st Pilot and Flight Lieutenant Goyan the aircraft captain. This means there was an issue of who was in command of the aircraft, the captain Flight Lieutenant Goyan or the squadron commander and 1st Pilot Wing Commander Moseley?

The second witness was Flight Lieutenant Leslie Lawrence Robert Burch service number 62349, a Signals Officer at RAF Invergordon. He also gave his evidence on 30 August 1942 and answered one question. He stated:

'I am the Signals Officer at RAF Station, Invergordon. At approximately 1000 hours on 25 August 1942, I examined the W/T briefing slips of Sunderland 'M' of No. 228 Squadron. I saw that they had all they required and everything was in order.'

Q. 'Was a W/T watch being maintained at Invergordon on the frequency that the aircraft was to use and if so, were any signals intercepted from it?'

A. 'Yes, a listening out watch was maintained on this frequency, but nothing was heard.'

The third witness was Donald Mackay Gunn, a civilian Meteorological Officer based at RAF Invergordon. He gave his evidence and answered one question on 31 August 1942:

'I am employed as a forecaster at RAF Station Invergordon. On 25 August 1942, at 0900 hours, a complete weather forecast was issued to the captain of the aircraft 'M' of 228 Squadron for the route from Invergordon to Iceland. This was followed by a discussion in the meteorological office at 0900 hours between the Met. Officer on duty and the captain of the aircraft. After the captain had boarded his aircraft, a supplementary forecast was sent out to him at approximately 1100 hours showing a further deterioration in the weather.'

Q. 'What was the cloud base and visibility at the time of the aircraft's take off at Invergordon?'

A. 'The general cloud base was 1,000 feet. There were some fragments at 200 feet. The visibility was from 2,200 to 4,400 yards.'

Once again, the detail of the actual weather forecast was not documented or discussed, neither was the content of the supplementary weather forecast and the only question the witness was asked, concerned the visibility at take-off.

The obvious clarifying question which should have been asked here is, 'Who was the aircraft captain?' The Court of Inquiry failed to check and corroborate the evidence of the earlier witnesses and to confirm the crew positions and the command structure on board the Sunderland.

Andrew Dryburgh, another Meteorological Officer at RAF Invergordon was the next witness. He gave his evidence dated 31 August 1942, he stated:

'I am employed as a forecaster at RAF Station Invergordon and was on duty from 0700 hours to 0900 hours on 25 August

1942. At approximately 0850 hours the captain, 1st Pilot, 2nd Pilot and navigator came into the Meteorological Office and discussed the 0200 synoptic chart. In the course of the discussion, I mentioned that in relation to the weather forecast, there was a risk of low cloud with a main base of about 800 feet spreading west of a line roughly from Lossiemouth to Wick.'

Q. 'Did the Captain of the aircraft ask what the conditions would be for flying at a height to clear the high ground over the north of Scotland?'

A. 'No.'

Once again, there appears to have been no question as to who was the captain and 1st Pilot etc. This may seem to be pedantic, but with the Form 412 showing a variation in 1st and 2nd Pilots, this should have been confirmed by the inquiry panel.

Yet again, there was no recorded comment from the witness giving precise details of the weather forecast or what the synoptic chart actually contained. They did however mention the risk of low cloud.

The one recorded question appears to have been a 'closed question', giving the witness little chance to reply with an expanded answer, but only with a simple 'yes' or 'no'. This, as we will see throughout this inquiry, is a continuous issue with the panel's line of questioning.

Flight Lieutenant Henry John Leonard Jones, service number 70437, was Permanent Duty Pilot at RAF Invergordon. He gave his evidence on 31 August 1942. He stated:

'I am the Permanent Duty Pilot at RAF Station Invergordon. I was on duty at West Pier, Invergordon on the morning of

25 August 1942. After the crew and passengers of 'M' No. 228 Squadron had embarked, the travelling Form 700, crew chit and receipt for the latest weather report had been handed to me, the aircraft slipped its moorings at approximately 1250 hours and became airborne at 1311 hours. It took off in a north-easterly direction and was lost to sight climbing steadily in that direction at a distance, I estimate to be 3,000 to 4,000 yards.'

No questions were asked of this witness by the inquiry panel.

The next witness was Flying Officer Norman Johnson Cryderman, service number C.8119, a Signals RDF Officer at RAF Oban. He gave his statement dated 1 September 1942:

'I am Signals RDF Officer of No. 228 Squadron. On 23 August 1942, I instructed Corporal Atherton to carry out a routine inspection of the Special Equipment (author's note: radar) on Sunderland 'M' of No. 228 Squadron.'

No questions were asked of this witness.

The next witness was Corporal James Atherton service number 98737, a Radio Mechanic on No. 228 Squadron at RAF Oban. He gave his statement dated 1 September 1942:

'I am Corporal in charge of the Special Equipment Section of No. 228 Squadron. At approximately 1000 hours on 2 August 1942, I carried out an inspection on the Special Equipment on Sunderland 'M' of No. 228 Squadron. Everything was satisfactory and I signed the Daily Inspection Form to that effect.'

Again, no questions were asked of this witness and it was clear the Court of Inquiry were satisfied the aircraft was airworthy and serviceable at the time of the fatal flight. Although no one gave technical or scientific evidence of examining the engines, the remains of the airframe or any instruments (if any were found), this is an important factor to consider. Just because an aircraft was in perfect working condition the day before the crash, does not mean there was no technical fault or a human issue in handling the machine immediately before the incident.

Surely a technical expert should have searched for and examined the wreckage for such issues. They could have explained their findings to the Court of Inquiry or at the very least, stated that they could not reach any conclusions due to the severity of the damage etc. This issue is exacerbated by the lack of any input by Sydney Vernon Brown and his team of accident inspectors.

The next witness was probably the most important in this case – Flight Sergeant Andrew Jack. The Form 412 states that his evidence, questions and answers are dated 29 August 1942, but as we have already seen, he was lying in a hospital bed in Lybster being visited by his family that day.

We already know from his family that on 29 August, they arrived to find a senior RAF officer and a senior Naval officer talking with Andrew Jack. The relatives were ushered away while the two men spoke with him and they saw Andrew being assisted by one officer in signing some sort of a document.

This is clearly how Andrew Jack gave evidence to the Court of Inquiry. His comments, the interviewing officer's questions and his replies, were then noted on the Form 412.

However, for veracity and openness, surely the Form 412 should have stated that Jack was interviewed in his hospital bed. It also raises questions about the evidence supplied by the other twelve witnesses, such as did they attend the Court of Inquiry and give 'live' evidence in person to a hearing, or did they just provide a verbal statement which was noted by an officer, signed by the witness and used in the final report?

Examination of the papers appears to indicate that evidence was probably not given at a live hearing at Invergordon, but gathered by visiting the witnesses and putting a bundle of their evidence together. This can be seen as the first five witnesses in the records attached to the Form 412, were based at RAF Invergordon (Alness), giving their evidence on 30 and 31 August 1942. Witness six and seven came from RAF Oban and gave their evidence on 1 September 1942, while Andrew Jack was the eighth witness, having given his evidence on 29 August 1942. He was followed by two witnesses on the same day from the Dunbeath area and then the final witness from Wick on 30 August 1942.

If Andrew Jack and the other witnesses did not give evidence in person to a formal hearing, it could lead to accusations of a cover-up. Witness evidence could possibly be omitted and witnesses could be selected and led through their evidence, with closed questions to obtain certain desired information. This would create an investigatory environment likely to miss crucial evidence.

Flight Sergeant Andrew Jack's evidence as presented in the Form 412 report states:

'I am an Air Gunner with No. 228 Squadron. On Tuesday, 25 August 1942, I was a member of the crew of aircraft W4026 which was on passage from Invergordon to Iceland. We were airborne at about 1300 hours and the height of the cloud was about 500 feet. The Captain, Flight Lieutenant Goyen, who was flying the aircraft, told us there would be a lot of cloud around, but he did not think it would last long. This was over the intercom. I was in the rear turret. As we proceeded, the cloud came down thicker. I felt the aircraft losing height after about twenty minutes, the pilot was apparently trying to get under the cloud base. I do not remember anything after this.'

Q. 'Do you know who was navigating the aircraft?'

A. 'I don't know.'

Q. 'Did you hear anything else over the intercom?'

A. 'No.'

Q. 'Do you remember who was in the 2nd Pilot's seat?'

A. 'No.'

Q. 'Did you think the aircraft climbed much before it started to come down again?'

A. 'No, not much.'

Q. 'Was the last thing you remember being in cloud?'

A. 'Yes.'

Jack clearly states that Flight Lieutenant Goyan was the captain and flying the aircraft. Why he was asked who was navigating the aircraft is a strange question, when there was only one dedicated navigator on board (Pilot Officer George Saunders), so why was he asked this question? Did the Court of Inquiry (or the two senior officers who met him in the hospital) suspect someone else was navigating the aircraft? Does this imply that the Court of Inquiry believed there was an issue with the navigation?

The fact the panel asked Jack if he heard anything else on the intercom is very interesting, especially as he replied 'No', but in later years he changed this account. In addition, the question about who was in the 2nd Pilots' seat is also odd.

Andrew Jack's comments about the pilot appearing to be trying to get under the cloud base are strange, especially as he stated the cloud was at 500 feet and was reducing further in height. If that was the case, surely any experienced airman would have climbed the aircraft and not tried to get under a cloud base of 500 feet which was allegedly getting lower – unless they expected to be over the sea. However, there were no further questions about what Jack saw or heard. In fact, again the line of questioning was 'closed' and prevented anything but yes, no and I don't know answers.

It is surprising Andrew Jack does not give details of what happened when he regained consciousness after the crash. There is no questioning about what he did or whether he examined his colleagues and the Duke of Kent. In addition, he was not asked his opinion about how the aircraft appeared to be performing prior to the crash. He was not asked about what he saw at the crash site and who was in what position and their physical condition. It is almost as if the Court of Inquiry had decided they only wanted certain details and these were who the pilot was, who was navigating and the weather conditions. This appears to be contrary to the explicit instructions in King's Regulations and repeated on Form 412.

As the sole survivor and primary witness, some might call Andrew Jack the 'star witness' and he should have been subjected to further probing questions.

Andrew Jack may well have been asked more questions in his hospital bed and this may have been noted by the attending officers, but we will never know as all we have is a typed copy of the final report. Why Jack's evidence was so curtailed and did not go into the pre-flight actions and his own subsequent observations and actions, is in my professional opinion as a former senior detective and case reviewing officer, a matter of great concern.

The next witness was Dr John Robert Kennedy, a medical doctor from Dunbeath. As we have seen from earlier civilian witnesses who were not called to give evidence by the Court of Inquiry, he arrived after being contacted by a postmistress and examined the body of the Duke of Kent. The duke's wristwatch had stopped at 1:42pm and the doctor kept it for safe keeping, believing it could be evidential.

Dr Kennedy noted that everyone at the scene was deceased, suffering multiple injuries and burns, but no mention was made of specific injuries to any individual person by the doctor. While this may have been difficult due to the number of casualties, the working environment and probably not having a pen and paper in his possession, surely he could remember the condition of the duke and possibly others such as Lieutenant Lowther in his distinctive naval uniform? Did he not make any notes when he returned to his surgery?

The next day, Dr Kennedy was called and informed of Andrew Jack's arrival at Elsie Sutherland's crofters cottage. He attended and treated his injuries before Jack was taken by ambulance to the Bignold hospital in Lybster.

In his evidence provided to the Court of Inquiry on 29 August 1942, the doctor stated:

'I am a Medical Officer for the Western District of the Parish of Latheron. At about 1400 hours on 25 August 1942, I heard casually on the telephone that an aircraft had crashed somewhere in the vicinity of Braemore. I immediately proceeded to Braemore by car with a small search party which I had organised. We proceeded down the Berriedale River for 2 ½ miles hoping to get in touch with a large search party under the control of Lord Titchfield. Owing to thick fog and rain, we were unable to contact this party. I sent three members of my search party ahead in a north-easterly direction where I thought the plane would be. They reached the plane which had been previously found by James Gunn, a shepherd from Braemore.

'They returned to where I was waiting and informed me that the occupants were all dead. I went back with them to the crashed aircraft and found eleven bodies in and around the wreckage and three trapped under burning wreckage. I examined all the bodies accessible and found that death was due to burning and multiple injuries in most cases. In all cases, death must have been instantaneous.'

Q. 'What do you estimate the visibility to be in the vicinity of the crash?'

A. 'About 30 yards.'

Why the doctor was not asked about specific injuries and the precise locations of the bodies is unfathomable. While the question about the visibility is viable, surely a doctor could have been asked some medical questions. This apparent lack of medical evidence from an expert witness is so shocking, it automatically leads one to suspect he did give exact details of injuries, but they were omitted from the record. However, this is a certified true copy of his evidence which was signed by him on 29 August 1942, so he appears to have never given such detailed evidence.

The omission of any details of casualty injuries is in contravention of section 4 of the forms notes for guidance and King's Regulations, which specifically state: 'Any special cause for particular injuries of any member of the crew should be brought out in evidence and recorded as under paragraph 1 of the report findings.'

To exacerbate this apparent omission, there is no mention of injuries entered in paragraph one of the findings, on page three of the completed Form 412.

Although he did not state it in his evidence, Dr Kennedy would later claim that he was the first to identify the duke's body, this conflicting with the two Special Constables claims.

The doctor later claimed he identified the duke's body from a monogrammed cigarette case and the inscription on his wristwatch. This information came in August 1985 from Kennedy's daughter Louise, when she was interviewed for the BBC Radio Scotland programme *The Crash of W4026* presented by Robin MacWhirter. However, according to Will Bethune's account, the Home Guard Sergeant, Bob Henderson, had found the wristwatch among the debris and handed it to Dr Kennedy, while the medic did not mention the duke's identity bracelet, unlike the special constable's account.

Dr Kennedy had attended a number of air crashes on the high-ground during the war. He was therefore very experienced in terms of what would be found at an air crash and I believe he should have been examined in more depth by the Court of Inquiry. There is no doubt in my mind that he could have given valuable evidence if examined in more detail.

The next witness was William Sutherland, a member of the Observer Corps and a local crofter from Ramscraigs near Dunbeath. In his evidence provided to the Inquiry on 29 August 1942, he stated:

'I am a member of the Royal Observer Corps. At approximately 1330 hours on 25 August 1942, I was in the post at Lower Newport, Berriedale, on duty. A plane was heard approaching from the south in cloud at an estimated height of 1,000 to 2,000 feet. After a short period, we lost the sound of the machine again. It was then disappearing in a north or north-westerly direction. This was the only aircraft going north within half an hour either side of 1330 hours.'

Q. 'What were the weather conditions at the time 1330 hours?'

A. 'Visibility was about 100 yards with cloud covering all the hill tops, wind was fresh from the south-east.'

William Sutherland, like other witnesses, was only asked about the weather conditions. He was not asked if the aircraft sounded like any other passing machine he had previously heard, whether he believed it was in trouble, or whether he can be certain of its general position and direction of travel in the cloud layer. Again, there is a clear lack of probing questions from the inquiry panel.

Flying Officer Kenneth Stanley Mullard, service number 101827, an RAF Medical Officer, was based at RAF Wick. In his evidence provided to the Inquiry on 30 August 1942, he stated:

'I am a Medical Officer in charge temporarily of RAF Station Wick. At about 1430 hours on 25 August 1942, I was informed by Flying Control that there had probably been an aircraft accident in the region of Scaraben. At approximately 1530 hours, we were informed that this news was definite and an ambulance party proceeded to Dunbeath.

'This party subsequently reported that Dr Kennedy of Dunbeath had seen the crash and that the crew and passengers were all dead. Further rescue operations were out of the question because the crash could not be found again in thick weather. Acting on the instructions of the Station Commander, the stretcher party was organised to go out at first light on 26 August.

'We arrived at the scene of the crash at approximately 0700 hours. I was taken by one of the soldiers forming the guard to the bodies and in the course of the next two to three hours, fourteen identifiable bodies were removed from the crash. The cause of death in all cases were multiple injuries. Some of the bodies had been burned, but in my opinion, burning took place after death, which was instantaneous in all cases.'

Considering this witness's position, rank and profession, he was not asked any questions. Here was another expert medical witness, someone who had probably seen air crash victims before, but he was not asked about individual body positions, details of their precise injuries or whether he knew the identities of each body etc. He would certainly have known which was the Duke of Kent, his entourage and the pilots from their uniforms and insignia, but no questions were apparently asked about this.

The next witness was Sub Lieutenant John Stanley Whitehead RNVR RNO Wick, a man we have already discussed. In his evidence provided to the Court of Inquiry on 30 August 1942, he stated:

'I am Watchkeeping Officer at RNO Wick. At approximately 1330 hours on 25 August 1942, I was fishing at the falls on Berriedale River to the west of Eagles Rock.

'A few minutes after this, I heard an aircraft approach from the sea. It was impossible to see the aircraft, but from the sound it appeared to be very low, so low in fact, that I half expected it to crash. The sound of the engines appeared to be quite normal. Immediately after this I heard a dull thud and the sound of the engines ceased and I assumed that the aircraft had crashed. I immediately packed up my tackle and proceeded towards Braemore. Owing to the thick mist, it was not until 1610 hours that I came upon the scene of the accident. In this search, I was accompanied by three shepherds. As it appeared that we were the first to find the crash a further search was made to see if there were any survivors in the immediate vicinity. None were found.'

Q. 'What were the weather conditions in the vicinity of Eagle Rock at the time of the accident?'

A. 'At 1330 hours, it was raining heavily with visibility approximately 100 yards. The mist was right down on the ground.'

The single question put to Lieutenant Whitehead appears to demonstrate once again that the panel were fixated with the weather conditions. As previously mentioned it is not known why this naval officer had not been questioned further about the crash scene. Although not an airman, he was another educated commissioned man, who could be relied upon to give structured and detailed evidence of what he found that afternoon. In addition, why did he not name the shepherds, or say he did not know their names? If he was the man who went to the gamekeeper MacEwan's home, why was this not mentioned in his evidence?

The final witness was Pilot Officer Joseph Edward Lewis service number 48155, an Assistant Signals Officer based at RAF Wick. In his evidence provided to the Inquiry on 30 August 1942, he stated:

'I am Assistant Signals Officer at RAF Station Wick. On the request of the Controller at 2215 hours on 25 August 1942, I visited the Squadron Special Equipment Section and made tests on equipment already set-up, and found that the Wick Responder Beacon at Harland was operating correctly.

I confirmed from the W/T Station at Harland that the beacon had been working correctly all day and that there had been no power failure. No requests were received from aircraft W4026 for W/T bearings on the H/F or N/F frequencies on which watch is normally kept at this station.'

Clearly satisfied the Wick Beacon was functioning correctly and had no bearing on this case, the inquiry asked Pilot Officer Lewis no further questions.

The Court of Inquiry members seemed to have been fixated with the weather conditions, visibility and who was flying and navigating the aircraft. However, no evidence was given from an engineer or other technical expert witness in relation to the aircraft's engines, its instruments or airframe; not even to state they were beyond examination due to damage sustained in the crash.

It seems odd that no effort was made to locate the positions of the bodies at the crash site, something that may have assisted with their deliberations. (A pilot could have still been strapped into a seat or pinned against the instrument panel.) It was as if the weather and pilot error had already been declared the cause of this fatal crash.

There is also the issue of who was in command of the aircraft, if Goyan was the captain and Moseley, a man who outranked him was flying the aircraft, who was making the decisions; or more importantly, who made the fatal decision to reduce height over land? Did they believe they were over the sea?

This was the second worst air crash in British history in 1942, with the Duke of Kent on board, but the Court of Inquiry appears, in my opinion, to have been cursory.

Royal Air Force Courts of Inquiry regularly move around to gather evidence, I have seen this in post war documents and witness statements.

It is clear the Inquiry opened on 28 August. The following day they received evidence from Andrew Jack (in Bignold hospital),

Dr Kennedy in nearby Dunbeath and the Royal Observer Corps man William Sutherland at Lower Newport near Berriedale. All three witnesses could have been visited within a few minutes' drive of one another. But this raises a significant question… if, as in the case of Andrew Jack, this was by a senior RAF officer and a Royal Naval officer, who were they? The three main Inquiry members were all RAF officers (Kay, Stacey and Lindsay).

On 30 August, evidence was received from the witnesses based at Wick and Invergordon. On the next day further evidence was heard from witnesses based at Invergordon and on 1 September, the witnesses from RAF Oban. Later that day, the Court of Inquiry completed their findings and gave the following findings and observations:

FINDINGS:

The cause of the accident was in our opinion due to the aircraft being flown on a wrong track at too low an altitude to clear the rising ground on the track.

The responsibility for this serious mistake in airmanship lies with the captain of the aircraft, F/Lt Goyan, who changed his flight plan for reasons unknown, in as much that he commenced the flight by climbing into cloud, and then started to descend, but failed to take the elementary precaution of making sure that he was over the water, and crashed in to the hillside whilst still in cloud.

In our opinion, the weather encountered should have presented no difficulties to an experienced pilot.

The examination of the propellors showed that the engines were under power when the aircraft struck the ground.

In the book *Double Standards – The Rudolf Hess cover-up*, there is a claim that on the Royal Air Force Station Oban website it is stated that 63 Maintenance Unit found the four engines to be at full throttle and their propellors at coarse pitch, indicating the aircraft had been climbing at the time of the crash. The website is sadly no longer available and I cannot confirm this. However, the available Court of Inquiry forms and the Forms 1180 and 765 do not give this detail, only that the engines were under power at the time of the crash.

The report concluded:

In accordance with Kings Regulations and A.C.I. para 1325 we find that all the occupants of Sunderland 'M' of No. 228 Squadron were on duty at the time of the accident.

RECOMMENDATIONS:

In view of F/Lt Goyan's previous experience, this sudden lack of judgement was quite unpredictable and in these circumstances the Court is unable to make any recommendations.

It is desired to bring to notice the magnificent work done by Dr Kennedy aged seventy-one of Dunbeath. In the last two years, he has been the first Medical Officer on the scene of the accident of six crashes, in this particular instance in appalling weather conditions, all over difficult terrain which would have taxed the endurance of a much younger person.

Interestingly, in section 9 of the form it states that 'The accident has been reported to the Accident Investigation Branch', although no other details were noted regarding this statement.

The form was dated 1 September 1942 and signed by Wing Commander A.W. Kay, Squadron Leader W.J. D'A Stacey and Flight Lieutenant Lindsay.

On 3 September 1942, Group Captain Edward F. Turner signed the Form as Station Commander, RAF Oban, making the following comment:

> 'I concur with the findings of the Court as to the actual cause of the accident, but I am of the opinion that, in the weather conditions pertaining at the time, a non-operational flight should not have been carried out.'

Was Group Captain Edward Turner criticising Wing Commander Moseley and Frank Goyan?

On 7 September, Air Vice-Marshal David Colyer the man who convened the Court of Inquiry added his own comment:

> 'I concur with the finding of the Court and consider that the weather conditions should have presented no difficulty to a crew of such experience.'

The fact the two senior commander's comments on the form were at odds with one another is very unusual. Turner was a very experienced pilot having flown transport aircraft in the 1920s, before flying boats with 201 and 202 Squadrons in the 1930s. If a man of his abilities and experience deemed the weather conditions to have been too dangerous for a non-operational flight, we should take notice.

However, what is often missed is the fact that Group Captain Edward F. Turner was not the RAF Oban Station Commander at this time according to the RAF Officer Lists, but a member of the No. 18 Group Air Staff. The commanding officer from 1938 was Group Captain John Hugh Oscar Jones, he departed in December

1943, so why was Turner signing and commenting on the report as the Oban Station Commander?

A WAAF Corporal – Dorothea Gray (nee Whyte) who was based at the RAF Station HQ in Oban – recorded her memoirs in 1996. She noted that the Officer Commanding was posted away with the Adjutant shortly after the crash. At the end of 1942, Turner was still shown as a member of the Air Staff on No. 18 Group, Coastal Command, so did he stand in as the Station Commander? Group Captain Jones, however, aged forty-eight in 1942, disappears from the RAF Officer Lists.

As we have seen, Air Vice-Marshal David Colyer seems to have had little experience flying large aircraft and apparently had never flown a flying boat himself.

The Form 765 (*Report on flying accident or forced landing not attributable to enemy action*) states the flight was a non-operational transit flight. This form was signed off by the acting commanding officer of No. 228 Squadron, Norman Eagleton, himself an experienced flying boat pilot, on 4 September. It was countersigned by Group Captain Edward F. Turner the 'new' RAF Oban commanding officer.

Form 765 also states that Frank Goyan, in addition to his 906 hours flying time on Sunderland aircraft, had 117 hours instruments flying and fourteen more in the Link trainer (a simple early form of flight simulator). Moseley had seventy-six hours instrument flying, but his Link trainer record was not known.

In section 11 of the Form 765 *(Report by appropriate specialist officers, airframe, engines, navigation etc.)* there is a short comment by a Flight Lieutenant J. McKay. It states: 'Technical failure not involved. Aircraft flew into hill in cloud.'

Who exactly Flight Lieutenant J. McKay was and his technical qualifications is unknown, nor whether he actually attended and inspected the crash site. Why he did not give evidence as a witness is similarly unknown. There is no other precise information regarding any examination of the engines, airframe or instruments etc. or the thoughts of any navigational expertise.

The Form 1180 (Accident card) repeated the data found on the other forms, but it was a little more direct in the cause of the crash, stating:

> 'Responsibility for serious error in airmanship lies with captain of aircraft, changed flight plan for reasons unknown and descended through cloud without making sure he was over the water and crashed. AOC concurs with findings and considers weather conditions should have presented no difficulties to a crew of such experience.'

In faint writing is added the comment: 'CIA no comments.' This clearly meaning the Chief Inspector of Accidents (Vernon Sydney Brown) had made no additional comments.

It is clear there was some doubt about who was flying the Sunderland at the time of the crash and who was the captain and in command. However, as the aircraft captain, Frank Goyan carried the blame as far as the Court of Inquiry and the Royal Air Force was concerned.

We shall look at the evidence and the possible causes of the crash later in the book, one of which could have been a disconnect between Frank Goyan and Thomas Moseley...

Chapter Eleven

The legal aspect to the Court of Inquiry

It is worth pausing at this juncture to consider the legal process for air crashes of this nature in 1942. All Courts of Inquiry were bound by the rules contained within King's Regulations, but in addition, in both wartime and peacetime Britain, there is a legal obligation for all deaths to be investigated to determine their cause and to record them.

For many years His Majesty's (or Her Majesty's Coroners) have been responsible for that process in England and Wales, while in Scotland, the Procurator Fiscal has overseen a slightly different process. We will look at this process in a moment, but we must consider the implications of a military death and in particular those within the Royal Air Force.

In 1942, commanding officers in the Royal Air Force had to deal with deaths in accordance with regulations contained within *Air Publication 1922: Notes on casualty procedure in war 1941/2*. This informed commanding officers that deaths caused by battle would not be referred to HM Coroner or the Procurator Fiscal. In such cases, the commanding officer of the airman's unit could issue a death certificate and release the body for a funeral.

The directive also stated that non-combat fatalities, either from accidents or natural causes, must be referred to the local Coroner or the Procurator Fiscal. In these cases, the officials would then decide if an inquest or a fatal accident inquiry (the latter in Scotland) was required.

In accordance with Air Ministry directive (Air Publication 1922), the deaths of those on board the Sunderland 'M' for Mother should have been referred to the Procurator Fiscal covering the Caithness area in August 1942.

Although the RAF conducted their own Court of Inquiry and supposedly informed the Chief Inspector of Accidents of their findings, there is no indication in the available papers that they ever informed the Procurator Fiscal, but conversely there is no evidence they failed to do so.

In an effort to establish whether the correct procedure had been followed, I contacted the Historical Search Room of the National Records of Scotland (NRS) in Edinburgh, and asked for their assistance in locating any papers concerning this incident. Unfortunately, they were unable to locate any record of a Fatal Accident Inquiry into the Duke of Kent's death or any of the men on board the aircraft.

They advised me that unlike England, Wales and Northern Ireland, there is no system of Coroner's Inquests in Scotland. The Fatal Accidents Inquiry (Scotland) Act 1895 provides for public inquiries by a Sheriff and jury upon petition from the Procurator Fiscal into fatal accidents occurring in industrial employment. The act was amended by the Fatal Accidents and Sudden Deaths Inquiry (Scotland) Act 1906 to include provisions for inquiries into any case of sudden or suspicious death in Scotland, in which it appeared that an inquiry would be in the public interest.

Following a sudden or suspicious death in Scotland, or deaths in public institutions, a report known as a 'precognition' should be submitted to the Procurator Fiscal. The Procurator, upon receipt of this report, will then decide whether they want a Fatal Accident Inquiry with a Sheriff and jury under this legislation.

The office of the Procurator Fiscal keep a register of all deaths and whether a precognition report was ever received in each case.

The Procurator's decision after reading the precognition report is then recorded in the *Register of Corrected Entries (RCE)*, but the report itself is not necessarily permanently preserved.

Where there is a 'Correction' entry in the Register of Corrected Entries that states 'as per verdict of a jury', this would indicate a Fatal Accident Inquiry had been held and therefore a precognition report had also been received from the relevant reporting authority such as the police, or in this case the Royal Air Force.

In addition to finding no trace of a Fatal Accident Inquiry or precognition report into the Duke of Kent's death, the Historical Research Room also made searches for the other Sunderland fatalities.

There was no trace of any of these names in the Register of Corrected Entries (RCE). Although it is possible there was an administration error, considering the magnitude of the case it is safe to assume no precognition report was sent to the Procurator Fiscal as required in Scottish law and therefore there was no Fatal Accident Inquiry.

All Fatal Accident Inquiry records held in the Record Office are listed individually by the deceased person's name. Searches of the National Records of Scotland catalogue for the Duke of Kent and the other deceased men failed to locate any fatal accident inquiry against any of the names.

I have personally viewed the entries in the register of deaths for each of the fatalities. The names of the deceased were all recorded by a registrar in the local district of Latheron in Caithness, but none of these entries have any associated correction that might indicate the matter was the subject of a precognition report to the Procurator Fiscal.

In addition, it appears there may have been further breaches of Scottish law in registering the deceased's details. In Scotland, a death should be recorded within eight days of the event. Usually, you cannot register a death if the matter has been reported to the

Procurator Fiscal and an investigation on their behalf is incomplete (i.e. a Fatal Accident Inquiry).

On 8 September 1942, a full two weeks after the crash at Eagles Rock, Group Captain Norman A. Pritchett, the Commanding Officer of RAF Wick, submitted information to the registrar at Latheron (Mr A.M. Gunn) to record some of the deaths. This was also a week after the Court of Inquiry had reached its own conclusion on 1 September 1942.

Why had it taken so long to register the deaths if the Procurator Thistle does not appear to have received a precognition report and requested a Fatal Accident Inquiry? Did the Court of Inquiry decide they did not need to inform the Procurator Fiscal contrary to Scottish legislation and the Air Ministry directive AP. 1922?

The names of Wing Commander Moseley, Flight Lieutenant Goyan, Pilot Officers Smith and Saunders, Sergeants Hewerdine, Catt, Blacklock, Jones, Lewis and Sweett were all recorded with the registrar; their cause of death being noted as being, 'Due to war operations, aircraft accident.' No specific cause of death injuries were recorded for any man.

There was no entry in the register of deaths for the Duke of Kent and his party until 22 September 1942, twenty-eight days after the event. The deaths were recorded on information laid by Squadron Leader R.T. Raw, an administration and special duties officer.

The Duke of Kent's cause of death was listed as, 'Due to war operations – compound fracture of the skull, flying accident.'

The entries for Pilot Officer Michael Strutt and Lieutenant (RNVR) John Lowther stated, 'Due to war operations, multiple injuries, flying accident.'

There was no entry for LAC John Hales, the duke's valet, until 22 October 1942, an inexcusable fifty-eight days after the incident, the information being once again being laid by Squadron Leader

R.T. Raw. The cause of death was again being as, 'Due to war operations – flying accident.'

There are apparent legal issues concerning this crash in terms of reporting the matter to the Procurator Fiscal and the late recording of the deaths. Why was the law and the Air Ministry directive regarding such deaths apparently not followed? This is in addition to the Court of Inquiry, apparently ignoring the fact the aircraft had been routed across land in contravention of another Air Ministry directive, which forbid such flight except in an emergency.

Some people have stated this was wartime and there were a great many deaths, but to repeat myself again, this was the second worst British air crash up to 1942, with the King's brother among the fatalities, this was no ordinary accident.

In addition to this, we have information (previously mentioned in an earlier chapter) that Police Scotland can find no reports, notebooks, or other documents relating to this incident. This is despite a number of regular and special constables attending the scene, guarding it and submitting their own reports.

Although over eighty years have passed since the crash, I know from personal professional experience that the police are sticklers for filing away major case files. Most cases will be kept for a number of years, but murder files, other significant investigations and those of public interest are stored away for eternity.

When I initially examined this case, I thought it likely the Procurator Fiscal had decided there was no need for a Fatal Accident Inquiry, because of the RAF's Court of Inquiry. Following my enquiries with the National Records of Scotland, it would appear the legislation was ignored and nothing was reported to the Procurator Fiscal; this being despite the Air Ministry's own directive and the long established requirement for a precognition report to be sent to the Scottish authorities. The only alternative is that the Court of

Inquiry and Air Vice-Marshal David Colyer were ignorant of the need to refer the case.

The lack of information regarding injuries sustained and where the bodies were found shows either a lack of investigative ability by the inquiry members or a desire to direct the evidence down a certain route, possibly to a pre-conceived finding. Some might say there is a possibility notes detailing this and other information were not copied and sent to Australia, being later destroyed, but this information should have been mentioned in the certified copies of Forms 412 and 765.

While the aircraft had broken up on contact with the ground, it was possible with some investigation to identify certain areas within the debris field, such as the cockpit, rear turret, engines and tail section. In addition, it was widely known that the cockpit area was fraught with danger in a crash and not just from the sea or earth. In his book *My Flying Boat War: Survival and Success over the Atlantic, Mediterranean and Pacific in WW2*, Wing Commander 'Vic' Hodgkinson DFC, Royal Australian Air Force states:

> 'About six feet behind him [the pilot] was the radio operator's position. This contained the Marconi transmitter and receiver attached to a metal frame. As with both pre-war and wartime items, they were large and heavy. The supporting framework always appeared fragile, no doubt weight saving. It was common knowledge amongst crews that in a crash it was advisable for the skipper to duck on a crash impact to allow this equipment to pass overhead, otherwise one would be decapitated.'

Injuries to the rear of the head and back of a pilot, may with the above information, have led to the identification of which seat they had been occupying at the time of the crash. Such small details can have major implications on a Court of Inquiry's findings.

In order to examine and evaluate the RAF Court of Inquiry for the loss of Sunderland 'M' for Mother, we must look at some other crash reports, some of which did not have a formal Court of Inquiry and were just recorded on Form 765 *(Report on flying accident or force landing not attributable to enemy action)*.

On the night of 18 August 1942, a week before the loss of Sunderland 'M' for Mother, an Avro Anson, serial number DJ178, of No. 20 Operational Training Unit at Lossiemouth, flew into the east side of the Scaraben, the high ground on the opposite bank of Berriedale Water from Eagle's Rock.

The pilot and another sergeant were seriously injured, while two navigators and a wireless operator were killed.

The sergeant pilot gave a statement and told his commanders that he had been given spot heights by one of the navigators of the ground beneath the aircraft. He admitted that he could not make out the ground as there was no moonlight, but he could see the flare path at RAF Wick and a nearby lighthouse. Despite being unable to see the ground, he decided to reduce his height with fatal results.

The Form 765 was signed by the Wing Commander (No. 20 OTU) who declared the accident to have been caused by the gross negligence of the surviving sergeant pilot. His flying log would be endorsed 'Gross negligence'.

The Station Commander agreed with these comments and recommended further disciplinary action be taken by the Air Officer Commanding.

Attached to this report were three separate copies of Form 551 *(Report on accidental or self-inflicted injuries or immediate death therefrom)*, each separately recording that each man had died from multiple injuries.

In the case of the Avro Anson, the pilot deemed responsible for the crash gave evidence which in effect *convicted* himself. For this reason, a Court of Inquiry was clearly not deemed necessary.

Many Court of Inquiry reports have been destroyed over the decades since the end of the Second World War, but some have been retained. They include the report into the B-24 Liberator crash at Gibraltar in which General Sikorski, the Duke of Kent's associate, was killed in July 1943, less than a year after the loss of the Sunderland.

The Court of Inquiry was convened by Air Marshal Sir John C. Slessor KCB, DSO, MC a few days after the crash and he appointed Group Captain John G. Elton DFC, AFC from RAF Turnberry as president. Other members included Squadron Leader D.M. Wellings DFC from HQ Gibraltar and somewhat surprisingly, Wing Commander Arthur Warren Kay – the President of the Duke of Kent's Court of Inquiry.

Arthur Warren Kay was still attached to Headquarters Coastal Command in 1943, but now he had been assigned to another Court of Inquiry. In December 1943 he was shown as working for HQ Coastal Command in Training (Accident Investigation). Does this mean he was undergoing training, or he was a tutor in that section? But more importantly, does this indicate Kay was a trained preliminary crash investigator in August 1942?

Two others in attendance on the Court of Inquiry were Wing Commander N.M.S. Russell from Headquarters Transport Command and Wing Commander Dudginski from the Polish Air Force, Inspectorate General in London.

Unlike the Court of Inquiry for the Sunderland investigation, this was a specialised team (taking Kay's experience of the previous year and possible training into account). They would call more than double the number of witnesses in the Sunderland inquiry, providing a lengthy and detailed report. (See UK National Archives reference AIR2/18812 and AIR2/15113.)

It is worth pointing out that the 1st Pilot and captain of Sikorski's Liberator aircraft, was a Czechoslovakian – Flight Lieutenant Eduard Prchal – while the 2nd Pilot was Squadron Leader Wilfred Stanley

'Kipper' Herring DSO, DFM. Herring was a very experienced bomber pilot and flying instructor on attachment to No. 511 Squadron from No. 10 OTU.

Despite his higher rank and his vast experience on many types of aircraft such as Hampdens and Manchesters, unlike Wing Commander Thomas Moseley, Herring did not assume the position of aircraft captain or that of 1st Pilot, leaving both roles to the experienced Liberator pilot – Flight Lieutenant Eduard Prchal.

Another important Court of Inquiry file is that concerning Avro York serial number MW126. That aircraft went missing on 14 November 1944 over Europe, with former Battle of Britain commander Air Chief Marshal Sir Trafford Leigh-Mallory, his wife and eight crewmen on board.

A Court of Inquiry was held on 23 November 1944, but the crash site and bodies were not found until after the war in Europe had concluded in June 1945.

In the UK National Archives, a detailed file (ref: AIR 2/10593) contains the weather forecast for the flight with charts, the inquiry terms of reference and a detailed list of nearly thirty witnesses.

The terms of reference from Air Marshal Roderic Hill (Air Officer Commanding in Chief Fighter Command) stated:

1. To enquire into the serviceability of the aircraft, aids to navigation carried, briefing, arrangements for the journey.
2. To investigate the procedure followed in making appointments of the crew.
3. To enquire especially into the meteorological aspects of the loss of the aircraft.
4. To investigate the adequacy of the measures taken before the flight to guard against tampering with the aircraft and any other form of sabotage.

5. To ascertain at what all-up weight the aircraft took-off and what was the highest all-up weight at which the pilot of the aircraft had previously flown a York.
6. To ascertain whether the load was distributed and stowed according to regulations.

These terms of reference could easily have been used to investigate the Sunderland crash, especially points one to five.

Over twenty pages of evidence from over thirty witnesses followed and there were then four typed pages of conclusions, findings and recommendations from the panel; and this was all for an aircraft that had still not been found! The Court of Inquiry was not only concerned about the fatal crash, but whether secret papers had been carried on the aircraft, something apparently not even considered with regard to the Duke of Kent.

The composition of this Court of Inquiry when compared to the Duke of Kent's, had a distinguished line-up including Air Vice-Marshal Scarlett-Streatfield of No. 38 Group as President of the Court, Group Captain P. Stevens of No. 11 OTU, Wing Commander Rupert H.S. Mealing from the Air Ministry and Wing Commander Eric E. Stammers from Fighter Command HQ. They were a highly respected and experienced group and it should be noted that even the most junior member was more senior than Acting Wing Commander Kay the President of the Duke of Kent's Court of Inquiry.

Based upon the Court of Inquiry files for the Sikorski and Leigh-Mallory cases alone, it would appear the Duke of Kent's Court of Inquiry was possibly understaffed in terms of experience and rank, maybe under-resourced, and certainly less intrusive with its examination of the witnesses, crash scene and other technical evidence.

Another case concerns a Short Stirling of No. 90 Squadron (serial number EF497), which crashed on 20 October 1943 at 1630 hours, near Benson in Oxfordshire.

The aircraft had taken off on a test flight and dived into the ground killing all seven crewmen. Without going into all the detail on the Form 765, the important fact is it states on page two: 'Cause of crash unknown. Crash being investigated by the Accidents Investigation Branch.'

In the book, *Air Crash* by Fred Jones, the author details a number of unexplained Short Stirling crashes in January 1944. One on 26 January 1944 was investigated by another Accidents Investigation Branch inspector...clearly the Accident Investigation inspectors were interested in this spate of apparent accidents, but Vernon Sydney Brown would not allow his team of inspectors to attend the Sunderland crash with the King's brother on board.

In his list of professional credentials and achievements, Vernon Sydney Brown is said to have solved the loss of a good number of Short Stirling aircraft when he deduced the pilots were uncomfortable in their harnesses. The pilots therefore released their harness after take-off, but when the aircraft dived, they fell forward over the control column, unable to recover the aircraft with fatal results. The Stirling from No. 90 Squadron would appear to be one of those investigated by Brown and his team. The expertise of this man and his team of inspectors would have been very valuable to the Sunderland investigation.

While the Duke of Kent's aircraft was lost in the middle of a conflict, and unfortunately there were many fatal accidents, the Courts of Inquiry for the Liberator and Avro York, which also occurred during the war, are much more in depth than that for the Sunderland.

In peacetime, Courts of Inquiry can be much more inquisitive, intrusive, in depth and complex.

In September 1970, a No. 5 Squadron Lighting jet-fighter with an American exchange pilot went missing off the Lincolnshire coast.

The subsequent inquiry called forty-four witnesses who gave a mass of detailed evidence. Many of them were technical experts as well as eye witnesses. The Court of Inquiry sat for over forty days and although I fully appreciate the times and conditions were totally different, I believe it underlines the fact the Sunderland investigation was perhaps sub-standard and curtailed.

This chapter raises some uncomfortable issues. The Court of Inquiry for the Sunderland appears to have been poorly staffed, possibly with pre-conceived ideas about the evidence, the cause and an ultimate finding. It is also unclear whether Kay was a trained preliminary crash investigator. If he was, he would, as President, have been a significant witness as well as the proverbial judge and jury! The Inquiry appears to have gone against Air Ministry directives and Scottish legislation, while the lack of any senior Accident Investigation Inspectors' involvement is particularly concerning, with Vernon Sydney Brown allegedly refusing to attend or assign an inspector to the case, unless the preliminary investigation did not find a cause. The apparent failure to utilise specialist technical experts in the evidence is also of concern.

Finally, having checked the registration of a number of fatalities from other air crashes in the Scottish Highlands in 1942, I found that on a number of occasions, some of the deaths were late in being recorded with the local registrar. This appears to have been a regular event and with the number of deaths in the area, this may be excusable, but that does not remove the other concerns raised in this chapter.

In the next chapter, we shall look at the political and royal response to the fatal crash.

Chapter Twelve

Royal and Political comment

By mid to late afternoon on 25 August 1942 it was clear Sunderland 'M' for Mother had been lost and it was initially believed all on board had perished.

In the UK National Archives file reference PREM 4/8/2A, there is a note to Winston Churchill from someone with the initials 'A.B.', almost certainly his Private Secretary Anthony Bevir. This informed the Prime Minister that the Air Ministry had 'rang up' at 9:55pm to say that:

'The Duke of Kent was flying to Iceland in his capacity as Inspector General of RAF Welfare… He left Invergordon at 1:30pm piloted by the Commanding Officer of No. 228 Squadron in a Sunderland. One hour later, aircraft reported crashed Dunbeath, twenty miles south of Wick. Twelve crew all killed. Not yet known whether fire occurred. Local doctor identified Duke of Kent. Head crushed, death instantaneous. Local weather not bad as a whole. Operational patrols have been flying.

'Secretary of State has informed Mieville at Balmoral. Mieville is informing Duchess and other royalties. Mieville ringing later about manner of announcement. Meantime stop being put on it.'

The note is to the point, but contains some interesting points:

1. This note does not contain a time of origin, but it must be after 9:55pm. If the crash occurred at 1:42pm and we know witnesses alerted the authorities within an hour or two, why did it take so long to inform the Prime Minister's office?
2. Twelve crew were claimed to have been killed, but there were no details regarding the royal party apart from the duke's death and his head injury.
3. Why was the issue of fire so important?
4. This is the first document (chronologically as far as I can determine) which details the fatal injury and the fact death was instantaneous.
5. Local weather was deemed to be 'not bad as a whole' with other operational patrols.
6. The King's Assistant Private Secretary, Sir Eric Charles Mieville was informed by the Secretary of State for Air (Sir Archibald Sinclair) at Balmoral, where the King was in residence.
7. Mieville was informing the Duchess of Kent and other members of the Royal Family.
8. No formal announcement had been made at the time of this note.

In his book *George and Marina, the Duke and Duchess of Kent*, author Christopher Warwick describes what happened when Sir Archibald Sinclair telephoned Balmoral Castle that evening.

Sir Eric Charles Mieville informed the King who was having dinner with Queen Elizabeth and the Duke and Duchess of Gloucester. When the King returned from receiving the phone call he was 'Grim faced and silent.' The King himself, later wrote: 'It came as a great shock to me and I had to break it to Elizabeth, Harry and Alice. We left Balmoral in the evening for London.'

Sir Eric Charles Mieville telephoned the Kent's home at The Coppins in Iver, Buckinghamshire. In his book, Warwick recounts that seven-weeks-old Prince Michael of Kent's nanny, Kate Fox, took the call, the Duchess being in bed. 'Numb with shock…she slowly climbed the stairs.'

The moment Kate Fox opened the bedroom door, the Duchess cried out: 'It's George, isn't it?'

Later that night, Sir Charles Portal the Chief of the Air Staff sent a Secret memorandum to Winston Churchill.

Once again, some of the details it contained were incorrect. Portal claimed that the aircraft had taken off from Invergordon bound for Iceland at 1:15pm with twelve people on board. 'The pilot was Wing Commander Moseley, an expert navigator and considered to be the best pilot in the squadron which he commanded.' While this once again appears to confirm Moseley was the 1st Pilot, the comment about his credentials as we have seen, is somewhat debatable. What is interesting is that even at this early hour with the initial exchanges of memoranda and messages, it is clear the official version had Thomas Moseley identified as the 1st Pilot, but there is no mention of him being the aircraft's captain and there is no mention of Goyan. Does this mean the hierarchy at Alness/Invergordon knew there was an issue with the piloting and captaincy of the Sunderland and had this been passed to Coastal Command HQ?

Portal's memorandum gave the weather conditions at the time and stated the Sunderland had struck high ground at about 2,300 feet – clearly an incorrect height.

The memorandum concluded by stating:

'Pending a full enquiry, the cause of the accident can only be surmised. It seems probable the pilot decided, in view of the bad patch round Wick, to climb through the cloud into the clear air above. While climbing through the cloud, he presumably drifted further to the west than he intended and hit the hill when he thought he was over the sea. All the occupants were killed, probably instantaneously.'

Just before midnight, an official announcement was made and the world was informed of the loss of Prince George, the Duke of Kent, his party and the aircrew. (Andrew Jack was still believed to be among the dead.)

On 27 August 1942, Winston Churchill wrote to the King. He wrote:

'Sir,

'Your Majesty's Ministers have asked me, on their behalf, to offer to your Majesties, to Her Royal Highness the Duchess of Kent and to all the Royal Family, their deepest sympathy on the death, on active service of His Royal Highness the Duke of Kent, and to express their sense of the grievous loss which the Nation and Empire have suffered thereby.

'With my humble duty, I remain, your Majesty's faithful and devoted servant and subject. W. S. C.'

The same day, the Duke of Kent's body was taken from Dunrobin Castle, where it had been held since its recovery from the crash site and taken by train to London Euston. The coffin, draped in a flag, was conveyed by road to Windsor Castle, where it was placed in the Albert Memorial Chapel.

Two days later, on 29 August, the duke's funeral took place in St. George's Chapel, Windsor Castle. The coffin was borne on the shoulders of two Air Marshals and four Air Vice-Marshals. The pall bearers were a who's who of senior commanders and included:

Air Vice-Marshal Frank McNamara VC, Air Officer Commanding Royal Australian Air Force overseas.

Air Marshal Harold Edwards Royal Canadian Air Force overseas.

Air Vice-Marshal George Ranald Reid DSO MC* from HQ Flying Training Command.

Air Vice-Marshal Arthur Clinton Maund DSO from HQ Technical Command (he would die with heart problems in December 1942).

Air Vice-Marshal Ronald Graham, DSO, DSC*, DFC from HQ Bomber Command.

Air Marshal Trafford Leigh-Mallory DSO* from No. 11 Group Fighter Command. (He would die in an air crash in 1944 and as we have seen, was subject of another Court of Inquiry examined later in this book.)

In retrospect, the speed with which the duke's funeral took place, just four days after the crash, may seem unusual, especially as the Court of Inquiry had not been completed and on the same day, Flight Sergeant Andrew Jack was being interviewed in his hospital bed.

On 30 August 1942, King George VI replied to Winston Churchill:

'My dear Prime Minister,

'I sincerely thank you for your kind letter of condolence which you, on behalf of my Ministers, have addressed to me and the

Members of the Family on the death, on active service of the Duke of Kent.

'The loss of my brother is, indeed, very grievous to us all, and we much appreciate your expressions of sympathy in our great sorrow.'

George R. I.

There has been throughout the documents and reports constant mention of the Duke of Kent and the crew being on active service. Even the post war memorial on Eagles Rock mentions active service and goes further mentioning a special mission to Iceland. What can this mean?

A modern definition, Section 48 (1) of the Coroners and Justice Act 2009 defines military 'active service' as:

1. An act or operation against an enemy,
2. An operation outside the British Isles for protection of life or property or
3. The military occupation of a foreign country or territory.

However, there has been some debate about whether in earlier years, the term merely meant being in a military role in a war zone. But what are we to make of the inscription on the memorial of a 'Special Mission'. Surely a welfare visit to Iceland is not a special mission, unless of course there was more to it than ever publicly acknowledged.

On 8 September 1942, Winston Churchill stood up in the House of Commons and begged to move two motions. The first was to express the deep concern of the House on the loss of the Duke of Kent while on active service. The second motion was to send the condolences of the House to the Duchess on her great loss.

A great number of MPs stood and made speeches commemorating the life of the Duke of Kent before the two motions were passed.

On 7 October 1942, Sir Archibald Sinclair, the Secretary of State for Air, made a statement to the House of Commons on the circumstances of the loss of the Sunderland, its passengers and crew. This was recorded in Hansard:

'The circumstances in which the tragic accident occurred have now been investigated by a Royal Air Force Court of Inquiry and the sequence of events as follows:

'The aircraft, which was proceeding from a Royal Air Force Station in Scotland to Iceland was airborne just after 1 o'clock in the afternoon of 25 August. Before departure, the correct procedure for briefing the captain as to the exact route to be followed and for providing full information about the weather conditions likely to be encountered was complied with. Local weather conditions were not good at the time of take-off, but the general indications showed a likelihood of improvement to the westward. The captain of the aircraft was a flying boat pilot of long experience and on the particular type of aircraft which he was flying that day, and of exceptional ability. About half an hour after take-off, the aircraft was heard approaching land from the sea at what appeared to be a low height and shortly afterwards it was heard to crash into the hills.

'The court found: First, that the accident occurred because the aircraft was flown on a track other than that indicated in the flight plan given to the pilot and at too low an altitude to clear the rising ground on the track; secondly, that the responsibility for this serious mistake in airmanship lies with the captain of the aircraft; thirdly, that the weather encountered should have presented no difficulties to an experienced pilot; fourthly, that the examination of the propellors showed that the engines were under power when the aircraft struck the ground; and fifthly, in accordance with King's Regulations and ACI paragraph 1325, that all the occupants of the aircraft were on duty at the time of the accident.

'The Chief Inspector of Accidents is in agreement with the findings of the Court.'

This statement carries two significant comments for our review. Firstly, Sir Archibald Sinclair is clearly talking about Flight Lieutenant Frank Goyan as an experienced flying boat captain with exceptional ability and not Wing Commander Thomas Moseley. The question is why, when all other material relates to Moseley being the pilot at the controls when it crashed? Secondly, Sinclair states the Chief Inspector of Accidents was in agreement with the findings of the Court of Inquiry. Was Vernon Sydney Brown aware of the full facts and did he really concur with the findings?

The politicians and the King were also involved in what seemed to be a simple case of recognition for services rendered. This was the award of a M.V.O. (Member of the Royal Victorian Order – Fourth Class) to Dr John Kennedy the Dunbeath doctor who attended the crash scene.

The doctor had attended a number of previous air crashes and rendered assistance, but the file in the UK National Archives (reference AIR 2/16973) seems to indicate some haste in sanctioning a reward.

As we have seen the doctor was called and attended the crash site with a number of others, but he was not the first person on scene and sadly, there was very little he could do for any of those at the crash site. His home and surgery in Dunbeath were used as a rendezvous point for the clear-up operations, but there is little else to differentiate his actions to that of the others who climbed the hill in a bid to give whatever assistance they could.

The Court of Inquiry in their final recommendations wished to bring the 'magnificent work' done by Dr Kennedy to the notice of others, not just for this incident, but for six other crashes he had attended over the previous two years.

On 28 August 1942, Group Captain Pritchett at RAF Wick sent details of the doctor's evidence and the Court of Inquiry's recommendation to his headquarters. He added his own comments stating:

'Shortly afterwards Dr Kennedy, Dunbeath, rang up the station and reported the crash as a Sunderland and that he had identified His Royal Highness the Duke of Kent. It is desired to bring Dr Kennedy to notice. He is an old man and his action in climbing up on the moor in cloud cover and finding the crashed aircraft and reporting it as soon as he could is most praiseworthy. Only two weeks ago, he climbed to within 200 feet of the top of Scaraben Mountain 1,900 feet to the assistance of the crew of an Anson. (Author's comment: probably Anson DJ178 discussed earlier in this book.) His action contributed very largely to saving the lives of two of the crew. Some months ago, it is understood, he was first out to the scene of a crashed Sunderland which occurred in the same area.'

Contained within the minutes of the file recommending an award, is a note to Sir Louis Greig at the Air Ministry. He was an old associate of the King and his brothers, having escorted the Duke of Kent on his tour of Canada and the United States the previous year. On 24 September 1942 the note asked him to read the reports and recommendations regarding Dr Kennedy. He then added:

'There are two routine possibilities. We could send a letter
of thanks as suggested by the AOC in C, but that seems
inadequate; or we could try to get Kennedy the MBE or
OBE in the New Year Honours List, but I am afraid that our
chances of success would be negligible.

'Do you think the Palace authorities would be willing to
recommend the award of an MVO to this doctor, who was the
first medical officer on the scene of the crash when HRH the
Duke of Kent tragically lost his life and who has been the first
on the scene of five other crashes during the past two years?'

There is also contained in the file a draft letter (with no date) from
the Permanent Under Secretary of State for Air (Harold Balfour)
addressed to Dr Kennedy. This states that the Air Council had their
attention drawn to his meritorious conduct.

It is clear that within days of the incident, efforts were afoot to
reward Dr Kennedy, but what about the other initial members of the
search party and the Special Constables?

The comment about the award of an OBE or MBE having a
negligible chance of success is interesting. Why was this the case?
Whatever happened, things moved very quickly and Dr Kennedy was
awarded the MVO. The award is given personally by the sovereign
for services to the Royal Family, so in this case it was awarded for
dealing with the Duke of Kent's crash and not necessarily the other
crashes, but what about the other rescuers?

The MVO was reportedly bestowed upon Dr Kennedy at an
investiture on or before 20 October 1942. An extract from Court
Circular of *The Times* newspaper on 21 October states that:

'Dr John R. Kennedy yesterday had the honour of being
received by The King, when His Majesty invested him with

the Insignia of a Member of the Royal Victorian Order (Fourth Class).'

On 21 October 1942, Sir Archibald Sinclair wrote to Dr Kennedy, congratulating him on the award of the MVO. It is worth remembering the doctor was one of his constituents in Dunbeath, the Sinclair family owning estates around Thurso.

I have been informed by someone in the Dunbeath area that Dr Kennedy was hardly invested with the MVO. According to local myth, he received a telephone call and was told to get on a particular train. At a named station, the carriage window dropped down and a hand, presumably the King's, handed the award to the doctor inside the train.

I cannot vouch for the validity of this story, but looking at the hasty manner in which the award was granted, not to mention the pace of the duke's funeral, it does give an impression of some impetuosity.

In the following weeks and months, the King and the Duchess of Kent visited the crash scene and met some of those involved in the rescue bid.

It is also said that in later years when Flight Sergeant Andrew Jack was posted to Gibraltar, the Duchess of Kent visited him. What was discussed in private was never revealed, but clearly there was an affinity between the pair.

As the years passed, the story faded from the minds of most people, but in time, a number would come forward and give information that was not known in 1942. In the next chapter we shall examine some of these accounts.

Chapter Thirteen

Those who came forward in subsequent years

Over the decades following the end of the war, there was the occasional mention of the Duke of Kent's crash in 1942, but most people accepted the official version of events. Many had suffered losses within their own families and it seemed the loss of the duke and his companions was just part of the millions lost during the tragic conflict.

The sole surviving witness to the event, Flight Sergeant Andrew Jack, was commissioned and reached the rank of Flight Lieutenant, continuing to serve until he retired in 1964. He rarely spoke about the event, and certainly not in public. As a serving officer, he was undoubtedly somewhat restricted in what he could say, but he did speak about the crash with close friends, colleagues and his family on a number of occasions.

We have already mentioned that in May 1961 the *Scottish Express* newspaper carried an article detailing the crash, together with a so-called 'exclusive' interview with Andrew Jack.

Jack who at the time was still a serving RAF officer, repeated the same old account about the crash and that he could remember very little. He then repeated his later comments about testing the intercom to the cockpit, adding, 'I had no conversation with any other member of the crew or captain again.'

Why Andrew Jack had suddenly spoken to the media after nineteen years of silence was not explained, but it soon became public knowledge that the day before the newspaper article was published, Marina, Duchess of Kent, had made a visit to the crash site with the couple's three children. Was this just a coincidence or had those in authority wanted to pre-empt any rekindling of public interest by getting Jack to repeat the same old account?

Despite the account in 1961, interest in the crash remained and even when he was posted to Prestwick airport, Jack was reluctant to discuss the matter with any stranger who asked about the incident. He eventually retired from the air force and went on to work as a telephone engineer in Sussex, but apparently suffered with depression, which brought on occasional bouts of heavy drinking.

In March 1978, Andrew Jack, having moved to Sussex, died in Brighton hospital. The causes of death were registered as cirrhosis of the liver and broncho-pneumonia, undoubtedly due to excess alcohol. At the time of his death, he was in his mid-50s. Was the burden of a secret too heavy to carry, too much to bear and what did he really know?

In his book *Scottish Mysteries* published in 1997, Donald Fraser says that before his death, Andrew Jack had stated that before the crash, he had been instructed to drop smoke floats, designed to gauge the drift of smoke and therefore the wind speed. (This was what Tim Wilson had also reported in his letter to *Aeroplane* magazine in 1996.) Jack did as he was ordered and informed the captain, but the response he received came from a voice he did not recognise (i.e. neither Flight Lieutenant Goyen or Pilot Officer Smith).

In a later conversation with Sergeant Ron Clayton of No. 210 Squadron, Jack is alleged to have gone further, stating that when he was instructed by the pilot to drop a smoke float to assist with navigation just before the crash, the voice on the intercom was not that of Goyan, but Wing Commander Moseley. In later years, it was apparently common knowledge at RAF Oban and RAF Alness /Invergordon that Thomas Moseley had control of the aircraft when it crashed.

These comments corroborate what Corporal Tim Wilson says he was told by Jack at RAF Aldergrove in 1943, when the rear gunner returned to the squadron having recovered from his injuries.

In 1982, *After the Battle* magazine carried an article about the crash and the following year, *Aeroplane Monthly* carried a similar account in January 1983. Both authors speculated about the cause of the crash, but at that time, the copy of the Court of Inquiry reports (Forms 412, 765 and even the Form 1180) were missing or unavailable. There was nothing in the Royal Archives, the Public Record Office, the RAF Museum, or the National Records of Scotland to assist the author's efforts and the copy of the reports in the Australian archives had yet to be discovered.

In 1988 the book *Hebrides at War* was published. It contained a history of RAF Oban and a section detailing the loss of Sunderland 'M' for Mother.

The book highlighted the account from Dorothea Gray (nee Whyte) who was a member of the WAAF and based at the RAF Oban Station Headquarters in Dungallan House, overlooking the bay. In her more detailed written memoirs held by the University of Leeds, Dorothea recalled that in late 1942, a rumour went around the station that a VIP was expected to arrive.

On the evening of 25 August, a friend named Jean came into her room and told her that she was going to tell her something, but she must not pass it on to a soul. Jean told her that the Duke of Kent had flown out that morning and the plane had crashed in the Highlands and everyone on board was dead.

The next morning (the twenty-sixth), they found that some of the bodies had been returned to the station and driven to the Catholic Cathedral in Oban, where they were given an honour guard by the WAAF. To use WAAFs for this guard was exceptional at the time.

On the morning of 27 August, Dorothea arrived at her office in the Station HQ at Dungallan House to be confronted by what she described as 'A heap of things on the floor, torn and blood-stained uniforms, pay books and a quantity of silverware – condiment sets, cutlery, plates, all with the duke's insignia on them.' She was told to list the items, something she found very difficult to do.

She recalled opening one pay book to find a piece of 'bloody flesh' adhered to it. In time, her uniform stank of smoke and she recalled having great difficulty in removing the smell from her hands and uniform, it was something she would never forget.

Dorothea Gray also recalled that 'In a time when men were basically protective and caring of women, it seemed to her that somewhere along the line, control had broken down and no one seemed to know what they were doing.'

Dorothea made the list of items and went off to lunch, but when she returned, the items had gone.

Later, the Officer Commanding (believed to have been Group Captain John Hugh Oscar Jones) dictated letters to her for various undertakers, these were to the effect that the coffins were under no circumstances to be opened, but left sealed when they were sent on from Oban. Why this unusual instruction was given is unknown, was it because very little remained of the aircrew and the remains in each coffin could have been any of the deceased? This latter reason seems unlikely considering the comments of the witnesses at the scene, but was there another reason?

Dorothea also claimed the Officer Commanding (Jones?) and his Adjutant were quickly posted away to South Wales, although official records do not seem to corroborate this. However, as we have already seen, Group Captain Jones did not sign the Court of Inquiry form as the Oban Station Commander – this was signed by Group Captain Edward F. Turner, a former member of the No. 18 Group Air Staff.

Dorothea Gray recalled a rumour that circulated at the time to the effect that the civilian meteorologists had given a wrong weather forecast for the fatal flight. After the crash, they were immediately placed in RAF uniform and became subject to King's Regulations. She added that this was done so quickly, one man wore other ranks uniform with officers insignia sown on to it. She recalled him complaining that the uniform did not fit him.

The issue with this comment about the Met. Officers, is this was at RAF Oban and the two men who later gave evidence at the Court of Inquiry were civilians from RAF Alness/Invergordon. I have checked RAF officer lists for these men and I have been unable to locate any named RAF Meteorological Officers at either base. Therefore, we must assume the two meteorological witnesses who gave evidence to the inquiry were the men concerned with the forecasts that day and Dorothea's rumour may have been a case of idle gossip.

In 1988, the book *Hebrides at War*, stated that Flying Officer George Gilfillan, an engineering officer at Oban, told the author that on the night of the crash, he was woken and told to gather all the technical and maintenance logs for Sunderland W4026 and take them to Kerrera (the location of the station HQ).

In consecutive editions of *Aeroplane Monthly* (January to March 1990), author and researcher Roy Nesbit recounted the story looking for possible causes and the mysteries that had grown around the loss of 'M' for Mother.

In the April 1990 edition of the magazine, the letters pages were full of comments regarding the crash. One of the most interesting came from Air Chief Marshal Sir Edward Chilton KCB CB.

In August 1942, he was a Group Captain and a specialist in navigation training. He was probably one of the most knowledgeable men in the RAF as far as air navigation was concerned at that time. In his letter, he told the editor he was a Group Captain at the time and immediately after the event, Group Captain Kelly Barnes and himself were warned to stand by for the Court of Inquiry. They were both 'freely available and were the RAF's two senior specialist navigators' at the time, but they were quickly told they would not be required.

Sir Edward then added, 'The senior officer of the Court of Inquiry was a Squadron Leader – all very low key, which was very odd in the circumstances.' (Clearly referring to Arthur Warren Kay who was an acting Wing Commander.)

Later in his letter, Sir Edward added that in 1949 he was Director of Personnel Services in the Air Ministry. He received a letter from a higher authority saying the Duchess of Kent had recently visited Eagles Rock crash site and was upset to find some debris remaining from the accident in 1942, so a further clean-up was embarked upon. This comment is interesting when we consider how the site was cleared in 1942 and the fact people are still finding debris into the twenty-first century – some of it now being housed in the Dunbeath Heritage centre.

In the same edition of the *Aeroplane Monthly* magazine, a Mr J.N.C. Richardson recounted a family holiday in August 1953 in Italy. As we have already seen earlier in the book, his family became friendly with another tourist who was called Mr I.F. Luckin. He claimed to have been a Radar Operator in 1942 and saw the Duke of Kent's Sunderland going off course and heading inland. He could not call the Sunderland as there was strict radio silence.

As mentioned earlier in the book, I examined the RAF officer lists and found a Flying Officer J.F. Luckin in July 1942, based at No. 14 Group (Fighter Command) on the Air Staff, based at the Drummossie Hotel near Inverness.

In March 1992, Roy Nesbit wrote another article for the *Aeroplane Monthly* called '*Duke of Kent update*'. This one covered a letter he had received from the RAF Alness station commander in 1942 – Group Captain Geoffrey Francis.

Geoffrey Francis explained that he had briefed the crew prior to the flight, instructing them to keep well clear of the east coast of Scotland and to climb until they reached sufficient height, by a margin, to clear any high ground as well as bad patch of weather before changing course. (This would therefore indicate that clearly, the plan was to cut across land to Thurso, contravening Air Ministry directives.)

A Mr Christopher Deansley also contacted Roy Nesbit claiming that he had been told by an unnamed officer who flew with the Duke of Kent, that the duke did not like flying in cloud and always asked to come out of it.

The family of Andrew Jack started to make media comments after his death, but the most challenging and controversial appeared in *The Times* newspaper on 24 March 1996.

Elspeth Jack, the widow of Andrew, claimed there was a cover-up and that the Duke of Kent had urged the crew to take-off in poor weather conditions. She also claimed that her late husband had told her the duke and many of the crew had been drinking champagne on board the aircraft before the flight. She added:

> 'For the rest of his life, Andy said it was a shame the pilot was blamed. He thought the Duke of Kent was at the controls, but he wasn't sure. It was a pretty miserable day, Andy thought the weather was too bad, very misty and foggy and he thought it was wrong to take off. But the Duke of Kent decided he still wanted to fly…drinking had started on board the plane before it took off.'

In addition, Richard Wigg, a former mechanic on No. 228 Squadron told *The Times* newspaper:

> 'When Andrew Jack came out of hospital, he said there had been a gigantic party on the aircraft and the duke had been at the controls when it crashed. They were all half-cut, there was a cover-up to spare the Royal Family's blushes.'

Jack's eldest son Ian also stated that his father said the blame did not lie with Frank Goyan. He said:

'My father did say that in no way was the pilot to blame, but there was nothing he could do about it as he was still in the RAF. He was very bitter about the way Goyan was treated.'

While it would appear from the evidence so far, that the Duke of Kent was not at the controls of the Sunderland (how could he fly with an attaché case attached to his wrist?), clearly there were some alcohol bottles found at the scene as mentioned by Special Constable Will Bethune.

The story in *The Times* caused outrage and author Roy Nesbit was quick to write another piece for *Aeroplane Monthly* in September 1996, denouncing the article in *The Times*. He was keen to repeat the old accounts, but he still could not access any part of the Court of Inquiry records.

Nesbit pointed out that any drinking of alcohol by the crew was a court martial offence and that Corporal Tim Wilson had previously stated Jack had told him that Moseley was in number one pilots' seat and Goyan in number two, with the duke stood between them. This, he added, must have been seen before take-off as Andrew Jack went to the rear turret and could not see anything else from that position.

Roy Nesbit added that Group Captain Geoffrey Francis, the Commanding Officer at Alness, had said in his letter to him, that some of the passengers probably had a drink in the Officers' Mess before take-off. Any bottles at the crash site were probably cargo for their destination and more likely to be Scotch Whisky than champagne.

Nesbit ended his article claiming that Andrew Jack had gone through an appalling experience and was physically and mentally scarred for life. With depression, it was not surprising if he felt a sense of bitterness and wanted to apportion blame for the accident. Nesbit added that it was unlikely Jack ever researched the subject with the documents not being available. This seems a little harsh, after all, he was on board the Sunderland and the only survivor from the disaster – surely he knew more than anyone alive until his death.

What are we to make of these claims? It is highly unlikely the Duke of Kent was flying the Sunderland for the reasons already outlined, but it is possible the passengers might have been drinking. Could some of the crew have also been given a drink while on board the aircraft? It seems very unlikely, but it is not impossible. Yes, the drinking of alcohol by aircrew during a flight was forbidden, but so too was the operation of flying boats over land except in an emergency!

As previously reported by Special Constable Will Bethune, bottles of alcohol were present at the crash site, but he did not state what type of liquid they contained or whether they were full, empty or broken; but as his son George explained to me many years later, they were probably all broken in the crash.

The weather claims are also interesting, especially when one considers the clear determination of the Court of Inquiry to hammer out the issue of weather as a possible cause for the crash. Then there is the apparent disagreement between Air Vice-Marshal David Colyer's comments and those of the station commander regarding the weather conditions and whether it was suitable for flying.

In the next chapter we shall consider the possible causes of the crash.

Chapter Fourteen

Possible Causes

There are a number of possible causes for this crash and we shall review each of them in turn.

The Rudolf Hess conspiracy:

The arrival of Rudolf Hess in Scotland in May 1941 has caused a great deal of debate for over eighty years. What his intentions were and whether he was working on the directions of Adolf Hitler is disputed to this day and remain a complete mystery.

Many people believe he was enticed by an MI6 operation, believing peace could be obtained through negotiation, but others believe it was his own flight of fantasy, a concoction of his own mind after consulting with a number of people who had previously liaised with the Duke of Hamilton. Whatever led to him arriving that evening in the spring of 1941, one element that is hardly touched upon is the alleged involvement of the Duke of Kent.

As we have already seen, there were strong connections between a number of people alleged to have been involved in a peace negotiation conspiracy. The Duke of Hamilton, General Sikorski and Tancred Bornius were all people familiar to the Duke of Kent, but whether that included a peace conspiracy is debatable.

In addition, we have the fact that the Duke of Hamilton was a member of the King's Privy Council, like Prince George and the disgraced Duke of Buccleuch; and there was a myriad of family links between a number of the alleged parties, including the Duke of Northumberland, the Duke of Gloucester and even Queen Elizabeth. However, familial links are not enough evidence for a conspiracy.

Historians and researchers have worked long and hard to identify where the Duke of Kent was on the night Rudolf Hess arrived in Scotland. However, no one has ever been able to say with any certainty where he was. Some believe he was in Scotland that evening, but there is no confirmatory evidence to corroborate such claims. He was, according to a number of sources, in Sumburgh in the Shetlands and at RAF Wick on the days either side of the day Hess arrived in Scotland, so it is safe to assume he probably was in Scotland.

To compound the conspiracy theories the Duke of Kent's diaries (if he ever kept one), cannot be located, therefore it is a complete mystery. How no one in the British Royal Family, the Air Ministry and the Royal Air Force cannot state with some certainty where the duke was that evening is quite surprising and only adds to the conspiracy theories.

In the book *Double Standards – The Rudolf Hess cover-up*, there are claims by the authors that a former employee at Dungavel House saw the Duke of Kent at the location on the night Hess arrived in Scotland. The woman, who would not give her real name, was given the pseudonym Mrs Baker, claiming, 'The Duke and his people were in the kennels.' When challenged with the fact the Duke of Hamilton had been confirmed as being at RAF Turnhouse, she promptly replied, 'Not the Duke of Hamilton, the Duke of Kent.'

This appears to be the only piece of evidence placing the Duke of Kent at Dungavel House the night Hess arrived, but what value can we place on information given by someone who will not allow themself to be identified?

The Duke of Kent knew a number of the parties allegedly involved in a peace negotiation, but that is as far as the hard evidence goes.

Then there is the second part of the Duke of Kent – Hess conspiracy, the claims the Sunderland carrying the duke and his entourage was on a secret mission. The conspiracists claim the the clandestine operation was to collect Hess from a location near Dunbeath and convey him to Iceland, or even Sweden, (depending on which version you prefer) for peace talks; and all without the knowledge of Prime Minister Winston Churchill.

It has been claimed that Hess had been housed at Braemore in a house belonging to the Duke of Portland, his son Lord Titchfield, being an associate of the Duke of Kent and the Chair of the Joint Intelligence Committee of the Chiefs of Staff.

It has also been claimed Hess was lodged in a cottage on the banks of Loch More to the north of the Eagles Rock crash site. This location was on the family estate of Sir Archibald Sinclair, the Secretary of State for Air, something conspiracy theorists also like to regularly point out.

It is claimed the Sunderland was heading inland towards Loch More, where it would land on the water, picking-up Rudolf Hess, before transporting him to a foreign location, although some believe Hess had already been collected and they were heading back towards the North Sea.

On 25 August 1942 the Sunderland was fully loaded and pretty much at its maximum take-off weight of 58,000lbs. It took an eternity to take-off from the calm lengthy waters of the Cromarty Firth and the Sunderland's already sluggish performance would be further handicapped by the extra weight of any passengers they picked-up.

Furthermore, Loch More was not long enough to allow the Sunderland to land, collect its extra passenger and take-off again. Most of its original load of fuel would still be in its tanks and therefore the conspiracy theory of collecting Rudolf Hess in secret is just not feasible.

The allegation of an extra body at the crash site is one that appears to have been created by poor communications, conflicting media reports and the late arrival of the survivor Andrew Jack.

Although the Duke of Kent cannot be categorically removed from the arrival of Hess in 1941, the evidence of him being involved in the 1942 crash, is at best, very thin.

Airmanship, pilot error or navigation:

One element that was clearly on the minds of the Court of Inquiry was that of airmanship and the actions of the pilot controlling the Sunderland.

As we have seen, Flight Lieutenant Frank Goyan was a very experienced flying boat pilot, one of the most experienced on the Sunderland, with nearly 1,000 flying hours on the type. Wing Commander Thomas Moseley was himself an experienced pilot, with many hours on flying boats and he was one of the finest navigators in the air force, having set up and managed navigation schools. However, Moseley had been on various ground staff assignments for a number of years before April 1942, when he was posted to command No. 228 Squadron.

Prior to joining No. 228 Squadron, Wing Commander Moseley underwent a refresher flying course and converted to the Sunderland, but by 25 August 1942, he had not flown a Sunderland as a captain or the 1st Pilot. In addition, his hours as a 2nd Pilot on the Sunderland were somewhat limited at best. In summary, Moseley was inexperienced on the Short Sunderland and had limited flying time on any type of aircraft in the years prior to taking command of the squadron – especially when compared to Flight Lieutenant Frank Goyan.

In addition, the third pilot on board the aircraft, Pilot Officer Sydney Wood Smith was a relative novice, who had only recently joined the squadron from flying training school. To exacerbate the impending problem further, the navigator, Pilot Officer George Saunders, was also a novice with very few operational flights under his proverbial belt.

Why Wing Commander Thomas Moseley went along on this fatal flight is unclear. Some people believe he went along because their passenger was the Duke of Kent, while others believe he could have gone along as a navigation expert to monitor and mentor the junior navigator.

This latter theory gathers some credence when one considers the squadron navigation officer, Archie Brember, had been selected for the trip, but the other navigators 'kicked up such a fuss', they had to draw lots and Saunders 'won' the role. Could it be Moseley, as commanding officer and expert navigator himself, was concerned and went along to check his junior navigators work at the plotting table? If that was the case, Moseley should have pulled rank and told the other navigators Brember would be the navigator for the trip to Iceland, or he perhaps should have taken on the role himself. The problem with this hypothesis is that it appears Wing Commander Moseley was flying the aircraft and therefore he could not monitor the junior navigator.

It is clear over eight decades later that there were some issues in the cockpit. The Court of Inquiry maintained that Flight Lieutenant Frank Goyan was the captain of the aircraft, but Wing Commander Moseley was the 1st Pilot. This is a major concern.

In the Royal Air Force during the Second World War, the pilot was always the captain of the aircraft. Even if there were two pilots, the 1st Pilot would be the captain – rather like those on a modern-day airliner. For example, in an Avro Lancaster, the only officer might have been the navigator, while the pilot was a sergeant. Regardless of rank, the pilot was in control of the machine and therefore he was the captain, despite being outranked by the navigator. Crews in RAF aircraft usually worked on first name terms when on operations, despite their various commissioned and non-commissioned ranks, it generated a good working environment, but the pilot was always the captain. On the ground, the crew would quickly revert to the disciplined rank structure and first names would be exchanged for sir or sergeant.

In the case of Sunderland 'M' for Mother, we have both a 1st Pilot and a different designated captain of the aircraft, so who was in ultimate command of the Sunderland? With an inexperienced navigator, an inexperienced third pilot and a royal passenger on board, this appears to have been the proverbial recipe for the impending disaster.

Frank Goyan was a very experienced captain and 1st Pilot on the Sunderland, so surely he should have taken command. Captain Ernest Fresson also stated he had heard there had been a change of captain prior to the flight, but how he knew this is unclear.

This issue may have led to a possible cause of the crash through conflict in the command of the aircraft. This is known in modern aviation circles as 'cross cockpit authority gradient' and any disagreement in the cockpit can lead to an 'adverse gradient', often with disastrous effects.

In an 'adverse gradient' situation, there is a conflict between two or more occupants of the cockpit or flight deck. In some cases, this originates through a senior officer going along as a passenger or second pilot, but wanting to take command due to his own perceived experience or rank etc.

In the airline business and military training today, this issue is widely recognised and junior pilots are trained to challenge any such behaviour. It is often known as the battle of the egos.

In 1942, challenging the commanding officer may have caused offence and if Wing Commander Moseley wanted to do something against the wishes of the captain Frank Goyan, it could have led to an 'adverse gradient' and ultimately the fatal crash. It is also possible

Frank Goyan did not challenge his commanding officer, thereby allowing the inexperienced Sunderland pilot to take the lead with fatal results.

If Wing Commander Moseley had taken full command of the flight and acted as 1st Pilot, this would have been the first time Moseley had flown a Sunderland as 1st Pilot and captain. If that was the case how did Goyan react to this?

We know this particular Sunderland was a brand–new machine and did not have any technical problems. The aircraft flew into the hillside in thick cloud, a term known in aviation circles as 'controlled flight into terrain'. In most cases like this, pilot error is the main cause.

There is also the element of navigation. Pilot Officer George Saunders was a relatively new and inexperienced navigator, having only a few operational trips in his logbook. If Moseley was the 1st Pilot and he was not overseeing the junior navigator's work, could this have resulted in a miscalculation and an incorrect bearing?

Sunderland W4026 was fitted with a distant-reading compass (DR), a relatively new instrument for this type of aircraft in August 1942. Most of the navigators on No. 228 Squadron had received training in its use, but their actual experience of using the device must have been limited by 25 August 1942. How much training and experience Pilot Officer Saunders had on the DR compass is therefore debatable and cannot be confirmed, but even Wing Commander Thomas Moseley may have had very little experience of this instrument as a navigator or pilot. In his book *Missing believed killed*, Roy Conyers Nesbit, himself a Coastal Command squadron navigation officer, pondered an incorrect setting of the DR compass, or even the P4A next to the 1st Pilot's knee, as a possible cause for the Sunderland being off track.

We have already examined how a DR compass was operated, but to repeat it one more time, the main compass was at the rear of the fuselage and needed checking and setting prior to a flight. An electrical cable passed from the main DR compass to the navigator's position in the cockpit where there was another device known as the Variation Setting Corrector (VSC). This was on the navigator's plotting table, allowing him to adjust the DR compass readings to allow for the local magnetic variation. (In this case a variation of thirteen degrees west.) Once set with the correct amount of deflection from true north, a course could be maintained and a repeater dial in the cockpit instrument panel gave the two pilots the heading according to the DR compass and the navigator's adjustment for the local magnetic variation.

The Sunderland was flying in thick, low cloud in close proximity to high ground, the pilot flying on instruments, so it was therefore imperative the setting of the DR compass and its variation setting corrector were correctly adjusted prior to take-off. The navigator would have been the crew member primarily responsible for carrying out these actions, but if the relatively inexperienced Pilot Officer George Saunders failed to carry out these functions, or carried them out incorrectly, a fatal accident was probably a foregone conclusion.

George Saunders had only joined the unit in July 1942. He had flown just three operational flights, two of them with a tutor navigator. All three operational flights had been with his captain Frank Goyen, but he had also undertaken a small number of VIP transit flights with the same Australian captain around the Hebridean islands. How often the DR compass was used on these short local flights is unknown, but if we assume it was used on the three operational flights, two of them were under the tutelage of a more experienced navigator who undoubtedly handled the DR and VSC devices.

The aircraft also had an ASV radar system fitted, used to trace and track surface vessels and surfaced U-boats. It could also be used in the hands of an experienced and capable pilot/navigator to identify a shore line, cliffs and even a valley. However, there was no evidence this system had been utilised during this final flight.

There is also the issue of whether Thomas Moseley misread or confused the navigator's instructions, the DR compass and or the magnetic P4A compass. Normally, the 2nd Pilot (Goyan in this case) should have been monitoring the 1st Pilot and the instruments to prevent any mistakes, but if there was an issue of authority, could Goyan have chosen to let his CO fly on without any input which might cause offence? For a seasoned, experienced captain like Goyan, this would seem unlikely. Even if he was angry with Moseley, it was a matter of safety.

The aircraft could also home in on beacons like that at RAF Wick, but again there is no evidence of their use, although they were checked by RAF personnel and evidence presented to the Court of Inquiry that the beacon was functioning correctly.

Then we have the distraction of the Duke of Kent and his entourage. While the three men in his party would have taken their places in the rest area in the lower hull/fuselage, we have evidence from Flight Sergeant Andrew Jack (although via a third party), that the duke was stood between the pilots before take-off. Had he remained there for take-off, the early part of the flight and even right up to the crash? If he had been in the cockpit, he would have been a distraction. In addition, the junior navigator would have been at the rear of the cockpit as well, possibly distracted by their royal guest.

The Court of Inquiry was quick to lay the blame for the crash on the shoulders of Flight Lieutenant Frank Goyan, something that clearly angered Andrew Jack. They were also quick, as was the Air Ministry and the politicians, to claim this was an experienced crew, when in reality, only Goyan could credibly take that mantle.

The Court of Inquiry failed to look at a number of wider issues and its members appear to have had closed minds and a predetermined finding in mind when examining the evidence.

Air crash investigators today claim that there is often more than one issue in the causation of a crash. With regard to the crew's experience, possible cross cockpit gradient authority and their handling of the DR compass and VSC, we have at least three possible causes. Then there is the possibility of passenger distraction and cutting the corner over land.

Corner cutting too early? And a breach of flying boat rules?

Although there was a long-standing Air Ministry/RAF directive that flying boats should only fly over water unless there was an emergency, we appear to have the Court of Inquiry being told by the first witness (Flying Officer Ronald McCallum) that the Sunderland crew were briefed to fly up the east coast to Clyth Ness and then over the low ground to Thurso (clearly cutting the corner instead of passing over Wick and John O'Groats). This also appears to have possibly been corroborated by Group Captain Francis in his letter to *Aeroplane Monthly* magazine.

In questioning by the Inquiry, the briefing officer, Flying Officer Ronald McCallum, was asked why in view of the low cloud the aircraft was routed overland and he replied, 'Because this was the normal route in any weather conditions.' He was also asked whether Moseley or Goyan had questioned this routing and he said they did not.

Bearing in mind the aircraft had transited from Oban to Alness via a mostly over water route via Loch Linnhe, Loch Lochy, Loch Oich and Loch Ness, why did the Court of Inquiry apparently not take issue with this flight plan and briefing?

George Bethune has asked a number of people over the years about this and those attached to the service admitted it was a standard flight path for flying boats as they were always trying to conserve fuel. This was the height of the Battle of the Atlantic and hundreds of thousands of tons of shipping were being sunk by

U-boats. The Sunderland and Catalina flying boats of RAF Coastal Command were dispatched to help protect convoys, so clearly the earlier directive was being ignored to allow for quicker movement of the aircraft and to preserve fuel.

Squadron Leader Rob Wilson, the former RAF Accident Investigation Inspector, told George Bethune that he had heard that a radar operator (possibly Mr Luckin who was mentioned earlier?), had stated the Sunderland was to fly along the coastline, then turn inland across the flat land of Caithness.

The fact the Observer Corps post at Lower Newport near Berriedale heard the Sunderland, but the post further up the coast at Dunbeath heard nothing, appears to confirm the Sunderland headed inland too early.

However, although a number of witnesses heard the Sunderland at the stated locations of Lower Newport, Berridale falls, and near Braemore, none of the witnesses could physically see the aircraft due to the low cloud. The two men at Ousdale also heard the aircraft, but were certain it was inland of their position.

This evidence changed slightly, when I visited Dunbeath and spoke to a number of people. Lewis Sinclair told me that his aunt – Georgie Mouat, was next to the towers on the headland at the mouth of Berriedale Water that day. She would always remember seeing the aircraft 'through the haze' passing over and past Langwell House. The question is whether it had passed over her from the sea and headed inland, or was she describing the fact it was already over the land and heading towards Eagles Rock? A line drawn from Ousdale to the crash side would pass within 1.5 miles of Langwell House and runs parallel to Berridale Water until it meets the crash site.

If correct, Georgie Mouat would be the only witness to see the aircraft over Caithness before it crashed. It is possible the aircraft was dropping down through the cloud base at about 1,000 feet to fix their position, before altering its course. Therefore, the Sunderland could have been momentarily seen from below, while the aircrew thought they were still in the cloud layer over the sea. If correct, they were about 3.5 miles and between 1-2 minutes from oblivion at Eagles Rock.

The interesting thing is the aircraft left an impression in the ground and a trail of wreckage in a rough NE–NNE direction which roughly aligns with the straight line from Ousdale.

It is possible the aircraft turned inland too early, but as we shall see in the next chapter, I feel there is a better explanation.

Sightseeing over Duke of Portland/Lord Titchfield's estate:

There have been suggestions that rather than going to Loch More to collect Rudolf Hess, the aircraft was flown over Berridale and towards Braemore for another prupose. George Bethune favours this as a possible reason for the Sunderland being over the land. This was a sightseeing detour or a fly-past over the home of the duke's friend, the Marquess of Titchfield, whether that be Langwell House or at Braemore Lodge further up the river.

The Marquess was in the area that day and formed part of the search party, but did he know more about this flight? Was he ever approached by the Court of Inquiry to give evidence or make a statement?

We cannot confirm anything which could corroborate the allegation of a fly-past, but this is a possibility and is akin to the allegation of alcohol being drunk on board the aircraft.

In both cases, such actions would probably lead to a court martial and should not take place, but we can never say these things did not take place. There are countless accounts of people drinking alcohol or being drunk while flying an aircraft. It is a legendary claim that

RAF fighter pilots would often attend the morning patrol severely hungover, but a few breaths of pure oxygen cleared their heads. There are also countless claims of fly-pasts over girlfriends and families, some with the girlfriend on the pilot's lap, so yet again, this may be a reason for the crash, but there is no hard evidence to substantiate it.

Chapter Fifteen

The unanswered questions

I shall now re-examine the issues and the unanswered questions in this case, before giving my own hypothesis of what possibly happened on 25 August 1942.

In my mind as a former senior investigating officer, a question mark sits over the evidence of Lieutenant John Stanley Whitehead, Royal Navy Volunteer Reserve. As we have seen, he claimed to be fishing at the waterfalls on the Berriedale Water/River, to the west of Eagles Rock, when in fact, the falls are to the south towards the village of Berriedale on the coast.

Lieutenant Whitehead said that after the crash he made his way to Braemore and on up to the crash site. If this was the case he must have followed the river up through the valley to Braemore and then assisted in the search.

In the *Daily Record* newspaper on 27 August 1942, David Morrison 'claimed it was James Sutherland, with James Gunn and a naval lieutenant who found the wreckage with him first.'

In the 1948 book *Caithness and the war 1939-1945*, an entry states, 'An angler plying his art three quarters of a mile away was first to gauge what had happened. He forsook his hobby and made for the home of Mr James MacEwan, gamekeeper, who communicated with police headquarters in Wick...'

Taking these comments together, it appears they clearly relate to Lieutenant Whitehead (as no other angler is mentioned by witnesses or the final report), but he never mentioned this in his evidence contained in the Court of Inquiry papers. Is it possible Lieutenant

Whitehead did not give all the information he held, or did the panel and their final report 'cherry pick' his evidence and only note the facts they wanted to be heard by a third party? Either way, evidentially and legally this is a major issue.

Lieutenant Whitehead's evidence also failed to identify the shepherds who attended the crash site with him or the gamekeeper. As an investigator, it is necessary to name these individuals and gather evidence from them, even if this only corroborates that of the naval officer. This apparent lack of further investigation tends to indicate an investigator or inquiry, trying to either reduce the amount of work they have to undertake OR they are trying to direct the course of the evidence.

If they were trying to reduce their workload this would be a major issue, especially when one considers the importance of this crash. If they were trying to direct the course of the evidence, that again would be of major significance and concern.

A search of Royal Navy Volunteer Reserve lists locates only one John Stanley Whitehead. Although the list does not state where he was based, the first mention of this officer is in April 1942, when he is shown as a temporary sub-Lieutenant since 19 February that year, attached to the Special Branch. This was a section often engaged in shore-based duties, such as the RNO at Wick, where Lieutenant Whitehead claimed to be based as a Watch Keeper in August 1942. It often included work such as Staff Officer's duties, Meteorological Office, Scientific, or Intelligence work. It is not linked to Special Branch Police duties.

By October 1942, Whitehead had been moved to Staff Officer shore duties, a role he remained in until last mentioned in April 1946. In August 1944 he was a lieutenant and still working on Staff Officer duties.

Like many of those linked to the Court of Inquiry, John Stanley Whitehead seems to have been non-operational and working within Headquarters and Staff Officer duties until the end of the war.

As an educated naval officer who attended the crash site, surely Whitehead could give excellent detailed evidence about what he found, including the position of bodies etc.; but none of this is in the record of his evidence.

In the Court of Inquiry records, his evidence is dated (Sunday) 30 August 1942, five days after the event and appears to have been taken down at Wick.

The Court of Inquiry members are also something of an issue. Wing Commander Arthur Warren Kay, who was appointed President of the Court of Inquiry, was a First World War pilot, but in August 1942 he was working on the Air Staff of Coastal Command Headquarters. Although shown on the Form 412 (Proceedings of the Court of Inquiry) as a Wing Commander this was only an acting rank and he was actually a Squadron Leader. This was an issue highlighted by Air Marshal Sir Edward Chilton in his letter to the *Aeroplane magazine* in 1990.

It also appears Kay had no actual personal experience of flying sea planes or flying boats like the Sunderland. According to documents held in the National Archives, Kay joined the Royal Naval Air Service (RNAS) in July 1916. He flew with the renowned No. 1 Squadron RNAS at Furnes, Belgium, for a few weeks under the famous Raymond Collishaw, but after less than a month he was deemed unfit for high altitude flying and sent to Eastchurch on the Isle of Sheppey to become a flying instructor.

With the rank of Captain in the new Royal Air Force, Warren left in April 1919. What he did in the 1920s and 1930s is unknown, but in 1938 he joined 908 Company of the Essex Barrage Balloon Squadron. He was recommissioned as a Flying Officer and commanded 'C' Flight in February 1939.

The barrage balloon unit was mobilised on 23 August 1939 with Warren now a Flight Lieutenant. A few weeks later he was with No. 30 Group Headquarters. He was apparently still with Balloon

Branch in August 1940, with the temporary rank of Squadron Leader by June 1941.

On 8 June 1942, less than three months before the fatal crash, Kay was made a substantive Squadron Leader on administrative duties at Coastal Command Headquarters.

For an inquiry of such importance and magnitude, these do not look like the credentials required to act as the President of the Court of Enquiry, although as we have seen he could have received some preliminary accident investigation training. As president it appears he had no personal experience of flying boats or their specialist navigational requirements. (This is of course assuming he did not fly such aircraft in the 1920s and 1930s.)

It could be argued that Kay could have been supported by the other members of the Court of Inquiry in making decisions, if they were themselves qualified.

However, it appears Kay made a name for himself by investigating the duke's crash and went on to permanent accident investigation work; he even sat as a member of the Court of Inquiry into General Sikorski's crash less than a year later in Gibraltar.

The second officer on the Court of Inquiry panel was Squadron Leader William John D'Amboise Stacey from No. 15 Group, Coastal Command. He joined the RAF in the 1920s flying a number of transport aircraft, as well as the Rangoon flying boat.

Stacey left the RAF in 1934 to join Imperial Airways with whom he gained valuable experience of flying boats. He joined the RAF Reserve list in January 1934, but joined the RAFO in September 1937, becoming a flying instructor and was promoted to Flight Lieutenant in September 1940.

In 1942, Stacey was posted as a temporary Squadron Leader (RAFO) to No. 15 Group Coastal Command. Therefore, like Kay, his rank was a temporary one, and in the case of both men not reflected on the Form 412, which did not indicate the two men held temporary or acting ranks.

The third and final member of the Court of Inquiry, was Flight Lieutenant Douglas Stuart Lindsay DFC, an Australian pilot attached to the newly forming No. 423 Squadron at RAF Oban (also flying the Short Sunderland).

Lindsay had joined the Royal Air Force in 1938 and been commissioned. He served with No. 201 Squadron flying the Short Sunderland in 1941, being awarded the Distinguished Flying Cross. He was promoted to Flight Lieutenant in August 1941 and joined 423 Squadron when it was formed at Oban. He was therefore the one member of the Court of Inquiry with up-to-date experience on flying boats and especially the Sunderland.

With Kay apparently having no experience of flying boat and Sunderland operations, he was also a Squadron Leader and not a substantive Wing Commander. Stacey was relatively inexperienced for the role on the inquiry and although it cannot be confirmed, it would be unlikely either man had prior experience of sitting on a Court of Inquiry and certainly not one of such magnitude.

If we ignore temporary or acting ranks, the panel consisted of a Squadron Leader and two Flight Lieutenants. With this apparent lack of experience and knowledge, it is very surprising they did not utilise any experts in navigation.

As we have seen, Air Chief Marshal Sir Edward Chilton, a navigation expert in 1942, says that together with his colleague Group Captain Kelly Barnes, he was warned to 'stand by' to assist the Court of Inquiry. In his own words they were both 'Freely available and were the RAF's two senior specialist navigators,' but they were quickly told they would not be required. Why was this never explained to either man?

Sir Edward also added that, 'The senior officer of the Court of Enquiry (Kay) was *a* Squadron Leader – all very low key, which was very odd in the circumstances.' Clearly, even in 1942, some officers thought something strange was going on.

Then we have the issue of the Air Accident Inspectors Branch not being directly involved in the investigation of the crash.

We have heard that crash inspector Rob Wilson recalled a signal and a phone call from the Under Secretary of State for Air (Balfour), requesting the services of the Air Accident Branch. Wilson claims he was called into the office of the Chief Inspector – Vernon Sydney Brown – and heard him not once, but twice, refuse to assist with the investigation. In addition, in 1992 Wilson was noted as stating the AIB had trained a number of Group officers to carry out preliminary crash investigation and Brown had agreed to assist if the local investigator found nothing. Although Brown reportedly mentioned eighty to ninety air crashes and that he was not going to investigate a Sunderland flying in to a hillside, regardless of whoever was on board, there remain several unanswered questions in relation to this:

1. Why refuse this particular investigation?
2. How did he know who was on board the aircraft?
3. Why did Balfour or his senior, Sir Archibald Sinclair, or even the Prime Minister, not order Brown to undertake an investigation?
4. Was Brown aware not only of the presence of the Duke of Kent on the Sunderland, but also the number of fatalities involved?
5. Did Brown not realise that this was the second worst air crash in British history up to that point in time?

As we have seen, the media reported that the Chief Inspector from the Air Accidents Branch was attending the crash site, but the evidence of Rob Wilson dismisses this. Did someone brief the media before Brown declined the request to attend the crash scene?

Later, the Court of Inquiry Form 412 and Sir Archibald Sinclair's statement to parliament in October 1942, both noted that the Chief

Inspector of Accidents had concurred with the findings of the Court of Inquiry. However, there is no evidence of what Sydney Vernon Brown had seen, heard, or read in relation to the crash of the Sunderland.

If Brown had concurred with their findings, what had he been told? I have made efforts to find a memoir of Vernon Sydney Brown which covers the crash and the deaths of these men, but I have been unable to find one. If, as appears to be the case, he did not attend the crash scene, nor any of his team for that matter, what involvement if any, did he have? If, as I suspect, he had none, what were his views on the public information and reports stating he concurred with the Court of Inquiry's findings?

The Court of Inquiry clearly did not know who was handling the Sunderland at the moment it crashed into Eagles Rock. However, they were quite clear with regard to Goyan being the captain of the aircraft and Moseley the 1st Pilot. From the available documents, there was apparently very little discussion about who was giving the commands on board the aircraft in the minutes leading up to the crash. The Court of Inquiry appears to have accepted that Flight Lieutenant Goyan, as captain, must have been giving the orders despite the 1st Pilot being two ranks higher and the squadrons commanding officer; Goyan must take responsibility for the crash.

Clearly, in 1942, there was no knowledge of cross cockpit authority gradient and there was no consideration of any possible conflict of command by the Court of Inquiry.

The apparent narrow-mindedness of the inquiry also appears to have led to a failure to consider the issue of possible errors in navigation. Although the full papers are no longer available, there were only thirteen witnesses and the Australian copy of the report would appear to contain all the evidence and the questions and answers of these people. The navigation is hardly mentioned, consideration was given to the planned flight path and flying overland, but there was no assistance given by navigation experts.

In addition, there is no mention of any instruments being located and examined (if they survived) at the crash site. Recovery of the P4A compass, the DR compass and its associated correcting device may have given some idea about what course the crew were actually flying, but there is no evidence of this – not even to say they looked, but could not find the instruments or any evidence.

This closing down of options and possible causes for the accident is unforgivable. If a police senior investigating officer did not explain why they had not considered something so apparently worthy of investigation in a matter like this, such as a compass being faulty or incorrectly set, they would be vilified and rightly so.

The Court of Inquiry also seemed either oblivious or chose to ignore the Air Ministry directive that flying boats should stay over water unless there was an emergency. The issue of drinking was not mentioned and does not appear to have been a possible issue in 1942, although to be fair, this was only raised in post war years.

Sunderland 'M' for Mother had already made its way via a series of interconnecting lochs to reach Invergordon/Alness from its home base at Oban. Admittedly, it had to fly over land for the odd minute here or there as they headed towards the next loch, but the course was clearly set to adhere to the official edict and also to avoid the high mountains. So, when the Court of Inquiry apparently seemed to ignore the revelation that a course had been briefed for the Sunderland to turn inland and cut the corner from Clyth Ness to Thurso, this surprisingly does not appear to have been challenged. Was this because everyone knew this was common practice and a means of saving precious fuel and time, or was it a case the panel were oblivious to the directive? I feel they chose to ignore it, having a current Sunderland pilot on the panel must have meant they were cognisant of this order.

There are also questions about who actually gave 'live' evidence to the full inquiry panel, and whether any witness actually did this or just gave a statement to visiting officers which was later summarised on the Form 412.

We know Andrew Jack did not give evidence to a live hearing or the full inquiry panel, as he was lying in his hospital bed on the date of his evidence according to the Form 412 summary.

Jack's family were present on the day of his evidence, stating the two officers attending him were from the RAF and the Navy, so clearly these were not the three members of the Court of Inquiry panel.

The evidence from Jack and his subsequent answers to their questions could only be obtained from him while he was lying in his bed suffering from burns and shock. The question is whether he was fit to be interviewed? Was he under some form of sedative or other medication that would hinder his memory of the event? Did they seek and receive the doctor's permission to interview Jack? None of this is covered in the Court of Inquiry record or even mentioned. If this occurred today it would be necessary to clear this questioning with the doctor caring for the patient and there would be concerns about the veracity of his statement.

We also know that William Sutherland at Lower Newport and Dr John Kennedy in Dunbeath gave their evidence on the same date as Andrew Jack (29 August). It appears they were probably visited by the same two officers and provided evidence in their own homes which were within a few miles of Jack's hospital bed.

The witnesses based at Invergordon all gave their evidence on the same day as those at Wick, making it appear the Court of Inquiry was moving around to receive evidence. While this is not unlawful or unheard of, it does raise the question of who the attending inquiry consisted of in relation to each witness? Was the full panel of officers present when these men gave evidence? Was legal representation present? Was there a note taker present? In the case of Andrew Jack, this does not appear to have been the case. In short, can we be certain the full evidence or the discussion was recorded verbatim and if not, why not?

Add to this the long-term relative silence of Flight Sergeant Andrew Jack and his alleged anger about Frank Goyan being blamed for the crash and it appears something is not quite right with this investigation.

The post war apparent loss or shredding of evidence is particularly disturbing, especially for such a prominent case as this. Why was this file shredded, yet those for the Sikorski and Leigh-Mallory Courts of Inquiry survived?

One element that I found particularly surprising was the apparent failure to engage with the Procurator Fiscal. If, as it appears, a precognition report was not sent to the Procurator Fiscal, this not only would breach Scottish law, but also Air Ministry directive Air Publication 1922 regarding the reporting and recording of military deaths, including those from accidents.

The legal follow-up for the recording of the deaths also seems to have been haphazard and somewhat clumsy. The No. 228 Squadron crew's deaths were recorded by the Commanding Officer of RAF Wick, but this was outside the legally required time frame for reporting a death in Scotland. I did note that other airmen killed in similar air crashes were sometimes recorded outside the legal time frame, so to be fair, this appears to have been due to the busy wartime period. However, it took even longer to record the death of the Duke of Kent, his equerry and private secretary. Then the poor valet, Airman Hales, was not recorded for many weeks – almost an afterthought or error.

There is no available medical evidence in relation to the cause of death in each man's case. On the death certificates, only the Duke of Kent has a precise cause of death (a compound skull fracture), while the others are shown as having multiple injuries from a flying accident.

There are no completed Forms 551 (*Report on accidental injuries or immediate death therefrom*) in the Australian copy of the Sunderland case papers, but according to the Air Ministry directive

Air Publication 1922: *Notes on casualty procedure in war 1941/2*, these were not required when a Court of Inquiry took place. The Forms 551 that I have seen from the air crash on nearby Scaraben on 18 August 1942, show the injuries to be described as 'multiple injuries.'

Although the use of the term 'multiple injuries' appears to have been common on crash reports, it might be expected that the significance of the duke's aircraft and the number of fatalities would lead to a more detailed and thorough description of their injuries.

There is an issue with how quickly the crash site was cleared. It has been claimed over the years that the RAF were desperate to clear the crash site, a location set on a difficult to access hillside. Many other similar sites had wreckage left in situ, any specialised equipment, bodies and personal effects being removed. Many other crash sites in Scotland, Wales and the Peak District can still be visited and wreckage observed from the Second World War, so why were the authorities allegedly so quick to clear it?

In some respects the removal of the wreckage is understandable. We know a great many of the local population attended the scene and picked over the debris, taking all manner of items from parts of machine guns to anchor chains and perfume bottles. This was despite a cursory guard being left at the scene overnight, but was it a case of the authorities wanting to stop souvenir hunting or some other reason? Despite their efforts, we have evidence of a further 'clean-up' being required after the war, while twenty-first century hikers are still picking up pieces of debris, which is often handed in to the nearby Dunbeath Heritage Centre where it is on display.

There is also the surprising and almost impetuous manner in which Dr John Kennedy was recommended for and awarded his MVO.

In addition, we have the local tale that he was invested with the honour through an open train window at a railway station. Whether this latter account is true or not, it appears from the records in the National Archives that there was high-level enthusiasm to award him the honour, although the papers suggest an OBE or MBE was unlikely and discounted. It therefore fell to King George himself to make the award.

While the recommendation mentioned Dr Kennedy's attendance at other recent air crashes, the award was specifically for his actions at the scene of the Duke of Kent's crash. These actions, while worthy of praise, are really no different to the actions of a number of other witnesses that day.

Finally, what are we to make of the comments of Leading Aircraftsman Arthur Baker? He claimed the Duke of Kent had a severe injury to his eyes and was holding a fan of playing cards, but he did not mention the attaché case or the scattered money.

We know other witnesses had already covered the bodies before the arrival of the RAF Regiment contingent, but the coverings may have blown off. While LAC Arthur Baker is one of a number of witnesses who recall the smell of scent in the air at the crash scene, he is the only known witness who mentions the body of a woman and female clothing, although Will Bethune did mention seeing pairs of ladies' shoes.

There have long been claims of an unidentified extra body at the scene, an issue that was exacerbated by the initial reports that all those on board the Sunderland had been killed. This in time blossomed into claims that the extra body was that of Rudolf Hess, but could there have been an unidentified female on board the aircraft? Special Constable Will Bethune was quite adamant, there was no female body at the crash scene when he arrived with his colleague and the RAF Marine tender men at Alness, including George Campbell, never mentioned any female passenger being present.

As we have seen, there have long been claims that the Duke of Kent had previously dressed in female clothes with Noel Coward, could the clothes have been his own? Or were they a present for an unknown female?

Then we have the claims, although hearsay from Mrs Margaret Harris, that her uncle Andrew Jack had told her father there had been a mysterious extra passenger on board the aircraft.

The claims of an extra deceased passenger appear to gain some credence when WAAF Dorothea Gray's statement about directing undertakers not to re-open the deceased's coffins is added to the story. It is likely this was to avoid the shock of seeing a deceased relative's injuries.

It is more likely the issue of an extra body is caused by the continuing confusion over reported numbers of passengers, bodies and their identities.

This is a summary of the issues I have identified with this case. The original Court of Inquiry papers are completely missing. In addition, the pages held in the Australian National Archives are typed copies and not a full set of case papers. Despite this, we can identify from those papers that are available and the other sources, the following points:

- Who was on the Court of Inquiry?
- Who ordered the Court of Inquiry?
- The date of the Court of Inquiry.
- Details of the aircraft.
- Aircrew and passenger details (these can be examined in more depth from other sources).
- The apparent condition and airworthiness of the aircraft.
- The names of the witnesses and their apparent evidence.
- The questions to some witnesses and their answers.
- The number of flying hours and experience of the three pilots.
- The navigator's experience and training.
- Details of the DR Compass and its operations.
- The involvement of the Air Accidents Inspectors Branch (or lack of it).

- The communications between politicians and royalty.
- Records pertaining to the recording of the deaths and procedures.
- The fact the Records of Scotland have no records from the Procurator Fiscal concerning this crash.
- Planned details of the agenda and travel for the Duke of Kent's party, before and after the flight.
- The fact Police Scotland no longer holds any records for this incident.

In the final chapter, I will give my own hypothesis on the cause of the crash and its aftermath...

Chapter Sixteen

My hypothesis

The following is my own hypothesis of what happened on the afternoon of 25 August 1942.

It is based upon the evidence contained within this book with some assumptions. The assumptions are based on some hearsay evidence, knowledge of events at that time and various other pieces of information.

It is clear that over the weekend before the fatal crash, No. 228 Squadron was preparing for a VIP flight. Although those outside the senior command group did not know who the special flight was for, they knew it was going to be something out of the ordinary. For that reason, Sunderland 'M' for Mother was made ready and serviced, while the Commanding Officer, Wing Commander Thomas Moseley decided he would also go along on the flight with a specially selected crew, under the experienced Flight Lieutenant Frank Goyan.

Although the initial selections appear to have been based upon ability and experience, as well as the fact most of Goyan's crew flew regularly together, this soon changed.

A junior pilot was initially to act as Goyan's second pilot – Pilot Officer Sydney Wood Smith. The navigator was to have been the squadron's navigation officer, Flying Officer (soon to be a Flight Lieutenant) Archie Brember, but that changed after a certain amount of agitation among the unit's navigators.

Frank Goyan and Archie Brember would have been more than capable, supported by Smith and the rest of the crew, in flying their VIP to wherever was required. The other seven members of the crew were a relatively experienced team of wireless operators, fitters and air gunners with many operations under their collective belts.

Why Wing Commander Thomas Moseley, a relatively new commanding officer, was going along is unclear. He was, as we have seen, an experienced pilot in terms of flying hours, but he was a bit of a novice on the Short Sunderland and he had spent most of the previous few years on ground instructional duties, which would have been mostly classroom based.

Who decided – and why – Moseley would be the 1st Pilot for this flight is also unclear, especially when his lack of experience on the Sunderland is taken into account.

Ernest Fresson claimed he was told there had been a last-minute change of captain on board the Sunderland which had delayed its departure. Who told him this was not explained or explored further by Fresson.

To compound this issue, it is difficult to explain or understand why Frank Goyan remained as aircraft captain for the flight, when Moseley became the 1st Pilot. As we have seen, in standard RAF crew formations of the time, or in most other cases with a multi-manned crew, the 1st Pilot was the aircraft captain regardless of their own rank. If Wing Commander Moseley was now the 1st Pilot, not to mention the fact he was senior in rank to any of the crew, why was he not the aircraft captain?

As we have seen, not only was Wing Commander Moseley's experience on the aircraft type limited, he only had twice the number of Sunderland flying hours of the junior pilot (Pilot Officer Smith), which he had accrued in the previous few weeks.

Flight Lieutenant Frank Goyan was a very experienced 1st Pilot and captain in his own right, whereas Moseley had no time as a Sunderland 1st Pilot since his arrival on No. 228 Squadron, less than three months before the final flight.

The 1st Pilot should have been the aircraft captain, a position Goyan had regularly filled on operations, so why did Moseley choose this flight to be the 1st Pilot and not the captain? On their repositioning flight from Oban to Alness, Moseley had been 2nd Pilot, so why was he suddenly the 1st Pilot? Was it because of the presence of Prince George, the Duke of Kent? Was it a case of wanting to be close to the duke?

Whatever Wing Commander Moseley's reasons were, it is clear there was a distinct possibility of a cross-cockpit adverse gradient incident. This would have led to a dislocated command structure on the aircraft's flight deck with disastrous results.

Wing Commander Moseley's decision to take command over a more experienced pilot probably caused the next crew issue – that of the chosen navigator Flying Officer Archie Brember.

Wing Commander Thomas Moseley, as commanding officer, should have managed the navigators and told them clearly that the Squadron Navigation Officer, Archie Brember, was going to undertake the role. Instead, he allowed a draw of lots to take place, resulting in one of the squadron's most inexperienced navigators (Pilot Officer George Saunders) taking his place at the plotting table.

As an expert navigator and instructor, Wing Commander Thomas Moseley possibly felt he could oversee the junior navigator, but he probably felt he could not order the other navigators to 'stand down' when he had already assigned himself to the flight. Add to this the fact he had now placed himself as the 1st Pilot on board 'M' for Mother above a more experienced man and these decisions may have been some of the fatal ingredients for the final recipe.

Once the crew of the Sunderland became aware of their royal guest and his entourage, the excitement and the want to be close to their prestigious passenger certainly spread among the wireless operator/air gunners. This led to another lottery by means of the tossing of a coin, Flight Sergeant Andrew Jack losing and having to take his position in the Sunderland's lonely rear turret.

This series of decisions, the drawing of lots and coin tossing, meant that a professional, dedicated and mostly experienced Sunderland crew had been chopped and changed to one led by a 1st Pilot who was not experienced in the role on the aircraft, a different captain, with an inexperienced navigator and what was probably an overly excited crew.

We also have Flight Sergeant Andrew Jack's alleged later comments that the Duke of Kent was stood in the cockpit between the two pilots, Moseley and Goyan, as they prepared for take-off on Cromarty Firth. Although the duke probably never meant to be a distraction, he most certainly would have been to the pilots and the inexperienced navigator sitting behind them next to the wireless operator.

Add to this equation, poor weather, a heavily laden 58,000lbs. Sunderland and a VIP passenger who allegedly disliked flying in cloud (although this does not sit well with the Jack family's assertion that the Duke of Kent had pushed the crew to take off despite the poor weather) and we have a number of issues.

The Sunderland's crew were briefed to take-off and fly to Tarbat Ness point, where they would set course for their next waypoint, north of Dunbeath at Clyth Ness lighthouse. They would then turn towards Thurso, effectively cutting the corner across the lowland of Caithness, contrary to official Air Ministry/RAF directives of the time, before heading to Cape Wrath, the Butt of Lewis and on to their final destination in Iceland.

With the aircraft flying in dense low cloud, it was imperative the Sunderland's instruments worked correctly and that the DR compass was set and adjusted prior to take-off. The VSC for the DR compass should have been adjusted to allow for the 13 degrees (west) magnetic declination variation from true north in that part of Scotland.

I believe the inexperienced junior navigator, possibly either failed to set the DR compass and the variation setting corrector (VSC) next to his plotting table, thereby giving the pilots an incorrect course, or it was not completed satisfactorily. He may have become distracted by the Duke of Kent standing next to him on the flight deck as they prepared for take-off. The two lead pilots were probably too engrossed with piloting the aircraft and liaising with their royal guest to notice while the 3rd Pilot probably kept out of the way in the crew rest area, ignorant of the situation developing on the flight deck.

There is also the possibility, no matter how unpalatable it may be to some, that there may have been the consumption of alcohol both before and after take-off. Whether this just concerned the passengers or possibly some of the crew we cannot say. Alcohol bottles were found at the crash site and the station commander at Alness, Group Captain Geoffrey Francis, has accepted that the royal entourage may have had a drink with lunch in the Officers' Mess. Others have also claimed there was an intake of alcohol on the aircraft. While we cannot confirm alcohol played any part in the crash, even the possibility that some of the guests were inebriated may have caused yet another distraction for the crew.

One other option that has previously been considered by some historical researchers is that the DR compass and the VSC had been demonstrated to the duke in the time he was on board, but not reset correctly post demonstration. I feel this is less likely, as the aircraft had only been in the air half an hour when it crashed and the weather situation was such that no competent pilot would allow themself to tamper with such a vital instrument in those prevailing weather conditions.

As a result of the issue with the DR compass and its associated VSC, the aircraft probably flew on a track from Tarbat Ness lighthouse, 13 degrees west of their planned flight path, along the coast of Caithness. I believe their cruising altitude was about 2,000 or maybe 3,000 feet at most, meaning they remained in the cloud layer throughout the trip missing higher ground. (N.B. Fresson recalled the top of the cloud layer being at 4,000 feet and the meteorologist who gave evidence – Andrew Dryburgh – said that in addition to the weather forecast, the crew were told of a risk of low cloud with a main base of 800 feet spreading west of a line roughly from Lossiemouth – to the east of Invergordon – to Wick.)

Having entered the thick cloud layer, the crew could not see the sea or the coastline and were navigating on the compass bearing, allowing for speed and time to identify their position.

The incorrect track of 13 degrees west of their intended course eventually took the Sunderland inland at a position to the south of Ousdale, over the high ground to the west of the Berridale River and past the settlements at Lower Newport and Berriedale. The aircraft narrowly missed a couple of peaks to the west of its track in the Scaraben range, before passing over the crest of Donald's Mount in the thick cloud and striking the ground on the opposite side of Berriedale Water at Eagles Rock. This occurred when the aircraft was making a gradual descent on a heading of about NNE.

The rate of descent was shallow, hence the reason the aircraft somersaulted after hitting the ground. Between Meall na Caorach and the crash site, the Sunderland's track would have passed over varying heights of 220 to 240 metres before it decreased to 200 metres near Donald's Mount, dropping down to Berridale Water and back up to the crash site at approximately 210 metres. The distance between the 240m and 210m (787-689 feet) locations, was just over a mile. Prior to this the height of the ground under the 13 degrees west track never exceeds 200 metres (656 feet) with most of the track lying below that height.

The witnesses at Ousdale heard the aircraft heading inland, while William Sutherland at the Royal Observer Corps post in Lower Newport and the Morrisons on the Berridale Water, also heard it fly over. None of these witnesses could say for certain whether the aircraft they heard was directly overhead or nearby, but all three locations lie within two miles of the 13 degrees west track from Tarbet Ness lighthouse to the crash site. In addition, Georgie Mouat is said to have momentarily seen the Sunderland in the haze of the cloud base as it passed Langwell House, but we cannot say whether she observed it above her head or in the distance above the house and in land.

It is difficult to apply any scientific logic to where the aircraft could have been in relation to the witnesses because the distance aircraft noise travels depends on its altitude, the local geography (i.e. hills, valleys and often buildings) and time. This latter point is particularly relevant if an aircraft is at a high altitude. On a sunny day, you may see an aircraft at over 30,000 feet with a contrail, but you may not hear it until it had passed overhead.

Some scientific studies have found that an aircraft passing directly overhead at 4,000 feet, will produce 100 per cent of its emitted sound. However, if the aircraft at 4,000 feet was a mile away this could drop to just 36 per cent of its sound and even 13 per cent two miles away. (These figures however, can be influenced by geographical factors with sound waves bouncing off hills, buildings and cliffs etc.)

We know the Sunderland was at an altitude of about 2,000–3,000 feet (609–914 metres) when it decreased its height and hit Eagles Rock at an altitude of about 900 feet, therefore anyone hearing the aircraft would have been relatively close to it.

Why the aircraft started to decrease its altitude is unknown, but it could either have been due to the duke's alleged dislike of flying in cloud, or more likely due to the DR compass and the crew believing they were still over the sea and approaching their turning point at Clyth Ness, north of Dunbeath. The pilot would therefore drop down below the cloud layer over the sea confirming their position, before making the turn inland. The pilot probably expected to exit the bottom of the cloud layer just below 1,000 feet – hence the shallow descent.

This appears to be backed up by Ernest Fresson's comment that Andrew Jack had allegedly said he had heard over the intercom, words to the effect of 'Let's go down and have a look', although we have no corroboration for this comment and we do not know how Fresson heard this. If correct, this could be possible evidence of the pilot going down below the cloud layer to fix their position. Sadly, the crew were unaware of their predicament and flew straight into the hillside at a shallow angle.

The Sunderland hit the hillside at Eagles Rock, leaving the impression of its lower hull before somersaulting and leaving a further impression of the wings' leading edge and the wing floats in the soft peaty ground.

As soon as it struck the earth, the forward somersault motion threw the detached tail section and rear turret containing Andrew Jack many yards ahead of the initial impact point. The remainder of the aircraft broke into hundreds, if not thousands of pieces, but a good number of larger components survived the impact, including the wing floats, engines, the tail section and larger sections of airframe, wings and flaps. The fuel burst from the tanks and immediately ignited, burning a good deal of the wreckage, many of the crew and the surrounding heather and bracken.

I do not believe the aircraft turned inland too soon as some people believe, although I can fully understand their reasoning. I think the Sunderland was on a wrong bearing and preparing to make the anticipated turn, thinking they were over the sea, when they flew into the hillside.

The Court of Inquiry may have been aware that alcohol had been consumed, but this cannot be confirmed.

The Court of Inquiry consisted of three officers unlikely to have been involved in such a process before and two of them were also lacking any recent flying boat experience. However, it appears the President, acting Wing Commander Kay, may have received some training as a preliminary accident investigator. They immediately suspected the weather and navigation as the probable causes, although they did not seek navigational expertise with their deliberations. With the death of the King's brother, this was a major embarrassment for the service.

Even if they did not know it immediately, the Court of Inquiry would have soon become aware of the make-up of the crew and the issue with Wing Commander Moseley acting as 1st Pilot, Goyan as the captain and the junior inexperienced navigator.

The RAF initially reported the matter to the Air Ministry and then requested the advice of the service's navigation experts – Group Captains Edward Chilton and Kelly Barnes and possibly Vernon Sydney Brown's team. The question is why Brown did not send an immediate team of Inspectors to the site, bearing in mind not only who was on board, but the number of fatalities; and who cancelled Chilton and Barnes?

Air Vice-Marshal David Colyer, the Commanding Officer of No. 15 Group, Coastal Command, possibly wanted this investigation completed as soon as possible. He therefore directed Acting Wing Commander Warren Arthur Kay from Coastal Command Headquarters to form the Court of Inquiry, Kay being the President and possibly a preliminary accident investigator, aided by Squadron Leader Stacey and Flight Lieutenant Lindsay. Stacey was also attached to No. 15 Group HQ and Lindsay a No. 15 Group Sunderland pilot with No. 423 Squadron.

Later, the final report was signed by Air Vice-Marshal Colyer and Group Captain Edward F. Turner, the latter, like Kay, another ex-pre-war Balloon Command officer and Air Staff Officer on Coastal Command since August 1939 (although he did have experience of flying sea planes in the early 1930s).

Group Captain Turner signed as the RAF Oban Station Commander, a position records show he did not hold at the time, so why did he sign as such, when he had been on the Coastal Command HQ Air Staff?

No. 63 Maintenance Unit (63 MU) were directed to attend the crash site, gather evidence, then clear the site as soon as possible, probably to prevent souvenir hunters, but also any media intrusion. Whether No. 63 MU gave an evidential report to the Court of Inquiry is unclear as no mention is made in the surviving report. The Court of Inquiry panel did sign the official forms stating they had visited the crash site. If that was the case, had there been an official written report from the 63 MU officer or did the panel deal with this from their own site visit and observations? Again, this should have been mentioned in the report.

Whether any aircraft instruments were recovered by No. 63 MU and if that included the DR compass and the attached VSC is unknown. The question is whether the recovery team found the DR compass and or the VSC and did those instruments display incorrect or correct readings? If they did, were the navigation experts Group Captains Edward Chilton and Kelly Barnes told to stand down because of this finding – whatever it was?

Then we have the issue of the Air Accident Inspectors Branch and the refusal of its Chief Inspector, Vernon Sydney Brown, to attend or send his team to the crash site.

We know Privy Council member and Under Secretary of State for Air, Harold Balfour, telephoned Brown twice requesting his help in investigating the crash. Despite this request, one of his Inspectors, Rob Wilson, who witnessed the telephone calls, said Vernon Sydney Brown refused to assist in the investigation.

It appears Brown knew who was on the flight according to Rob Wilson's comments, as well as the number of fatalities, so why did he refuse to assist with such a major accident? Are we to believe the second worst air crash in British history at that time, with the King's brother on board, was not important enough to warrant a full investigation and it was left to a preliminary investigator? Surely Harold Balfour and by extension his seniors (Sir Archibald Sinclair and Winston Churchill) could have ordered Brown to attend and investigate the site?

There is, however, the possibility that Harold Balfour was working in an independent role as a Privy Council member and liaising directly with the King, but Sinclair and Churchill were too embarrassed by the loss and wanted the RAF to start a smaller low-key investigation. Did Sinclair, Churchill, or one of their staff contact Vernon Sydney Brown and tell him not to engage with the RAF and Balfour's request? Did this then extend to cancelling Chilton and Kelly?

The media comments about the attendance of the Chief Inspector of Accidents may have been speculative on their part, based on expected post incident protocols. However, what are we to make of the claims on the Court of Inquiry papers and by Sir Archibald Sinclair in parliament that the Chief Inspector of Air Accidents concurred with the inquiry's findings?

Then there is the issue of not apparently making a so-called precognition report to the Procurator Fiscal as per Scottish law and the Air Publication 1922 Air Ministry directive on accidental deaths. Why was this not submitted? The only possible reasons are the Court of Inquiry did not know this was a requirement or they chose to ignore it. This in itself begs the question did they seek any legal advice on the issue?

Then there is the issue of the deaths being registered late and why no one in authority did not link the registrations to the fact no precognition report was ever received by the Procurator Fiscal. Could someone have spoken with the local Procurator Fiscal and the registrar, who then decided no further action was needed after the conclusion of the Court of Inquiry?

Although some of this is conjecture based on the available evidence, desperation at the thought of killing a prince of the realm, due to a possible navigation failure, poor weather and or an inexperienced crew member or members, could have led to an attempt to cover-up the crash.

One question I have been asked was whether the authorities could have known it was a crew and navigational error that led to the crash?

I believe it was evident straight away that there was a probable issue of 'cross cockpit authority gradient' between Moseley and Goyan, not to mention the close proximity of the duke. They were also aware of the junior navigator, picked by lots, operating in an unusual environment with new DR compass technology.

The recovery team may have found some remains of the DR compass and its associated parts as well as the navigator's charts, issues that would have caused acute embarrassment. I believe this is the case because of the lack of evidence from a crash scene examination and its findings. Even the most catastrophic of air crashes have parts that can be salvaged and examined. Why did no one give evidence from the recovery team detailing what they had found (or not found)? Why were the two navigation experts cancelled without explanation and why did the Chief Inspector of Air Crashes refuse to attend or send his team?

Although we cannot say anything for certain due to the missing papers, the lack of any mention of such witness evidence or an examination report in the Australian papers points to this issue being ignored or removed from the investigation file.

However, one thing appears to be certain – this was an accident. There was no Rudolf Hess or an unknown female on board the aircraft when it crashed in to Eagles Rock. The conspiracy claims have sprouted from snippets of evidence and confusion surrounding the initial number of dead at the scene, and the finding of female clothing and perfume. In many ways, I believe the authorities may have been only too happy for the conspiracy theories to develop and flourish; acting as a form of disinformation, they have diverted attention away from the real issues.

The aircraft and its occupants were clearly on their way to Iceland when tragedy struck and with most of the relevant paperwork missing and the witnesses no longer alive, we will probably never know exactly what happened that afternoon on 25 August 1942.

If, as I suspect, the crash was due to the factors outlined above, the blaming of Flight Lieutenant Frank Goyan is a travesty of justice. This appears to have caused depression and stress for Flight Sergeant Andrew Jack, a man who took that anger to his grave at a relatively young age. Maybe, just maybe, the Royal Air Force and another inquiry could reinvestigate the matter, perhaps removing the blame from Goyan's shoulders. However, with papers missing and witnesses no longer alive, that is unlikely to ever happen.

Finally, it is worth considering the Court of Inquiry into the death of Air Marshal Trafford Leigh-Mallory, his wife and the Avro York's crew in 1944. Not only did it avoid the dreaded shredder, it went on to recommend that specialist flight crews and aircraft be used for the transportation of members of the Royal Family and other dignitaries…. In effect, The Royal Squadron was about to be born…

Post script

As part of my enquiries I approached the Air Accident Investigation Board (AAIB), asking if they had any records relating to this case and any investigation. I was informed that they have no records and as a military crash, they referred me to the RAF Air Historical Branch and the RAF Museum at Hendon. Subsequently, both the RAF AHB and the museum were contacted and they informed me they held no records relating to this incident, apart from the Form 1180 accident card.

In October 2023, having completed a good part of my enquiries I decided it would be useful to get an expert air investigator's opinion on the matter. I therefore made two approaches on identical lines, one to the Air Accident Investigation Board and another to an academic specialising in air crash investigation. In both emails I explained who I was, what I was doing and gave a brief synopsis of the case:

'Dear Sirs,

'I am a retired police senior investigating officer who now works as a researcher and writer.

'I am currently completing a review of the air crash which killed the Duke of Kent in 1942 and will publish a book on the subject in 2024.

'From my extensive enquiries to date, I have found what I believe to be a lack of post-crash detailed investigation. The crash site was cleared within a few weeks and the Court of Inquiry completed its investigation and findings within a week of the incident.

'The evidence that still survives today gives plenty of information about the aircraft, its crew and flight plans, but there is little evidence of the scene examination and inspection of any wreckage and or instruments etc. There is no evidence of what wreckage was found.

'I was wondering if there was anyone (at the AAIB/University) willing to give me an expert opinion about what should have occurred post-crash in 1942? At the time, this was the second worst air crash in British history with fourteen fatalities, one of which was the King's brother the Duke of Kent.

'If you can assist me I would be very grateful and I look forward to hearing from you.'

The academic replied, asking me to send them the data set, so I duly sent a much longer synopsis with a number of the images contained within this book.

A few days after first contacting the academic, the Air Accident Investigation Board CC'd me into an internal email, in which the author asked another employee for their view on the fact this was a military issue, and whether they should not make any comment on the case. They also suggested the matter be referred to the DAIB (Defence Accident Investigation Board) as it was a military incident.

A few days after receiving the AAIB email, the academic, having read my longer synopsis, emailed me to say his original understanding was that this had not been investigated. Working closely with the organisation (Author's note: they meant the AAIB) who investigated the original case, the academic said they were now uncomfortable carrying out a historic critic of the event. (Author's note: even though this was now over eighty-one years ago!) The academic therefore referred me to the Air Accident Investigation Board.

It was clear to me that no one wanted to give an opinion on this case, the question is why, well over eighty years after the event?

In October 2023, I decided to contact the Defence Accident Investigation Board (DIAB) myself with the same request, although I did not expect much of a response. I was not surprised when I did not receive a response.

After a failure to obtain any assistance from three different areas of professional air crash expertise, I now had a perception there was a lack of interest or a willingness by the authorities to reconsider this event and any suggestion that something was wrong with the official history. This perception only exacerbates the conspiracy theories, but the issue is, as I have explained, the more outlandish theories appear to be incorrect.

I believe that on the balance of probabilities this was sadly a tragic accident, caused by a combination of issues in terms of flight deck command, navigation, inexperience, aircraft instruments and the weather conditions.

Although I cannot completely prove my hypothesis, one cannot help but think for over eighty years now the authorities have been content to allow the more outlandish Rudolf Hess theories to flourish. Although the authorities have never entertained the Rudolf Hess theories and totally deny them, I believe the theories have distracted people from the real issues at the heart of this tragic event.

The authorities have never made a full public explanation of the crash investigation, what was at the scene etc. and probably never will if the original case file is no longer available. However, I believe there are enough issues contained within this book to cast a major doubt over the findings of the 1942 Court of Inquiry.

Sadly, we may never get to the bottom of this tragic case...

Flying hours of pilots/navigator
in May-August 1942

WG CDR Thomas Lawton Moseley flying hours From 228 Squadron ORB May-Aug 1942:				Total hrs. as 2nd Pilot
02.05.1942	Took Command of 228 Sqn.			
03.05.1942	Flew on air test as a spare	14:45–17:30	2 hours 45 mins	
04.05.1942	Flew with Goyen (as 2nd Pilot?) to Lochboisdale, South Uist to review fatal crash. Goyen and a/c returned but Moseley returned by boat.	15:30–??	30 mins???	
09.05.1942	Flew as spare D/C practice off Mull	09:52–10:33	41 mins	
18.05.1942	Flew on photo recce as spare	09:15–16:55	7 hours 40 mins	
21.05.1942	Flew as 2nd Pilot with Goyen on A/S search. Attacked U-boat with D/Cs	12:00–22:37	10 hours 37 mins	10.37 2nd
11.06.1942	Flew as spare on A/S escort	16:25–04:05	11 hours 40 mins	
13.06.1942	Flew as 2nd Pilot on A/S escort	09:00–19:25	10 hours 25 mins	21.02 2nd
08.07.1942	Flew as spare – transit to Lough Erne	10:25–12:25	2hrs	
08.07.1942	Flew as spare on convoy escort	16:15–05:15	13 hours	
23.07.1942	Flew as spare transit to Lough Erne	10:58–12:40	1 hour 42 mins	
24.07.1942	Flew as spare on A/S escort	17:28–06:15	12 hours 47 mins	
27.07.1942	Flew as spare on transit to Oban	14:07–16:00	1 hour 53 mins	
16.08.1942	Flew as 2nd Pilot with Goyen in W4026 on A/S escort	11:35–17:37	6 hours 12 mins	27.14 2nd
23.08.1942	Flew as 2nd Pilot with Goyen to Invergordon/Alness for pick-up of Duke of Kent & party.	15:35–16:30	55 mis	28.09 2nd
25.08.1942	Fatal flight as 1st Pilot??	13:12–13:42	30 mins	28.39 2nd
		Total hours = 72 hours 40 mins*		

*In nearly 4 months Moseley had not flown as a 1st Pilot and only **28 hours 39 mins** as a second pilot. He had been on board aircraft as a spare for a total of **44 hours 1 mins**.

According to the Form 412 (proceedings of the Court of Inquiry), he had flown 104.05 dual and 55.05 hours solo.

Therefore, we can surmise, his refresher flying course in March/ April 1942 had included 55.05 hours solo and about 30 hours dual flying.

FLT LT Frank Goyen flying hours From 228 Squadron ORB May–Aug 1942:				Total hrs. as a 2nd Pilot
04.05.1942	Flew as captain on transit	15:30–1640	1 hour 10 mins	
04.05.1942	Flew as captain on transit	20:00–21:00	1 hour	
07.05.1942	Flew as captain on transit	14:26–22:20	7 hours 54 mins	
11.05.1942	Flew as captain on trials with RN	07:32–11:03	3 hours 31 mins	
14.05.1942	Flew as captain on transit	18:05–18:35	30 mins	
18.05.1942	Flew as captain on A/S search	21:00–08:12	11 hours 12 mins	
21.05.1942	Flew as captain with Wg Cdr Moseley as 2nd Pilot on a sweep	12:00–22:37	10 hours 37 mins	10hr 37 min
15.06.1942	Flew as captain on transit	15:30–16:42	1 hour 12 mins	
15.06.1942	Flew as captain on transit	18:15–19:27	1 hour 13 mins	
16.06.1942	Flew as captain on local flight	17:45–19:34	1 hour 49 mins	
18.06.1942	Flew as captain on patrol	17:46–04:25	10 hours 11 mins	
23.06.1942	Flew as captain on convoy escort	04:30–16:22	11 hours 52 mins	
25.06.1942	Flew as 2nd Pilot on an air test.	15:53–17:00	1 hour 7 mins	11 hours 44 min
28.06.1942	Flew as 2nd Pilot on an air test.	15:40–17:24	1 hour 44 mins	13 hours 28 min
29.06.1942	Flew as captain on transit	14:43–15:35	52 mins	
29.06.1942	Flew as captain on transit	16:35–17:45	1 hour 10 mins	
19.07.1942	Flew as captain with Smith on local flight	16:35–16:57	22 mins	
23.07.1942	Flew as captain with Smith on local flight	15:20–16:02	42 mins	

24.07.1942	Flew as captain with Smith on transit	20:02–21:33	31 mins	
29.07.1942	Flew as captain with Smith on transit	13:48–17:20	3 hours 32 mins	
04.08.1942	Flew as captain with Smith & Saunders on convoy escort	03:28–15:42	12 hours 14 mins	
05.08.1942	Flew as captain with Smith on transit	11:10–12:04	56 mins	
07.08.1942	Flew as captain with Smith on local flight	15:55–16:31	36 mins	
11.08.1942	Flew as captain with Smith & Saunders on transit flight	17:02–18:55	1 hour 53 mins	
13.08.1942	Flew as captain with Smith & Saunders on transit flight	12:14–13:50	1 hour 41 mins	
14.08.1942	Flew as captain with Smith on local flight	15:36–15:50	14 mins	
16.08.1942	Flew as captain with Moseley (2nd Pilot), Smith & Saunders on A/S escort	11:35–17:37	6 hours 2 mins	
20.08.1942	Flew as captain with Smith & Saunders on convoy escort	12:56–19:25	7 hours 29 mins	
23.08.1942	Flew as captain with Moseley (2nd Pilot), Smith & Saunders to Invergordon/Alness.	15:35–16:30	55 mins	
25.08.1942	Fatal flight	13:12–13:42	30 mins	
		Total hours = 112 hours 48 mins +		

N.B. Mostly as first pilot/Captain (**99 hours 2 mins & 13 hours 28 mins** as the 2nd Pilot).

PO Sydney Wood Smith RAAF flying hours From 228 Squadron ORB May–Aug 1942:			
19.07.1942	Flew as 2nd Pilot with Goyen local flight	16:35–16:57	22 mins
23.07.1942	Flew as 2nd Pilot with Goyen local flight	15:20–16:02	42 mins
24.07.1942	Flew as 2nd Pilot with Goyen on transit	20:02–21:33	31 mins
29.07.1942	Flew as 2nd Pilot with Goyen on transit	13:48–17:20	3 hours 32 mins
04.08.1942	Flew as 2nd Pilot with Goyen & Saunders on convoy escort	03:28–15:42	12 hours 14 mins
05.08.1942	Flew as 2nd Pilot with Goyen on transit	11:10–12:04	56 mins
07.08.1942	Flew as 2nd Pilot with Goyen local flight	15:55–16:31	36 mins
11.08.1942	Flew as 2nd Pilot with Goyen & Saunders on transit	17:02–18:55	1 hour 53 mins
13.08.1942	Flew as 2nd Pilot with Goyen & Saunders on transit	12:14–13:50	1 hour 41 mins
14.08.1942	Flew as 2nd Pilot with Goyen local flight	15:36–15:50	14 mins
16.08.1942	Flew as spare pilot with Goyen & Moseley (2nd Pilot), Saunders A/S escort	11:35–17:37	6 hours 2 mins
20.08.1942	Flew as 2nd Pilot with Goyen & Saunders on convoy escort	12:56–19:25	7 hours 29 mins
23.08.1942	Flew as spare pilot with Goyen & Moseley (2nd Pilot), & Saunders to Invergordon/Alness.	15:35–16:30	55 mins
25.08.1942	Fatal flight	13:12–13:42	30 mins
		Total hours =	37 hrs 44 mins

Mostly as 2nd Pilot (**30 hours 47 mins and 6 hours 57 mins** as a spare pilot).

PO George Saunders RAFVR flying hours From 228 Squadron ORB May–Aug 1942:		Navigator	
04.08.1942	Flew as navigator with Goyen as captain & Smith on convoy escort	03:28–15:42	12 hours 14 mins
05.08.1942	Flew with Goyan & Smith on transit flight	11:10–12:04	56 mins
07.08.1942	Flew with Goyan & Smith on local flight	15:55–16:31	36 mins
11.08.1942	Flew with Goyan & Smith on transit flight	17:02–18:55	1 hour 53 mins
13.08.1942	Flew with Goyen & Smith on transit flight	12:14–13:50	1 hour 41 mins
14.08.1942	Flew with Goyen & Smith on local flight	15:36–15:50	14 mins
16.08.1942	Flew with Goyen, Moseley (2nd Pilot), & Smith on Anti Sub escort	11:35–17:37	6 hours 2 mins
20.08.1942	Flew with Goyan & Smith on convoy escort	12:56–19:25	7 hours 29 mins
23.08.1942	Flew with Goyan, Moseley (2nd Pilot), & Smith to Invergordon/Alness	15:35–16:30	55 mins
25.08.1942	Fatal flight	13:12–13:42	30 mins
		Total hours =	32 hrs 39 mins

Appendix B

List of witnesses mentioned in this book

Those called as witnesses by the Court of Inquiry:

- Flight Sergeant Andrew Jack (Rear gunner of Sunderland)
- Lieutenant John Stanley Whitehead RNVR
- William Sutherland (Royal Observer Corps)
- Dr John Kennedy (Dunbeath doctor)
- Flying Officer Ronald McCallum (Air Traffic Invergordon)
- Flight Lieutenant Leslie Burch (Signals Invergordon)
- Mr Donald Gunn (Met. Officer Invergordon)
- Mr Andrew Dryburgh (Met. Officer Invergordon)
- Flight Lieutenant Henry Jones (Duty Officer Invergordon)
- Flying Officer Norman Cryderman (Signals officer Oban)
- Corporal James Atherton (Radio Mechanic Oban)
- Flying Officer Kenneth Mullard (Medical Officer Wick)
- Pilot Officer Joseph E. Lewis (Signals Wick)

Senior Officers involved in the Court of Inquiry:

- Air Vice-Marshal David Colyer
- Wing Commander Arthur Warren Kay
- Squadron Leader William A. Stacey
- Flight Lieutenant Donald Lindsay RAAF
- Group Captain Edward F. Turner
- Group Captain John Hugh Oscar Jones

Other known professional witnesses:

- Vernon Sydney Brown (Chief Air Crash Inspector)
- Rob Wilson (Air Crash Inspector)
- Sir Arthur Balfour (Assistant Secretary of State for Air)
- George Campbell (RAF Alness)
- Flying Officer Archie Brember (No. 228 Squadron)
- Sergeant James Swanson (RAF Police Wick)
- Corporal Tim Wilson (RAF Aldergrove)
- Ron Clayton (No. 210 Squadron)
- Arthur Baker (No. 2847 Squadron RAF Regiment)
- D.G. Jubb (RAF Regiment)
- Air Vice-Marshal Edward Chilton
- Group Captain Kelly Barnes
- Richard Wigg (No. 228 Squadron)
- Group Captain Geoffrey Francis (RAF Alness)

Civilian witnesses:

- Jean Jack
- Robert Jack
- Elspeth Jack
- Sandra Young
- Dick Ross
- Will Bethune (Special Constable)
- James Sutherland (Special Constable)
- Robert Sutherland (Ousdale)
- George Grant (Ousdale)
- David Morrison (Braemore)
- Hugh Morrison (Braemore)
- James Gunn (Shepherd)
- James Sutherland (Crofter)

- Minnie Gunn (Postmistress)
- Betty Kennedy (Police constable's daughter in Dunbeath)
- Sergeant Bob Henderson (Dunbeath Home Guard)
- PC Tom Carter
- PC Edward Carter
- Elsie Sutherland
- Alice Gunn (Hospital Matron)
- Captain Ernest Fresson
- John Angus Miller (aged eight in 1942)
- Zena Sutherland
- David Sinclair (Home Guard)
- Bert Gunn
- Addie Gunn
- John MacDonald
- Iain MacDonald
- Margaret Harris
- Mr J.K. Luckin

Appendix C

ROYAL AIR FORCE.

R.A.F. Form 412.

PROCEEDINGS OF COURT OF INQUIRY OR INVESTIGATION.

FLYING ACCIDENTS.

The inquiry (or investigation) opened on (date) 28.8.42.
at (place) INVERGORDON.
by order of Air Vic Marshal D. Colyer, C.B., D.F.C.
with instructions to inquire into the circumstances connected with the accident on (date) 25.8.42.
at (place) Eagles Rock. (nearest town) Wick.
involving :

Aircraft.		Engine.				
Type and Mark.	Extent damaged, e.g. totally, seriously, slightly.	Type and Series.	No.			Extent damaged, e.g. totally, seriously, slightly.
			A.M. No.	Makers' No.		
Sunderland. Mk.111	Totally	Pegasus XVIII.	240608 240435 240631 240674	S.13519 F. S.13346 F. S.13542 F. S.13585 F.	))) Seriously.	

			Occupants.		
Name.	Rank.	Unit.	Duty, e.g. 1st Pilot, A.G. passenger, etc.	No. of aircraft in which he was occupant.	Extent injured, e.g. totally, seriously or slightly.
Moseley, T.L.	W/Cdr.	No.228 Sqdn.	1st Pilot.	W.4026	Fatally.
Goyen, F.M.	F/Lt.	"	Captain.	"	"
Smith, S.W.	P/O.	"	2nd Pilot.	"	"
Saunders, G.R.	P/O.	"	Navigator.	"	"
Sweet, L.E.	Sgt.	"	F/Eng.	"	"
Jones, W.R.	F/Sgt.	"	FME/AG.	"	"
Hewardine, E.J.	F/Sgt.	"	WEM/AG.	"	"
Blacklock, E.E.	Sgt.	"	W/OP/AG.	"	"
Lewis, E.N.	F/Sgt.	"	P/MECH.AG.	"	"
Catt, A.R.	F/Sgt.	"	W/OP.AG.	"	"
Jack, A.S.W.	F/Sgt.	"	AG.	"	Seriously.
H.R.H. Duke of Kent.	A/Comm.		Passenger.	"	Fatally.
Hon M. Strutt.	P/O.	"		"	
Lowther, J.	Lt/RNVR/	"	Passenger.	"	Fatally.
Hales, J.	LAC.	"	"	"	"

In attendance	F/Lt.		D.S. LINDSAY.		No. 423 Squadron.

LIST OF WITNESSES.

Rank.	Name.	Unit (if civilian say so).	Rank.	Name.	Unit (if civilian say so).
F/Sgt.	Jack, A.S.W.	228 Sqdn.	MR.	Gunn, D.M.	R.A.F.Invergordon.
Dr.	Kennedy, J.R.	Civilian	MR.	Dryburgh, A.	-do-
MR.	Sutherland, W.	"	F/Lt.	Jones, H.J.L.	-do-
F/O.	Mullard, K.S.	R.A.F. Wick.	F/O.	Cryderman, N.J.R.	A.F.,Oban.
Sub-Lieut.	Whitehead, J.S.	RNO.Wick.	Cpl.	Atherton,J.	-do-
F/O.	Lewis, J.E.	RAF.Wick.			
F/O.	McCullum, R.A.	RAF.,Invergordon.			
F/Lt.	Burch, L.L.R.	-do-			

The first page of the Court of Inquiry report, clearly showing Wing Commander Moseley as 1st Pilot and Goyen as Captain. (*National Archives of Australia. NAA: A9300, Smith S.W.*)

CERTIFIED TRUE COPY.

(Sgd.) ??? F/O Adjutant

ROYAL AIR FORCE.

R.A.F. Form 412.

Encl 28 A

PROCEEDINGS OF COURT OF INQUIRY OR INVESTIGATION.

FLYING ACCIDENTS.

The inquiry (or investigation) opened on (date) ....28.8.42....

at (place) ....INVERGORDON.

by order of ....Air Vic Marshal D. Colyer, C.B., D.F.C.

with instructions to inquire into the circumstances connected with the accident on (date)....25.8.42.

at (place)....Eagles Rock. (nearest town)....Wick.

involving :

Aircraft.		Engine.			
				No.	
Type and Mark.	Extent damaged, e.g., totally, seriously, slightly.	Type and Series.	A.M. No.	Makers' No.	Extent damaged, e.g., totally, seriously, slightly.
Sunderland. Mk.111	Totally	Pegasus XVIII.	240608 240435 240631 240674	S.13519 F. S.13346 F. S.13542 F. S.13585 F.	)Seriously.)))

	Occupants.				
Name.	Rank.	Unit.	Duty, e.g., 1st Pilot, A.G., passenger, etc.	No. of aircraft in which he was occupant.	Extent injured, e.g., fatally, seriously or slightly. (See Note 4, para 2.)
Moseley, T.L.	W/Cdr.	No.228 Sqdn.	1st Pilot.	W.4026	Fatally.
Goyen, F.M.	F/Lt.	"	Captain.	"	"
Smith, S.W.	P/O.	"	2nd Pilot.	"	"
Saunders, G.R.	P/O.	"	Navigator.	"	"
Sweet, L.E.	Sgt.	"	F/Eng.	"	"
Jones, W.R.	F/Sgt.	"	FME/AG.	"	"
Hewardine, E.J.	F/Sgt.	"	WEM/AG.	"	"
..cklock, E.E.	Sgt.	"	W/OP/AG.	"	"
E.N.	F/Sgt.	"	F/MECH.AG.	"	"
	F/Sgt.	%	W/OP.AG.	"	Seriously.
..ent.	F/Sgt. A/Comm	"	AG. Passenger.	"	Fatally.

the purpose of :—
) Establishing the facts called for in the findings on page 3 of this form.
) Enabling the Court or Investigating Officer to state, on page 4 of this form, an opinion as to the cause of the accident, the degree of responsibility of any person concerned (see K.R. & A.C.I., para. 1319 (3)), and to make recommendations for the future.
(iii.) Inquiring specially into *

...N OF THE COURT (OR NAME OF INVESTIGATING OFFICER).

Rank.	Name.	Unit.
W/Cdr.	A.W. Kay	H.Q., C.C.
S/Ldr.	W.J. D'A Stacey.	15. Group.
F/Lt.	D.S. LINDSAY.	No. 423 Squadron.

In attendance ....

LIST OF WITNESSES.

Rank.	Name.	Unit (if civilian say so).	Rank.	Name.	Unit (if civilian say so).
F/Sgt.	Jack, A.S.W.	228 Sqdn.	MR.	Gunn, D.M.	R.A.F.Invergordon.
Dr.	Kennedy, J.R.	Civilian	MR.	Dryburgh, A.	-do-
MR.	Sutherland, W.	"	F/Lt.	Jones, H.J.L.	-do-
F/O.	Mullard, K.S.	R.A.F. Wick.	F/O.	Cryderman, N.J.	R.A.F.,Oban.
Sub-Lieut.	Whitehead, J.S.	RNO.Wick.	Cpl.	Atherton,J.	-do-
F/O.	Lewis, J.E.	RAF.Wick.			
F/O.	McCullum, R.A.	RAF.,Invergordon.			
F/Lt.	Burch, L.L.R.	-do-			

RECORDED FOR STATISTICAL TABULATION
P/P 113 Serial No. .... Initials. ....

(*9391) Wt. 52713—3576 10,000 6/42 T.S. 700

30 MAR 19..

2

Notes for the Guidance of Courts of Inquiry or Investigations into Flying Accidents.

(1) The findings which the Court or Investigating Officer are called upon to make (on pages 3 and 4 of this form) should be kept clearly in view in conducting the inquiry.

(2) It must be borne in mind that the findings (including an opinion as to the cause of the accident and the degree of responsibility and any recommendation for the future) must be based upon and supported entirely by the recorded evidence of the witnesses or by additional facts ascertained by the Court themselves or by the Investigating Officer, which are to be recorded in items 8 and 9 of the findings.

(3) The Court or Investigating Officer will therefore not omit to see that the necessary witnesses are called and that their evidence on all material points is ascertained and recorded. If the Court or Investigating Officer have not considered it necessary or feasible to visit the scene of the accident or to examine log books they will state these facts in items 8 and 9 of the findings.

(4) Any special cause for the particular injuries of any member of the crew should be brought out in evidence and recorded as under para. 1 of the findings.

(5) Investigation should be made to determine whether the failure of any part of the engine or aircraft, or the inefficient working of any accessory was a contributory cause of the accident, and an opinion recorded under item 9 of the findings.

(6) It should be stated under item 9 of the findings whether there is any evidence that the occupant(s) of the aircraft attempted to make use of parachute(s).

(7) Where the injuries to any person involved in the accident are such as preclude his evidence being available when the Court or Investigation is held, it will be so stated in item (B) of the findings.

(8) The evidence of every witness may be recorded by hand or type-written. This will be done on ordinary foolscap sheets. Both sides of the sheet should be used; the use of a fresh page for each witness is unnecessary. The pages of these sheets (after being signed as described below) must be consecutively numbered and securely fastened.

(9) Each witness must sign each page of the evidence upon which his own evidence is recorded, but the signature of the president or investigating officer is not necessary in addition.

(10) The questions put to witnesses should be as simple as possible, and the Court or Investigating Officer should see that the recorded evidence of each witness is free from ambiguity, although it may not agree with the evidence of another.

(11) When it appears that the inquiry affects the character or professional reputation of an officer or airman compliance with the provisions of paragraph 1318 of King's Regulations and Air Council Instructions is to be ensured.

(12) If no recommendations are made, the Court or Investigating Officer should specifically state that they have no recommendations to make.

(13) All printed sections of the form must be accurately completed. The instructions contained in A.M.O. A 88/31 will be followed when they are applicable to the accident being investigated, and to A.M.O. A 98/39 as to evidence on matters which are shown in the relative R.A.F. Form 700.

(14) Attention is invited to Section VII of A.P. 837 (Manual of Administration in the Royal Air Force).

THE HEADINGS OF THE FINDINGS have been framed so as to meet the case where more than one aircraft is involved in the accident, and care is to be taken to see that the findings clearly indicate to which aircraft they refer.

7 (b).   The flying experience of the pilot(s) prior to this flight was :—

Pilot.	Type of aircraft.	Time flown on each type : hours.					
		Total.		Night flying included in previous columns. (c)		Within the six months previous to the accident.	
		Dual.	Solo.	Dual.	Solo.	Dual.	Solo.
Name W/Cdr. MOSELEY	Avro) Tutor) Atlas)	70.35	60.35				
Trained at Cranwell.	Hart.) 28 types various.						
Date awarded flying badge 13.7.33.				1075.25	243.00	104.05	55.05
(d) Total hours flown by instruments 1146.00							
(d) Hours on Link Trainer 303.35.	TOTALS	70.35	60.35	1075.25	243.00	104.05	55.05

Page 2. (*Courtesy of the National Archives of Australia. NAA: A9300, Smith S.W.*)

3

FINDINGS OF COURT.

An inquiry (or investigation) has been conducted on the instructions set forth on the first page of this form, and at the place and on the date thereon stated.

The evidence of the witnesses is recorded on the pages inserted inside this form.

(A) We (I) find from the evidence that the following facts have been established :—(*See* page 2, para. 4)

1. The description of the pilot(s), aircraft and engines and of the extent of injury to them is as set forth on the front page of this form, with this exception that

2. The purpose of and instructions for the flight(s) were as follows :—

Aircraft.		Who ordered the flight and for what purpose? Were any special instructions given? State if one occupant was instructing the other.
Type.	No.	
Sunderland.	W.4026	A.O.C., 15 Group. Transit Flight to Iceland. No Special Instructions.

3. The accident occurred at...................hours at the place and on the date set forth on the front page of this form.

4. The aircraft ~~were~~ was controlled as follows :—

Aircraft.		No. of seats.	Whether fitted with single or dual control.	Names of occupants of seats.		
Type.	No.			Front.	Back.	Other.
Sunderland	W.4026	2	Dual	1st Pilot. F/Lt. Goyen	2nd Pilot W/Cdr. Moseley P/O. Smith. P/O.Saunders. Sgt. Sweet. F/O. Jones. F/S.Hewardine Sgt. Blacklock Sgt. Catt	Sgt.Lewis Sgt. Jack(Tail Turret). HRH. Duke of Kent. P/O.Hon.M. Strutt. Lt. LoWther LAC. HALES.

5. The aircraft took off as follows :—

Aircraft.		Time	Weather conditions where aircraft and also, if ascertainable, at the time of the accident.
Type.	No.		
Sunderland.	W.4026	1311	Wind.East 10 m.p.h. Visibility 2200-4400 yds Cloud.10/10 at1000 ft. Fragments at 200 ft.

6. Condition of aircraft at commencement of flight(s)   (*See* note 13 on page 2.)

Aircraft.		When last examined.				Whether aircraft and engine fit for flight in question.
		By fitter.		By rigger.		
Type.	No.	Date.	Hour.	Date.	Hour.	
Sunderland	W.4026	25.8.42	A.M.	25.8.42	A.M.	Yes.

7 (*a*).   The flying experience of the pilot(s) prior to this flight was :—

Pilot.	Type of aircraft.	Time flown on each type : hours.					
Note :—Finding 7 (*b*) at foot of page 2 will be used for the second pilot involved		Total.		Night flying included in previous columns. (c)		Within the six months previous to the accident.	
		Dual.	Solo.	Dual.	Solo.	Dual.	Solo.
Name F/Lt. GOYEN. Trained at EFTS.30 EFTS, 15 FTS Date awarded flying badge 4.10.39 (d) Total hours flown by instruments 1026.35 (d) Hours on Link Trainer 324.25	Avro. Magister Tiger Moth Oxford Singapore. Sunderland.	13.15 Nil 35.05 56.15	24.55 08.15. 35.20 32.40	14.40 907.20	10.30 212.45	264.30	
	TOTALS	104.35	101.10	922.00	223.15	264.30	

(c) only to be quoted if accident occurred at night.
(d) To be quoted only if loss of control at night or in bad visibility or cloud by day was sole or contributory cause of accident.

Page 3. (*Courtesy of the National Archives of Australia. NAA: A9300, Smith S.W.*)

4

8. We (I) (have)/(have not) examined the following aircraft, engine and pilot's flying log books and form 700 and have ascertained :—

Description of book and form	Remarks, including material facts supplementing or confirming evidence of witnesses.
Engine Log Books, Air Frame Log Books Form 700. Pilots. Log Books. Special Equipment Maintenance Form.	All found correct and up to date.

9. We (I) (have)/(~~have not~~) visited the scene of the accident (before)/(~~after~~) aircraft (was)/(~~were~~) removed and have found the following material facts :—(*See* page 2, paras. (5) and (6).)

1) The engines were under power at the time of the crash

2) Parachutes were not used.

(B) We (I) have been unable to obtain the evidence of the following material witnesses :—

Name.	Rank.	Unit.	Reasons precluding obtaining of evidence.	How concerned with accident.

(C) The cause of the accident was in our (my) opinion   See attached findings.

(D) This accident (has)/(~~has not~~) been reported to the Accidents Investigation Branch.

Signature of president of court   **(Sgd.) A.W. KAY W/Cdr.**
(or investigating officer)

Do.   member of court   "   **W.J.D'A STACEY. S/Ldr.**

Do.   Do.   "   **D.S. LINDSAY. F/Lt.**

Date of signing

REPORT OF COMMANDING OFFICER.

I concur with the finding of the Court as to the actual cause of the accident, but I am the opinion that, in the weather conditions pertaining at the time, a non-operational flight should not have been carried out.

Date of signing   3.9.42   Signature of C.O.   (Sgd.) E.F. TURNER.G/C

: Commanding   R.A.F.Station. OBAN.

REMARKS OF GROUP COMMANDER.

. I concur with the finding of the Court and consider that the weather conditions should have presented no difficulty to a crew of such experience.

Signature (Sgd.) ????
Air Vice Marshal.

Date of signing   7th September, 1942.   Commanding. No.15.   Group.

Page 4 showing the conflicting comments of AVM Colyer and Group Captain Turner. (*Courtesy of the National Archives of Australia. NAA: A9300, Smith S.W.*)

Encl 28E

Certified True Copy.   (Sgd.) ???   F/O. Adjutant.

PAGE NO. FIVE.

(Continued.)

SIXTH WITNESS:-

Flying Officer NORMAN JOHNSON CRYDERMAN, No. C. 8119 of
R.A.F. Station, Oban, states:-

                I am Signals R.D.F. Officer of
No.228 Squadron , On the 23rd August, 1942,
I instructed Corporal ATHERTON to carry out
a routine inspection of the Special Equipment
on Sunderland "M" of No. 228 Squadron.

                  (Signed.) N.J. Cryderman. F/O.

                1.9.42.

SEVENTH WITNESS:-   PAGE No. SIX.

No. 98737, Corporal ATHERTON, JAMES, Radio Mechanic
of No. 228 Squadron, R.A.F. Station, Oban, states:-

                I am Corporal in charge of Special
Equipment Section of No. 228. Squadron. At
approximately 1000 hours on the 23rd August,
1942, I carried out an inspection on the Special
Equipment on Sunderland "M" of No. 228 Squadron.
Everything was satisfractory and I signed the
Daily Inspection Form to that effect.

                (Signed.) J. Atherton. Corporal.

                1.9.42.

EIGHT WITNESS:-   PAGE NO. SEVEN.

No. 970168 Flight Sergeant JACK, ANDREW SIMPSON WILSON,
Air Gunner, No.228 Squadron, R.A.F. Station, Oban states:-

                I Am an Air Gunner with No.228 Squadron.
On Tuesday, 25th August, 1942, I was a member of the
crew of aircraft W.4026 which was on passage from
Invergordon to Iceland. We were airborne at about
1300 hours and the height of the cloud was about 500
feet. The Captain, Flight Lieutenant Goyen, who was
flying the aircraft, told us there would be a lot of
cloud around but he did not think it would last long.
This was over the inter-com. I was in the Rear Turret.
As we proceeded the cloud came down thicker. I felt
the aircraft losing height after about 20 minutes.
The pilot was apparently trying to get under the cloud
base. I do not remeber anything after this.

                (Signed.) A. Jack,

                29.8.42.

Part of the 'transcript' of the evidence to the court detailing evidence from
survivor Flight Sergeant Andrew Jack. (*Courtesy of the National Archives
of Australia. NAA: A9300, Smith S.W.*)

<u>Certified true copy.</u>   (Sgd.) ????? F/O. Adjutant.

                                                    PAGE No. SEVEN.

                                                        (Continued.)

<u>QUESTION ONE:-</u>   Do you know who was navigating,
                          the aircraft ?

<u>ANSWER ONE:-</u>   I don't know.

<u>QUESTION TWO:-</u>.   Did you hear anything else over
                          the inter-com?

<u>ANSWER TWO:-</u>   No.

<u>QUESTION THREE:-</u>   Do you remember who was in the
                          2nd Pilot's seat ?

<u>ANSWER THREE:-</u>   No.

<u>QUESTION FOUR:-</u>.   Did you think the aircraft climbed <u>PAGE NO EIGHT</u>
                          much before it started to come down
                          again ?

<u>ANSWER FOUR:-</u>   No, not much.

<u>QUESTION FIVE:-</u>   Was the last thing you can remember
                          being in a cloud ?

<u>ANSWER FIVE:-</u>   Yes.

                              (Signed.) A. Jack.

                                          29.8.42.

<u>NINTH WITNESS.</u>

Doctor JOHN ROBERT KENNEDY, Medical Officer at Dunbeath,
Caithness, states:-

              I am a Medical Officer for the Western
        District of the Parish of Latheron. At about 1400
        hours on 25th August, 1942, I heard casually on the
        telephone that an aircraft had crashed somewhere in
        the vicinity of Braemore. I immediately proceeded
        to Braemore by car with a small search party which
        I had organised. We proceeded down the Berriedale
        Riverfor 2 - 1/2 miles hoping to get into touch with
        a large search party under the command of Lord
        Litchfield. Owing to the thick fog and rain we were
        unable to contact this party. I sent three members
        of my search party ahead in a North Easterly direction
        where I thought the plane would be. They reached the
        plane /////

                        (Signed) John R Kennedy.

        //// which had been previously found by   <u>PAGE NO NINE.</u>
        James Gunn, Shepherd, Braemore. They returned
        to where I was waiting and informed me that the
        occupants were all dead. I went back with them
        to the crashed aircraft and found 11 bodies in
        and around the wreckage and 3 trapped under burning
        wreckage. I examined all the bodies accessable
        and found that death was due to burning and multiple
        injuries in most cases. In all cases death must have
        been instantaneous.

                        (Signed.) John R. Kennedy.

                                    29.8.42.

The simple questions and answer attributed to the examination of Flight
Sergeant Jack by the Court of Inquiry and the evidence by local medical
officer – Dr John Kennedy. (*Courtesy of the National Archives of Australia.
NAA: A9300, Smith S.W.*)

Certified True Copy.   (Sgd.) ???? F/O. Adjutant.

FINDINGS.

The cause of the accident was in our opinion due to the aircraft being flown on a wrong track at too low an altitude to clear the rising ground on the track.

2.   The responsibility for this serious mistake in airmanship lies with the Captain of the aircraft, F/Lt. GOYEN, who changed his flight plan for reasons unknown, inasmuch that he commenced the flight by climbing into cloud, and then started to descend but failed to take the elementary precaution of making sure that he was over the water, and crashed into the hillside whilst still in cloud .

3.   In our opinion the weather encountered should have presented no difficulties to an experienced pilot.

4.   The examination of the propellors showed that the engines were under power when the aircraft struck the ground.

5.   In accordance with K.R. & A.C.I. para 1325 we find that all the occupants of Sunderland "M" of No.228 Squadron were on duty at the time of the accident.

RECOMMENDATIONS.

In view of F/Lt. GOYEN's previous experience this sudden lack of judgment was quite unpredictable and in these circumstances the Court is unable to make any recommendations.

It is desired to bring to notice the magnificent work done by Dr. KENNEDY, aged 71, of DUNBEATH. In the last 2 years he has been the first Medical Officer on the scene of the accident of six crashes, in this particular instance in appalling weather conditions, all over very difficult terrain which would have taxed the endurance of a very much younger person.

                        (Sgd.) A.W. KAY.   W/Cdr.
                                W.J.D'A. STACEY. S/Ldr.
1.9.42.   D.S. LINDSAY.   F/Lt.

The Court of Enquiry's findings and recommendations. (*Courtesy of the National Archives of Australia. NAA: A9300, Smith S.W.*)

Resources used in this book

UK National Archives:

The following references have been used in this book under version 3.0 of the Open Government Licence. The UK National Archives may, from time to time, issue new versions of the Open Government Licence. If you are already using Information under a previous version of the Open Government Licence, the terms of that licence will continue to apply.

These terms are compatible with the Creative Commons Attribution Licence 4.0 and the Open Data Commons Attribution Licence, both of which licence copyright and database rights. This means that when the Information is adapted and licenced under either of those licences, you automatically satisfy the conditions of the OGL when you comply with the other licence. The OGLv3.0 is Open Definition compliant.

AIR 2/5452 File on HRH Duke of Kent's one year with RAF as Inspector General of Welfare

AIR 2/10593 Loss of Avro York MW126 & ACM Leigh-Mallory in 1944.

AIR 2/16973 Recommendation for award Dr John Kennedy

AIR 2/18812 and AIR2/15113 (Sikorski inquiry)

AIR 25/418 No. 18 Group (Coastal Command) Operations Record Book.

AIR 27/1415 No. 228 Squadron Operations Record Book (ORB)

AIR 28/402 RAF Invergordon/Alness Narrative Sept. 1939-Dec 1942

AIR 28/620 RAF Oban Operations Record Book (ORB)

AIR 28/915 RAF Wick Operations Record Book (ORB)

AIR 29/1013 56 Maintenance Unit (MU) Operations Record Book (ORB)

AIR 29/1019 63 Maintenance Unit (MU) Operations Record Book (ORB)

AIR 81/17336 File relating to loss of Anson DJ178 Berriedale on 19 Aug 1942

FO800/313 & FO800/316

HO 45/20275 Condolences to Royal Family

PREM 4/8/2A Prime Minister's correspondence on death of HRH Duke of Kent.

National Archives of Australia:

Pilot Officer Sydney Wood Smith RAAF ref: A9300 item 5253132 Smith S.W.

Royal Archives Windsor:

Letters and correspondence in preparation to the flight on 25 August 1942

George Bethune:

Presentation: A very Human story (from Feb 2013)

Various records of testimony from witnesses

Nucleus Archive, Wick:

Caithness Police air crash reports from the Second World War

Newspapers:

The Scotsman newspaper, article by Robin MacWhirter, August 1985

The Scotsman newspaper, 7 September 1985 (Richard Fresson's letter
    to editor)
Caithness Courier, 31 August 2005 article (Duke of Kent memorial
    makes up for lost time) by Alan Hendry
    August 2002 article by Alan Hendry (Eagles Rock collision course)
Edinburgh Evening News, Page 1, 26 August 1942
Aberdeen Press & Journal, Page 1, 27 August 1942
Birmingham Mail, Page 2, 27 August 1942
Daily Record, Page 1, 27 August 1942
The Scotsman, Page 5, 27 August 1942
Birmingham Daily Post, Page 3, 27 August 1942
Bradford Observer/Daily Herald/Liverpool Daily Post, 27 August 1942
Scottish Daily Express, 18 May 1961
The Times, 24 March 1996
Daily Mail, 9 November 2007
Mail on Sunday, 10 July 2021
John O'Groats Journal & Caithness Courier, 21 August 2022

Magazines & Periodicals:
After the Battle No. 37, 1982
Aeroplane Monthly, January 1983
Aeroplane Monthly, January 1990
Aeroplane Monthly, February 1990
Aeroplane Monthly, April 1990
Aeroplane Monthly, March 1992
Aeroplane Monthly, September 1996

RAF Air Historical Branch:
Accident Card Form 1108 for Sunderland Mk III W-4026
Air Publication 1234 – Manual on air navigation
Air Publication 1922 – Notes on casualty procedure in war from
    1941/1942

Bibliography:

RAF officer lists July 1942

The Hebrides at War, by Mike Hughes, published by Birlinn Ltd 2003

Air Crash by Fred Jones, Hale Publishing 1985

Double Standards (the Rudolf Hess cover-up) by Picknett, Prine & Prior, Time Warner paperbacks, 2001

George & Marina, The Duke & Duchess of Kent by Christopher Warwick, Weidenfeld & Nicolson 1988

Great Mysteries of the Air by Ralph Barker, Pan Books 1966

Secret and Personal by F.W. Winterbotham, William Kimber books 1969

The Nazi Connection by F.W. Winterbotham, Weidenfeld and Nicolson 1978

Rudolf Hess: Treachery & Deception by Harris & Wilbourn, Jema publications 2016

Rudolf Hess a new technical analysis of the Hess flight, May 1941, by Harris & Wilbourn, Spellmount publications 2014

Rudolf Hess: The British illusion of peace by John Harris, Jema publications 2010

Missing Believed Killed, by Roy Conyers Nesbit, Sutton Books 2002

Scottish Mysteries by Donald Fraser, Mercatt Press 1997

My Flying Boat War: Survival and Success over the Atlantic, Mediterranean and Pacific in WW2 by Wing Commander 'Vic' Hodgkinson DFC, RAAF Air World Books, Barnsley, 2023

Mask of Treachery by John Costello, Warner Books 1990

Caithness and the War 1939-1945, by Norman M. Glass, originally published by North of Scotland newspapers, Caithness 1948

Imperial War Museum:

Private papers of Air Marshal David Colyer CB DFC

National Records of Scotland:
Scottish/Caithness Death records 1942

Miscellaneous:
Hansard

BBC News website, 23 Dec 2003 (Secret of Duke's plane)

BBC Scotland Radio Progamme 1985 'The Crash of W-4026' *The London Gazette*

Leeds University Library (memoirs of Dorothea Gray nee Whyte) Caithness.org

Index

If you have enjoyed this book, please view my website
msmorganbooks.co.uk.

Other books by this author include:

The Hurricane Pilot who became a Gestapo Agent
&
Hitler's RAF Collaborators
(Agents or traitors the RAF PoWs alleged to
have assisted the Nazis)